W9-DGY-024

# Letters to Doubting Thomas

# Letters to Doubting Thomas

## *A Case for the Existence of God*

### C. STEPHEN LAYMAN

*Seattle Pacific University*

New York ◆ Oxford
OXFORD UNIVERSITY PRESS
2007

Oxford University Press, Inc., publishes works that further Oxford University's
objective of excellence in research, scholarship, and education.

Oxford      New York
Auckland   Cape Town   Dar es Salaam   Hong Kong   Karachi
Kuala Lumpur   Madrid   Melbourne   Mexico City   Nairobi
New Delhi   Shanghai   Taipei   Toronto

With offices in
Argentina   Austria   Brazil   Chile   Czech Republic   France   Greece
Guatemala   Hungary   Italy   Japan   Poland   Portugal   Singapore
South Korea   Switzerland   Thailand   Turkey   Ukraine   Vietnam

Published by Oxford University Press, Inc.
198 Madison Avenue, New York, New York 10016
http://www.oup.com

Oxford is a registered trademark of Oxford University Press

**Library of Congress Cataloging-in-Publication Data**

Layman, Charles S., 1950–
    Letters to Doubting Thomas : a case for the existence of God / by C. Stephen Layman.
        p. cm.
    Includes bibliographical references and index.
    ISBN-13: 978-0-19-530814-3 (cloth)
    ISBN-10: 0-19-530814-X (cloth)
    ISBN-13: 978-0-19-530815-0 (pbk.)
    ISBN-10: 0-19-530815-8 (pbk.)
    1. God—Proof. 2. Theism. 3. Naturalism—Religious aspects. I. Title.

BL200.L39 2006
212'.1—dc22

                                                                    2006040083

9 8 7 6 5 4 3 2 1

Printed in the United States of America
on acid-free paper

# Contents

*v*

# Preface

Some people never doubt the existence of God. And they may find a discussion about the existence of God puzzling or useless (or both). We may call them *true believers*.

For some other people, the belief that God exists is a relic of the past and completely irrational—a stubborn superstition nurtured by ignorance and fear. We may call them *true disbelievers*.

This book is likely to be of little interest to either true believers or true disbelievers. I hope it will be of interest to that very large group of people, believers, agnostics, and atheists, for whom the existence of God is a vital issue worthy of our best thinking.

In the course of my adult life, I have held widely different opinions about the evidence for God's existence. Early in my undergraduate years, before I studied philosophy, I was impressed with several arguments for the existence of God. A few years later, during my graduate studies, I thought that all of the arguments for God's existence failed badly. I was for some years tortured by doubts, shifting opinions so rapidly that I fell into deep confusion. In short, I am among those who have found it extremely difficult to sort through the various lines of reasoning about God's existence and to come to any sort of considered view.

In the past fifty years, philosophers of religion have done an enormous amount of work on the question of God's existence and nature, with the result that the philosophical "landscape" has changed dramatically. Many very fine contributions have appeared, and they have been tried in the fire of vigorous debate. My goal in this book is to set forth a case for the existence of God that incorporates some of the best of the new developments—as many of them as I know how to mold into a coherent, sustained argument.

In part, then, this work attempts to synthesize a number of arguments developed by others. I make no apology for relying on the excellent work of others in building a cumulative case for theism. But I think those who know the literature will see many points at which I have approached the issues in a new way or introduced significant refinements.

Philosophy is never easy, but I have tried to write a book that can be read by those without philosophical training. Perhaps I can best indicate the level of difficulty in this way: I believe any university student or college-educated person can read and understand this book if he or she is willing to proceed at a moderate pace, ponder the key concepts, and occasionally reread closely reasoned paragraphs. I have developed my arguments in the form of a correspondence because I think this approach is engaging and breaks the material down into manageable bits.

It is often claimed that arguments are of little value where religion is concerned. I believe this claim to be false. Of course, people seldom change their minds immediately upon hearing an argument about an important religious issue. But the same can be said for arguments about controversial issues in general, for example, in politics or morality.

The analogy with politics is worth exploring a bit further. Obviously, people are influenced by many things besides arguments in regard to their political beliefs, e.g., upbringing, social status, and temperament. But over the course of their lives, many people change or develop their political beliefs significantly, at least in part because they hear arguments on radio or TV, read them in editorials, or encounter them in discussions with friends. I think argument plays a similar role where religion is concerned, or at least it does when people are exposed to it with some regularity.

In my line of work as a philosophy teacher, I frequently hear people confess to being at a loss as to how to approach the question of God's existence. And often, when people first encounter an argument for God's existence, it raises more questions than it answers. My goal in this book is to provide at least one way of approaching the issue of God's existence—a way to organize what can seem a chaos of claims and concepts. If I have provided a helpful framework for thinking about the existence of God, one that brings some clarity to matters that often cause confusion, then I'll have achieved my purpose.

# Acknowledgments

In the final chapters of this book I have made use of previously published material. In Chapters 7 and 8, on the problem of evil, I have borrowed both argumentative strategies and occasional brief passages from "Moral Evil: the comparative response," *International Journal for the Philosophy of Religion*, v. 53, n. 1 (February 2003), 1–23, and from "Natural Evil: the comparative response," *International Journal for the Philosophy of Religion*, v. 54, n. 1 (August 2003), 1–31. In Chapter 9 ("A Moral Argument"), I have borrowed the main argument and several paragraphs from "God and the Moral Order," *Faith and Philosophy*, v. 19, n. 3 (July 2002), 304–16. I thank all of the publishers and editors in question for permission to use this material.

I owe a great debt to the philosophers who have commented on and critiqued the various chapters of this book. Andrew Jeffery provided me with extensive written comments on every chapter of the first draft. Phillip Goggans, Kenneth Einar Himma, and Patrick McDonald not only read most of the chapters, but also met with me to discuss them. Terence Cuneo read drafts of many of the chapters and sent me thoughtful responses via email. Whatever the value of the book, it is much better for having undergone the careful scrutiny of these friends and colleagues.

I also wish to thank the students in my philosophy of religion class, spring of 2004, for reading the manuscript in its entirety and for making many helpful suggestions about ways to improve it.

I am grateful to Seattle Pacific University for a sabbatical in the fall of 2003 that enabled me to complete an initial draft of this book.

Special thanks are due to the editors at Oxford University Press, Robert Miller, Sarah Calabi, and Emily Voigt, for their support and advice throughout the project. I also wish to thank the reviewers who provided me with both encouragement and helpful suggestions for improving the manuscript: Michael Beaty, Baylor University; James W. Eiswert, Northwest Missouri State University; Noel Hendrickson, James Madison University; Ian Markham, Hartford Seminary; Wesley Morriston, University of Colorado-Boulder; Thomas Senor, University of Arkansas; and William Sweet, Saint Francis Xavier University.

I would like to take this opportunity to acknowledge a special debt to the teachers through whom I came to love the philosophy of religion: Alvin Plantinga, Nicholas Wolterstorff, Marilyn Adams, and Robert Adams. I hope that this work honors these remarkable teachers and philosophers. I owe them a lot.

It remains for me to dedicate this book to my siblings, John, Daun, and Rick, who gave me my first lessons in the art of argument.

# Introduction

Are there any good reasons to believe that God exists? That's the question this book attempts to answer. But in my experience, it's unwise to plunge directly into arguments for and against the existence of God. To avoid inevitable misunderstandings, we must first tackle certain preliminary issues.

For example, what counts as a "good argument" in this context? Many people become disappointed with philosophy because they demand *proofs*. By a "proof" I mean an argument with these two features: (1) Its premises are acceptable to all rational people, and (2) its conclusion follows logically from its premises. Proofs in this sense are rare or nonexistent in philosophy. *The defense of virtually any major philosophical position will involve controversial premises at some point, i.e., premises not acceptable to all rational people.*

Is it then pointless to argue about philosophical matters? Well, many people seem to think so. They have a low regard for philosophy, at least in part because "It never settles anything." Now, I can understand why someone might feel this way. We'd all like to have definitive answers to philosophical questions, but in the absence of proofs, no answer seems definitive. So, isn't one opinion just as good as another? And if so, what's the point of philosophical argument, anyway?

Look at it this way—you've got two options:

1. Just ignore reasoning altogether.
2. Take reasoning seriously and accept whatever guidance it can give (even if the amount of guidance is less than one would like).

Some people go with option 1. They may regard feelings or intuitions as better guides than reason. Or they may depend wholly (no questions asked!) on alleged authorities, e.g., priests, pastors, or sacred writings. Others may take option 1 because they are in general careless—they just don't think much about their own lives or about life in general. But a great many people are not content with option 1; they are thoughtful and wish they could sort through major religious and ethical issues in a rational way. They must take option 2.

Still, if philosophy can't really *settle* the issues, why expend all the effort required to think things through? Fair question—I answer as follows. First, many suppose that arguments are no good unless they persuade all rational people. Let me suggest that the first order of business, when we are thinking, is not to persuade others, but to clarify our own views. Instead of worrying about the fact that I can't persuade everybody, perhaps I should start simply by trying to find a line of thought that seems genuinely insightful to me. And of course the same goes for you.

Second, all of us hold positions on controversial matters, e.g., abortion, euthanasia, the death penalty, vegetarianism, the treatment of animals, or the best political candidate. And we have *reasons* for holding what we hold—even though we know that our reasons won't convince all rational people. Moreover, our reasons matter a lot to us. We would consider our views *arbitrary or irrational* in the absence of such reasons. So each person is very familiar with the business of holding positions based on reasons that (a) he or she finds convincing but that (b) leave many apparently rational people unconvinced. Most of us aren't too troubled by this as regards moral and political issues—why not religious issues too? Which leads to my next point.

Third, beware of a double standard in the area of religion. It is common for people to demand a higher standard of reasoning in religion than they do with regard to other areas of controversy, such as morality and politics. I suspect that this double standard is a major source of religious skepticism.[1]

Fourth, even if reasoning cannot fully settle an issue, we may nevertheless by reasoning come to understand the issue much better. The various alternative answers may become clearer, we may be able to construct a kind of "conceptual map" of the intellectual territory, we may unmask certain tempting errors, and we may be able to see that one or more answers really do not stand up well under scrutiny. In short, we can make progress in our thinking even when we cannot settle an issue.

An illustration may be helpful here. In a democracy, there will normally be a national debate before the country goes to war. And surely it is important that such debates take place. But do those entering such debates (for or against war) suppose that their arguments will convince all rational people? Only very naïve persons would make that assumption. Nevertheless, such debates are not useless; they serve to make the pros and cons explicit, to identify key points of agreement and disagreement, to highlight areas of uncertainty, to sort out central and peripheral arguments, and so on. But if we think a consideration of arguments, pro and con, is important in the case of going to war, what should we say about the case of our ultimate commitments in life? Even if we think it's unlikely that arguments for or against God's existence will settle the issue, in so important a matter shouldn't we at least try to discover what the main arguments are and to weigh them carefully? I think we should if we are able to and more pressing duties do not require our attention.[2]

Before taking up the issue of God's existence, another key preliminary matter requires our attention. In the course of our discussions, we will frequently encounter a certain type of argument, what philosophers call an **argument-to-the-best-explanation**. This type of argument is fairly common but is often misunderstood, and some clarifications are in order before we plunge into deep waters.

In an argument-to-the-best-explanation, there is a description of a **phenomenon** or fact to be explained. The argument proceeds by giving reasons for supposing that one hypothesis explains the phenomenon better than rival hypotheses do. Here's an example.

> **Phenomenon**: My TV is missing from my apartment. The door to my apartment is wide open, and the lock is broken. My apartment has been "trashed." Earlier today, Clarence Busby (a person unknown to me) was seen standing on a ladder, looking into the front window of my apartment. The police have found my TV in Busby's car.

Many hypotheses could be put forward to explain this phenomenon. Let's consider just three (H here stands for "hypothesis"):

H1: Busby stole my TV.
H2: A friend borrowed my TV.
H3: Busby, assisted by poltergeists, stole my TV.

How do we determine which of these hypotheses is the best? We have to ask two main questions. First, "If we temporarily assume the hypotheses to be true, do they do an equally good job of *leading us to expect* the phenomenon? Do some of the hypotheses, assuming they are true, make the phenomenon *more likely* or *less surprising* than others?" This is the question of **explanatory power**—we are asking how *probable* the phenomenon is *on the condition (or assumption) that* each hypothesis is true. For example, compare H1 and H2. The phenomenon is just what we would expect if Busby stole my TV (i.e., if H1 is true). But if a friend borrowed my TV, would we expect the lock to be broken and the apartment to be "trashed"? No, those aren't actions typical of a friend. Also, if we assume H2 is true, we're not led to expect that the TV will be in Busby's car. Of course, it's *possible* that a friend of mine has decided to play a bizarre practical joke and so has borrowed my TV and put it in Busby's car, but in the absence of further evidence that seems unlikely. So H1 seems to do a better job of leading us to expect the phenomenon than does H2.

How about H3? If we assume H3 is true, does it lead us to expect the phenomenon? *Yes, it leads us to expect the phenomenon just as well as H1 does.* But surely the clause regarding poltergeists somehow makes H3 inferior to H1. This points us to the second main question we need to ask when comparing hypotheses: "*Prior* to considering the phenomenon, how probable are the hypotheses? That is, leaving aside any support the phenomenon gives to the hypotheses, what is their relative likelihood?" Logicians refer to this as the *prior probability* of the hypotheses. The **prior probability** of a hypothesis is its probability *independent of (or apart from)* the facts referred to as "the phenomenon." In other words, to compare the prior probability of two hypotheses, you ask how likely they are without taking the phenomenon in question into account.

The prior probability of the hypotheses is evaluated in terms of the background evidence. The **background evidence** consists of *whatever can reasonably be assumed in the context other than the phenomenon*. In our example that would include such things as physical generalizations (e.g., "TVs don't simply evaporate"), facts about human behavior (e.g., "Burglary is not uncommon"), and principles of logic. Presumably, the background evidence provides no support for "Poltergeists sometimes assist burglars." And at least partly for this reason, H3 has a significantly lower prior probability than H1 does.

According to many philosophers, the background evidence, properly understood, includes the **Principle of Simplicity**, which says that, when comparing two hypotheses, *other things being equal*, the simpler hypothesis is more probably true. (Put negatively, the principle says that, when two hypotheses are otherwise equal, the more complicated hypothesis is less probable.) We will discuss the Principle of Simplicity in detail in Chapter 1. But intuitively, "Busby, assisted by poltergeists, stole my TV" is a more complicated hypothesis than "Busby stole my TV." So, if we include the Principle of Simplicity in the background evidence, we have an added reason to prefer the latter hypothesis.

Arguments-to-the-best-explanation come in more than one form. To argue that H1 ("Busby stole the TV") is superior to H2 ("A friend borrowed the TV"), we might use this form:

**Premise 1**. In regard to their prior probability, H1 and H2 are equal. (On the basis of the *background evidence*, we have no good reason to regard one as more likely than the other.)

**Premise 2**. H1 does a *much* better job of leading us to expect the phenomenon than H2 does.

**Conclusion**: H1 explains the phenomenon better than H2 does (hence the phenomenon is evidence that favors H1 over H2).

Note that one premise makes a claim about the *prior probability* of the two hypotheses, while the other premise makes a claim about their *explanatory power*. (Of course, each premise would have to be defended with detailed arguments, and I have not provided such a defense. I am merely illustrating the general strategy involved in this type of argument.) The foregoing argument illustrates the following principle: If two hypotheses are equal in their prior probability but differ in their explanatory power, then the one with greater explanatory power is the better hypothesis.[3]

To argue that H1 is superior to H3 ("Busby, assisted by poltergeists, stole my TV"), we might use a slightly different form of argument-to-the-best-explanation:

**Premise 1**. H1 does as good a job of leading us to expect the phenomenon as H3 does.

**Premise 2**. The prior probability of H1 is significantly greater than the prior probability of H3.

**Conclusion**: H1 explains the phenomenon better than H3 does (hence the phenomenon is evidence that favors H1 over H3).

Again, one premise concerns the prior probabilities of the two hypotheses, and the other premise concerns their explanatory power. This argument illustrates the following principle: If two hypotheses are equal in explanatory power but differ in their prior probability, then the one with the higher prior probability is better.

Arguments-to-the-best-explanation naturally provoke a number of questions. First, couldn't a hypothesis be the best available explanation (in the terms indicated by the premises) and yet be false? After all, as I just noted, it's at least *possible* that Busby didn't steal the TV and that the phenomenon is *correctly* explained by the activities of a friend playing a rather extreme practical joke. Indeed, even if a true hypothesis is among those being considered, the available information regarding prior probabilities and explanatory power might lead us *reasonably* to conclude that some false hypothesis is best. Moreover, we can never have an absolute guarantee that a true hypothesis appears among the hypotheses we are considering. And the history of science abundantly illustrates this point. For example, prior to Walter Reed's famous experiments in 1900, virtually no one had considered the possibility that mosquitoes transmit yellow fever.[4]

So we can conceivably be right in arguing that a certain hypothesis is the best among known rivals, and still that hypothesis might be false. Unfortunately, this sometimes happens in courts of law. Perhaps at the time of the trial "The defendant is guilty" is the best available hypothesis. New evidence might change the picture entirely and point to a hypothesis that was not even considered at the time of the trial (e.g., the very respectable twin brother of the defendant, whom no one suspected at the time of the trial, is guilty of the crime). This underscores the need for intellectual humility when deploying arguments-to-the-best-explanation, but it's not a good reason to dismiss all such arguments as weak; they are often quite strong and are commonly used in science as well as in daily life.

Here's a second question about arguments-to-the-best-explanation: "Such arguments only give us reason to prefer one hypothesis over another, but we can go on producing hypotheses to explain any phenomenon *indefinitely*. For example, as regards the 'missing TV phenomenon,' we can easily add new hypotheses to our earlier list:

H4: Busby, assisted by a corrupt policeman, stole the TV.
H5: Extraterrestrials removed the TV.
H6: In hopes of collecting some insurance money, I removed the TV and put it in Busby's car.

Since there seems to be no end of hypotheses, how can we ever have any assurance that we've identified the best hypothesis? Furthermore, if so many hypotheses can be formulated in connection with a relatively simple matter, such as a missing TV, how many hypotheses would need to be considered where the deep and complex issues of philosophy are concerned?"

I do not think, however, that the number of possible hypotheses should deter us. For each of the major questions of philosophy, after some dialogue, two or three main positions usually emerge as far more plausible than the others. At least that's how most philosophers tend to see it. True, there are usually numerous possible *variations* on the two or three main positions; but the primary objects of interest are those main positions. Of course, there's still plenty to get confused about in philosophy. But I don't think we need to see philosophy as just a hopelessly long list of more or less equally plausible positions. Far from it.

Here's a third question that the use of arguments-to-the-best-explanation may provoke: "Can everything be explained in a scientific fashion? And is that being assumed if we approach the issue of God's existence via arguments-to-the-best-explanation?" I certainly do not assume that everything can be explained scientifically. **Scientific explanations** are given in terms of laws of nature. (That's an oversimplification, but it will do for present purposes.) A **law of nature** is a *generalization about the behavior of physical objects*. For example, a scientist might explain the path of a falling object in terms of Newton's law of gravity or explain the presence of ice by appealing to the law that water freezes at 32° Fahrenheit. But there seems to be at least two other fundamental types of explanation. Let me try to characterize them briefly.

**Personal explanations** are given in terms of the beliefs, purposes, powers, and choices of agents. (An *agent* is an entity who can perform actions.) For example, the oven is turned on because I had the purpose of baking cookies, I believed that turning the oven on was a means to this end, I had the power to turn the oven on, and I chose to turn it on.

It's a matter of debate whether scientific explanations can (in principle) replace personal explanations. I think the answer is no, but this is a complex issue. Key questions include: "Can science fully explain mental phenomena, such as beliefs and purposes? Can free choices be fully explained in terms of laws of nature?" These are fun questions, but big ones and tough ones.[5]

**Conceptual explanations**—very common in philosophy—are given in terms of necessary connections between properties or propositions. Such necessary connections can be expressed as necessary truths. A **necessary truth** is one that cannot be false under any possible circumstances. For example, "No circles are squares," "Nothing can be red all over and blue all over at the same time," "Whatever has a color has some size," and (in my opinion) "It is always wrong to torture a person for fun." The opposite of a necessary truth is a **contingent truth**, i.e., a proposition that is true but could have been false under different circumstances. For example, "I exist" is a contingent truth; it is actually true but it would have been false (I assume) if my parents had never met. And since "I exist" could have been false, it is not a necessary truth.

So I'm suggesting that there are three fundamentally different types of explanations: scientific, personal, and conceptual. I believe we need all three types of explanation in order to develop a comprehensive understanding of the world and of our place in it. Accordingly, by offering arguments-to-the-best-explanation, I am not assuming that the best explanation is always scientific in nature.

Here's a fourth question that may be provoked by the use of arguments-to-the-best-explanation, especially when the nature of ultimate reality is at issue: "Is it possible to explain everything?" I don't think that any theory or hypothesis can explain everything. Suppose we explain A in terms of B, B in terms of C, and C in terms of D, and so on. *In the end, we have to get back to some definite hypothesis, which will involve the claim that some object or objects have such and such properties, and for this we will have no explanation.* In short, we have to acknowledge something as ultimate in our attempt to explain as much as we possibly can.

Let us consider one last question about the use of arguments-to-the-best-explanation: "Does it make sense to argue that the existence of God is the best explanation of any phenomenon? What sense does it make to appeal to the existence of God to explain something when the question is, 'Does God exist?'" Let me answer this question a bit indirectly. Do you believe that subatomic particles such as electrons and quarks exist? Would you at least agree that it's reasonable to believe that such entities exist? (I assume you would answer yes to one or both of these questions.) Well, electrons and quarks cannot be seen. They cannot be directly observed at all. But by postulating or hypothesizing that such entities exist, physicists can explain many things that can be seen or observed. Philosophers of science call these types of entities *theoretical entities* because the only evidence for their existence is the fact that, if we assume they exist, we get the best explanation of a wide range of physical phenomena. In outline form, the argument for the existence of quarks would go something like this:

**Premise 1.** The existence of quarks has a low prior probability, but not so low as to justify our dismissing it outright.

**Premise 2.** Physical theories involving quarks do a very good job of leading us to expect a wide range of physical phenomena, far better than known or conceivable alternatives.

**Conclusion**: Physical theories involving quarks explain the relevant phenomena much better than the alternatives do (and hence are more likely true).

This is just an outline, of course, but the main point is that, even though there is no *direct* empirical evidence for quarks and electrons, it is reasonable to believe that they exist. Put simply, it is reasonable to believe that they exist because, if we assume they do, we get far and away the best explanation of a wide range of physical phenomena.

Similarly, theists may hold that if we assume God exists, we get the best explanation of a wide range of phenomena. The phenomena here are the raw materials out of which theistic arguments have often been constructed down through history: the very existence of physical reality, the fact that the universe supports life, the presence of beings (such as humans) who have moral responsibilities, and so on.

This introduction would not be complete without an explanation of two structural features of the work. First, unlike most books in the philosophy of religion, this one constantly compares two large-scale metaphysical hypotheses: Theism and Naturalism. I'll describe these views in detail in Chapter 1, but speaking in very rough terms, Theism is the view that an almighty and perfectly good God exists, while Naturalism is the view that physical reality is the ultimate reality (there is no God). As I see it, these are the leading, major metaphysical hypotheses of our time. We will need to consider other views on occasion, but these views will be the main focus of attention.

Why compare Theism and Naturalism? Why not simply set forth arguments for God's existence, as is customary? Because philosophy is inherently a comparative enterprise. Few if any important philosophical positions are problem free. Put negatively, one is looking for the view with the fewest or least pressing problems. Put positively, one is looking for the view that holds up best under scrutiny. For this reason, in a discussion of God's existence, it is helpful to compare Theism constantly with the most defensible alterative available. Philosophers can (and do) raise objections to all philosophical positions. And most any position can be made to look implausible if one dwells on its difficulties without considering the difficulties of its rivals. To assess the true strength of any philosophical position, we need to consider whether alternative views fare better over a relevant range of challenges.

The second main structural feature of this work is that it takes the form of a correspondence. I hope this makes the present work a bit easier to read than the typical philosophy book, but misunderstandings are apt to occur if nothing is said about the correspondents, Thomas and Zachary. Thomas and Zachary were roommates in their university days. They got along well and were constantly discussing all sorts of issues in politics, art, ethics, and religion. Thomas, a computer science major, is now a computer programmer in mid-career. Zachary, a philosophy major, went on to study philosophy at the graduate level and now teaches at a university in the United States. For some time, work schedules and geography kept the friends apart, but about five years ago Thomas initiated a correspondence on an issue that had been on his mind for some time: the existence of God. During the intervening years, the correspondence grew into the wide-ranging discussion you find on the pages that follow.

CHAPTER 1

# Theism and Naturalism

Dear Zachary,

I know it has been a long time since you've heard from me—much too long! But I think of you often and often wish I could talk with you. I miss our discussions and regret that we live so far apart.

I've decided to write you some letters. If you don't have time to reply, I'll understand. But, to make a long story short, I've been doing a lot of thinking about religion lately—more specifically, about the existence of God. And I'm not too happy with the thoughts I've been having. They seem disorganized and muddled. To be honest, I don't know where to start.

Recently it occurred to me that I should write my old friend Zach! He's been teaching courses in philosophy for some years now, and he can probably help me put my thoughts into some sort of order! Hence this letter.

My basic question is simply this: "Are there any good reasons to believe that God exists?" If you have any time to write, I'd love to hear your thoughts on that subject. (In case you're wondering, as things stand I don't believe there's a God, but I'm not exactly an atheist. I'm just not sure what to think.)

I hope things are going well.

Your friend,
Thomas

Dear Thomas,

Good to hear from you! I too wish we didn't live so far apart. I certainly welcome your letters and will gladly respond as best I can.

I see philosophy as very much an exercise in comparing views. To evaluate the strengths and weaknesses of a view, we have to keep in mind its rivals—some of them at least. So what do you see as the main *positive* alternative to the belief that God exists? I mean, if we deny that God exists, what should we affirm? I'm just asking for your opinion.

I hope this note finds you in good health and good spirits.

All my best,
Zach

Dear Zach,

I'm not sure I understand your question. If there's no God, I guess the fundamental reality is the physical universe. We humans evolved from simpler forms of life by means of purely natural causes. Our lives are difficult and we need help from others; so we live together in groups. But we can't live together in groups without rules, such as "Don't kill," "Don't steal," and "Don't lie." We call those rules "ethics." Death is inevitable. There is no life after death, so whatever fulfillment we obtain must be obtained prior to death.

Is that the sort of thing you had in mind?

—Thomas

Dear Thomas,

Yes, exactly. You've described a version of what philosophers call Naturalism, which, very roughly, is the idea that the fundamental reality is physical reality operating via entirely natural causes (there is no God or any other supernatural agency). We agree, then, that Naturalism is one of the main rivals of Theism (the belief that God exists). I happen to think that Naturalism is *the* leading (i.e., most defensible) alternative to Theism. Perhaps, then, our first task is to describe both Theism and Naturalism more clearly and precisely.

Once we've got clear and explicit formulations of Theism and Naturalism, we can begin to compare them. These views offer competing explanations of many things, such as the existence of the universe, the existence of a universe that supports life, the moral life (or aspects thereof), and suffering. One crucial question, then, is which of these two views provides the best explanation of these features of the world and of human life?

—Zach

Dear Zach,

Sounds like a reasonable way to proceed, although I'm not sure we need to spend much time formulating Theism and Naturalism. These views are pretty familiar, aren't they?

—Thomas

Dear Thomas,

I believe that many discussions of Theism and Naturalism get derailed because of insufficient clarity about exactly what's involved in each of them. There's a tendency for people to "read things into" both views. And if we are going to treat these views as explanatory hypotheses, it's very important to be explicit and clear about their content.

That reminds me. I've written up some lecture notes on what philosophers call "arguments-to-the-best-explanation." I believe this type of argument is crucial for an evaluation of Theism and Naturalism. The principle underlying such arguments is that the best explanation of some phenomenon is probably true. Most of the work in advancing an argument-to-the-best-explanation comes in arguing that one explanation is best (or better than some salient alternative). I'll send you my lecture notes—I think they'll help you understand why I think it's important to begin with explicit formulations of Theism and Naturalism.[1]

Now I'm going to forge ahead and spell out the claim or hypothesis that God exists. I'll call it the *theistic hypothesis* or *Theism*.

> **Theism**: (1) There is exactly one entity that is (2) perfectly morally good and (3) almighty and that (4) exists of necessity.

Some clarifying comments are in order.

*Exactly one entity.* Judaism, Christianity, and Islam are monotheistic religions. In accord with these traditions, our theistic hypothesis postulates one God rather than many.

*Perfectly morally good.* If God is morally good, then God is a personal entity. A personal entity is one who has beliefs, purposes, and the power to make choices. And if God is *perfectly* morally good, then God has the moral virtues of wisdom, love, and justice. If God is wise, then God knows what is important and how to achieve it. If God is loving, then God cares about the long-term best interests of any persons he creates. If God is just, then God will act in accord with certain moral principles; e.g., God will not fail to keep any promises he makes.

*Almighty.* An almighty entity is one that has maximal power, but I assume that maximal power has logical limits; e.g., it does not include the power to make contradictions true. For example, can God make himself both exist and not exist at the same time? Or *force* a person to lie while making her tell the lie *freely*? Or remain perfectly good while breaking a promise to his creatures? Surely not. At least since the time of Aquinas, this understanding of God's power has been typical among Christian theologians and philosophers. Furthermore, in the present context, in which we are thinking of Theism as an attempt to *explain* certain things, it would obviously be a liability to suggest that God can make contradictions true—a hypothesis containing that feature is too confusing to explain anything.[2]

*Exists of necessity.* If God exists of necessity, then the entity who is God cannot fail to exist under any possible circumstances. So if God exists of necessity, God is eternal. Philosophers and theologians have differing views of divine eternality. The most common interpretations of "God is eternal" are (a) God is everlasting and (b) God is timeless. God is everlasting if God existed at each past moment, exists now, and will exist at each future moment. God is timeless if there is no sequence, no "before and after," in the divine life. It is of course a matter of debate among Theists whether God is everlasting or timeless, but for present purposes we need not be detained by this "family quarrel."

Let me know if this is unclear, OK?

—Zach

Dear Zach,

Thanks for sending along the lecture notes on arguments-to-the-best-explanation. I'll read them as soon as possible.

In regard to your formulation of the theistic hypothesis, aren't you taking a lot for granted? We want to find out what God is like, if there is a God, right—as opposed to assuming we know what God is like in advance? In short, doesn't your formulation of Theism **beg the question**, i.e., assume the point to be proved?

—Thomas

Dear Thomas,

In my last letter I was formulating a specific theistic hypothesis. I was describing the content of the hypothesis, *not claiming to know that the hypothesis is true*. If we are going to consider Theism as a hypothesis, we have to have something definite to consider, as opposed to a vague idea. Obviously, a vague hypothesis isn't going to explain much of anything.

So in my last letter I was not making claims about what God is really like. Instead, I was spelling out the central elements of Theism as traditionally understood by Christians, Jews, and Muslims. OK?

—Zach

Dear Zach,

OK, but if you are trying to describe traditional Western Theism, it seems to me that you've left out some key points. For example, you didn't mention that God is all-knowing or omniscient. And you didn't mention that God is not a physical entity.

—Thomas

Dear Thomas,

You are of course right to say that God is traditionally regarded as both omniscient and nonphysical. But I think that both of these attributes are implied by the claim that God is almighty (together with some relevant background evidence). Let me explain.

First, a maximally powerful being must be extremely knowledgeable, for *knowledge is a form of power*. And this being so, a maximally powerful being knows all propositions that can be known. We can underscore this point with what I call a "philosophical cartoon." Imagine a true/false quiz that includes all propositions (except for any whose truth or falsity is absolutely unknowable—I'll explain the restriction momentarily). Either a being can infallibly obtain a perfect score on the quiz or it cannot. If it cannot, then it is not *maximally* powerful, for we can readily describe a being that would have more power (in the sense of being able to *do* more), namely, one that *can* infallibly score "perfect" on the quiz.

Now, why do I say that a maximally powerful being would know all propositions *that can be known* instead of simply "all true propositions"? How could a true proposition be unknowable to a maximally powerful being? In a nutshell, the answer is this: Propositions such as "An infallible being foreknows that Al Bloggs will *freely* lie at noon next Friday" may imply a contradiction. Many philosophers, including many who are Theists, claim that if God has infallible foreknowledge of future human acts, then the acts cannot be free. Suppose God believes today that Bloggs will lie at noon next Friday. Then if Bloggs has the power (next Friday, at noon) to refrain from lying, Bloggs apparently has the power to make God's belief false—but that can't be if God is infallible. As a corollary, if any human acts are truly free, then God cannot infallibly foreknow that they will occur. But note that, by saying that a maximally powerful being would know all propositions *that can be known*, we avoid getting bogged down in this issue, for if an infallible being *can* know future free acts, the description still works.[3]

Second, a maximally powerful entity will be nonphysical, since an entity counts as physical only if it is governed by laws of nature (such as the law of gravity); and a maximally powerful entity is not governed by the laws of nature. Some clarifying comments about the laws of nature are needed here.

- Strictly speaking, laws of nature are generalizations about (i.e., statements describing) the behavior of physical objects. But presumably these laws are grounded in the powers (or capacities) of physical entities, such as the negative charge of an electron. These powers are specific and have limits. So when I say that a maximally powerful being is not governed by laws of nature, I am speaking a bit loosely; the point is that a maximally powerful being is not limited by the *powers* of physical entities. And "Physical objects are governed by laws of nature" is shorthand for "The behavior of physical objects occurs within limits set by the inherent powers of the fundamental physical entities (whatever those are)."

- Traditionally—at least in the West—God is regarded as the creator of the physical universe: God brought physical entities into existence and endowed them with the powers they have. God is also traditionally regarded as able to perform miracles, such as raising a person from the dead, and miracles are events that cannot be produced by merely natural causes. (Laws of nature tell us what happens when only natural causes are operative; they do not tell us what happens if and when supernatural causes are operative.) So if our theistic hypothesis is to reflect a traditional Western understanding of God, then a maximally powerful being must be able to create physical reality, endow it with the powers by which it normally functions, and also work miracles.[4]

- Laws of nature are not laws of logic. A maximally powerful being can create a physical system that normally operates in accordance with laws of nature and yet can intervene in that system on occasion, i.e., work miracles. But a maximally powerful being cannot produce events or situations that are contrary to the laws of logic. To illustrate, a maximally powerful being can enable a person to walk on the surface of a lake; but a maximally powerful being cannot cause a person to walk on the surface of a lake *while simultaneously* not walking on its surface. Most philosophers assume that events contrary to (true) laws of logic simply cannot occur; they are absolutely impossible. My characterization of an almighty or maximally powerful being accords with this assumption.[5]

To sum up, in formulating the Theistic hypothesis, I did not explicitly mention that God is omniscient and nonphysical. But for the reasons I've just given, I think these attributes are implicit in God's almightiness (together with relevant background evidence), and if that's correct, there is no need to make explicit mention of these attributes in formulating the Theistic hypothesis.

—Zach

Dear Zach,

You have formulated Theism as follows: "There is exactly one entity that is perfectly morally good, almighty, and exists of necessity." But every clause in your definition of Theism reminds me of how many different God hypotheses there are. For example, there might be many gods, God might be morally imperfect, less than almighty, and so on. Don't these rival forms of Theism complicate matters?

—Thomas

Dear Thomas,

Yes, and we'll have to consider these rival forms of Theism whenever they are relevant. But—and I think we agree here—for those of us living in a culture heavily influenced by science, the most serious rival to traditional Theism is probably not some other form of Theism, but Naturalism. The really big metaphysical dispute of the day, in our culture, is surely the dispute between traditional Theism and Naturalism. So I think that the rivalry between Theism and Naturalism should be our central concern.

—Zach

Dear Zach,

I agree that what you call Naturalism is an important view; indeed, I sometimes find it *very* attractive. At this point I suppose we need an explicit formulation of Naturalism to compare with our formulation of Theism. How exactly would you state the naturalistic hypothesis?

—Thomas

Dear Thomas,

I think Naturalism can be boiled down to three key theses:

**Naturalism**: (1) There is a self-organizing physical reality (i.e., there is a physical reality whose nature is not imposed by a god or by any other force or agent), (2) physical reality exists either necessarily, eternally, or by chance, and (3) leaving aside possible special cases (see later), all entities are physical entities.

Again, some clarifying comments are in order.

*There is a self-organizing physical reality.* What is meant by the word
*physical*? Its meaning has been stretched over the history of science. As Thomas Nagel remarks,

> New properties are counted as physical if they are discovered by
> explanatory inference from those already in the class. This re-
> peated process starts from a base of familiar, observable spatio-
> temporal phenomena and proceeds to take in mass, force, kinetic
> energy, charge, valence, gravitational and electromagnetic fields,
> quantum states, antiparticles, strangeness, charm, and whatever
> physics will bring us next.[6]

Definitions of *physical* are controversial. I think the following partial
characterization will be adequate for our purposes. Start by thinking
about subatomic particles such as electrons and protons. These particles have certain built-in tendencies to behave in relation to each
other (and to other physical particles). When certain conditions are
met, the built-in tendencies of an electron are triggered and the electron behaves automatically, mechanistically (e.g., it circles the nucleus of the atom). In saying that electrons behave **mechanistically**, I
mean that *they do not act with a purpose or make free choices; their built-
in (or inherent) tendencies are deterministic or probabilistic in nature.*
(That's why scientists can describe their behavior in terms of those
generalizations we call laws of nature.) Now, I suggest that if an entity is **physical**, then either (a) it is composed entirely of entities
whose only built-in tendencies are mechanistic or (b) if it is a fundamental entity (i.e., one not composed of others), then its only built-in
tendencies are mechanistic.[7]

The idea that physical reality is *self-organizing* is the heart of the
Naturalistic hypothesis. I have already noted that physical things
have inherent (or built-in) tendencies. But according to the Naturalist, these inherent tendencies are not bestowed or imposed from
without by a god (or by any other nonphysical force or agent);
rather, it is simply the nature of physical reality to be organized.

*Physical reality exists either necessarily, eternally, or by chance.* Naturalists must have some explanation for the existence of physical reality and I will just leave the options open at this point. They could
say that physical reality in its entirety popped into existence uncaused. They could say that physical reality (in some form or
through various phases) is eternal and without beginning. Or
they could say that physical reality exists of necessity, i.e., could
not fail to exist. (Of course, if physical reality exists of necessity,
then it is eternal. But if it's eternal, it doesn't follow that it exists of

necessity. Conceivably, something could be eternal even though it *could* fail to exist.)

*Leaving aside possible special cases, all entities are physical entities.* There are no nonphysical agents, e.g., souls or gods, according to the Naturalist. Some Naturalists think that sets and numbers are nonphysical objects, but with the understanding that these entities cannot cause events.

Let me add here one point of contrast between Theism and Naturalism. For Theism, personal explanation is more ultimate than scientific explanation, in this sense: The factors involved in scientific explanation are due to God's creative activity; that is, God creates the physical universe and it is due to God that physical reality behaves in those patterned ways that can be formulated as laws of nature. Thus, the factors involved in scientific explanations are themselves susceptible to personal explanation, given Theism.

Naturalism reverses this picture: Scientific explanation is more ultimate than personal explanation. We explain that the oven is on because Fred chose to turn it on. But we can explain the very existence of Fred (i.e., of human beings in general) by way of evolutionary theory, and evolution is a process governed by laws of nature. So the presence of persons is to be explained by way of a more ultimate, scientific explanation. Many Naturalists would add that this scientific explanation needs to be accompanied by a philosophical (conceptual) explanation of the specifically mental factors, e.g., purposes, desires, and choices. But the point, again, is that scientific explanation accounts (fully or partially) for the very presence of the factors involved in personal explanation—and not the other way round.

More radically, many Naturalists hold that human behavior itself can be *fully* explained in terms of laws of nature, so we could *in principle* do without personal explanations—for there is always a deeper, scientific explanation of why people behave as they do. We'll have to consider this type of Naturalism in due course.

I must stop here for today.

—Zach

Dear Zach,

Naturalism seems to be a very "natural" position for scientists to take. Are scientists always (or at least typically) Naturalists?

—Thomas

Dear Thomas,

Many scientists are in fact Theists. To cite some famous historical figures: Newton, Mendel, Faraday, Asa Gray, Planck, and Maxwell.

One study I've seen states that, in 1996, about 42% of American biologists and 29% of American physicists believed that God exists.[8]

It is true, however, that science can increase the credibility of Naturalism. For example, before Darwin developed his theory of evolution, Naturalists were hard put to explain the extraordinary diversity of forms of life on earth. Darwin's theory provided an explanation of the diversity of life in terms of purely natural causes. Thus, Darwin's theory increased the explanatory power of Naturalism. It's not that Darwin's theory disproves Theism, of course. Indeed, many Theists accept Darwin's theory. But Darwin's theory gave Naturalists a credible explanation where previously they had had only rather dubious speculations.

It *is* extremely important to distinguish Naturalism from science. Confusion can occur here because most scientists, including scientists who are Theists, are **methodological naturalists**. This simply means that, *when doing science*, they leave theological factors out of account. In other words, most scientists think of science as an attempt to explain things in terms of natural as opposed to supernatural factors (such as God, angels, miracles). I hope it's clear that Naturalism as I've defined it is distinct from methodological Naturalism. *Methodological Naturalism is a thesis about how science should be conducted, while Naturalism is a metaphysical position—a view about what's real.* And note that Naturalism involves many claims that cannot be verified scientifically. For instance, no scientific experiment could possibly show that the inherent tendencies of physical entities are *not* put there by God. And we cannot determine via observation that all entities are physical. We may by observation discover that a particular physical object is present at a certain location or that it is not present, but such observations could not show that nonphysical entities—e.g., souls, gods, or angels—don't exist. Naturalism is clearly a philosophical position, not a scientific theory.

—Zach

Dear Zach,

All right. We now have explicit formulations of both Theism and Naturalism. Our next step, I take it, is to consider which of these hypotheses *best* explains certain phenomena. And I have now read several times the lecture notes you sent me: To determine that one hypothesis is better than another, we need to compare their *prior* probability as well as their explanatory power. But how can we determine the prior probability of Naturalism relative to Theism? To be honest, when I consider that question, I "draw a blank."

—Thomas

Dear Thomas,

Good question—the answer is of course controversial!

Remember that prior probabilities are determined with reference to whatever background evidence is available, that is, what can reasonably be assumed other than the facts referred to as "the phenomenon" (i.e., what we are trying to explain). What sorts of phenomena are Theism and Naturalism supposed to explain? Here's a partial list.

1. *The presence of contingent beings*: A **contingent being** is an entity that actually exists but might not have existed. A vast number of entities seem to fall into this category. For example, humans in general would seem to be contingent beings. (Had one's parents never met, one presumably would never have come into existence at all. And it is not logically necessary that one's parents should ever meet; e.g., they might have died in infancy.) Indeed, most things we know of come into existence at some point. And unless the processes that bring such things into existence are logically necessary, those processes might not have occurred, and so, presumably, the entities in question might not have existed.

2. *The appearance of design in the world*: Our universe supports life. But scientists tell us that many precisely specifiable factors must be present in order for life (as we know it) to exist. Just to cite one of many examples: If the force of gravity were weaker or stronger by one part in $10^{40}$, stars could not exist and so there would be no Sun. In short, it *looks as if* our universe were designed to support life.

3. *The presence of consciousness*: Our world contains beings that have mental states, such as desires, beliefs, purposes, intentions, volitions, sensations, pains, and pleasures.

4. *The presence of morality*: Our world seems to include moral value and moral agents—a kind of moral structure.

5. *The apparent presence of moral and natural evil in the world*: Moral evil is the wrongdoing for which humans are responsible *and* the suffering (and loss) that results from it. Natural evil is the suffering (and loss) due to nonhuman causes, e.g., earthquakes, disease, tornadoes, animal attacks.

This brief, partial description of the phenomena vividly raises the question of the prior probabilities of Theism and Naturalism. What sort of background evidence can we appeal to? Both hypotheses are trying to explain very general, pervasive features of the world, so what counts as background evidence? Such evidence cannot of course presuppose the phenomena one is trying to explain. Let me try to describe the main categories of background evidence.

1. The principles of logic are part of the background evidence. These principles will assign a low prior probability to any hypothesis with *internal* logical deficiencies. Such internal deficiencies can occur in two ways: First, when the statements within the hypothesis are logically inconsistent; second, when some statement within a hypothesis is *improbable* given some other statement(s) in the hypothesis. The principles of logic won't take us too far with regard to the issue of prior probability, but they do enable us to eliminate immediately a host of logically deficient hypotheses that might otherwise bog us down.

2. Mathematical truths, if known, are part of the background evidence. Again, this won't take us too far, but it enables us to eliminate any hypotheses that involve mathematical absurdities.

3. Necessary truths are part of the background evidence—or, more accurately, what are *reasonably taken to be* necessary truths. (Recall that necessary truths are ones that cannot be false in any possible circumstances.) Most philosophers regard the truths of math and logic as necessary, so 1 and 2 can be viewed as falling under the more general category of "truths reasonably taken to be necessary." But many necessary truths lie outside the realms of math and logic. And philosophical arguments very frequently employ such necessary truths. For example, formulations of the problem of evil often employ some version of the following premise: "If a perfectly good God exists, then there is no evil, *unless there is a reason that would justify God in permitting it.*"[9] The basic idea here is that a perfectly good God won't allow any evil without having a good reason for doing so. Theists as well as non-Theists usually accept that some such principle is necessary.

4. Well-confirmed scientific results will normally count as background evidence (assuming they do not presuppose the phenomenon in question). There is of course some vagueness here in the term *well-confirmed* as well as in the word *science*. As regards *science*, I'm here thinking primarily of the natural sciences, such as physics, chemistry, and biology. As regards the term *well-confirmed*, I have in mind roughly what would be presented as firmly established in reputable science textbooks, as opposed, for example, to what might be hypothesized by a scientist writing a speculative piece for *Scientific American*.

5. More generally, reasonable claims (that do not presuppose the phenomenon) can count as background evidence. Items belonging to so-called "common sense" (e.g., "There are physical objects," "There are people other than me") will normally count as

background evidence, as will many plausible and defensible philosophical claims. My use of "Knowledge is a form of power" in arguing that a maximally powerful entity would know all propositions that can be known is, I hope, a good example.

I'd like to take this a step further, but I've got to stop for now.

In haste,
Zach

Dear Zach,

OK, you made a list of phenomena, that is, a list of facts Theism and Naturalism try to explain. That gives me some idea of where you are headed. Also, you offered a partial breakdown of what counts as background evidence. The breakdown helps—it clears up a few questions I've had. But your last category, category 5, includes claims of common sense and "plausible and defensible" philosophical principles. That's a bit vague, isn't it?

—Thomas

Dear Thomas,

I agree that category 5 leaves a lot open, but I see no way to avoid that, short of laying down highly dubious rules of rationality. I think we just have to consider various claims as they turn up in the discussion and consider arguments for and against them. As I've said before, whether we are Theists or not, at the end of the day we cannot expect that all rational people will find our premises acceptable. I'm afraid we simply have to face that fact.

That said, our arguments will of course be more interesting as they show promise of appealing to a wide audience. Put negatively, the more an argument "preaches to the choir," i.e., is apt to appeal only to someone who already accepts the conclusion, the less interesting the argument will be, from a philosophical standpoint.

—Zach

Dear Zach,

Fair enough. But you said you'd like to go a "step further" in your discussion of background evidence—what did you have in mind?

—Thomas

Dear Thomas,

I think we can also reasonably include the Principle of Simplicity in our background evidence:

**The Principle of Simplicity**: When comparing two hypotheses, *other things being equal*, the simpler hypothesis is more probably true.

This principle is admittedly controversial, so, I must do some explaining here. Let me refer to the "missing TV case" in the lecture notes I sent you some time ago. (As you'll recall, my TV is missing, the door to my apartment has been forced open, and the police have located my TV in the car of a man named Clarence Busby.) Various hypotheses were considered as explanations for the missing TV, including these:

H1: Busby stole the TV.
H3: Busby, assisted by poltergeists, stole the TV.

Now, part of the problem with H3, relative to H1, is that it is very doubtful that poltergeists assist burglars. But there is another problem too, namely, that the clause regarding poltergeists is an unnecessary complication, for H1 does *just as good a job as* H3 does in leading us to expect the phenomenon of the missing TV. So the principle of simplicity tells us to prefer H1 in this case. Nothing about the phenomenon of the missing TV invites us to postulate poltergeists.

Yet another hypothesis will help us to isolate the role of simplicity:

H4: Busby, assisted by a corrupt policeman, stole the TV.

While I doubt that poltergeists ever assist burglars, I don't doubt that corrupt cops sometimes do. Nevertheless, nothing in the phenomenon suggests that there was an accomplice, so H4 is unnecessarily complicated. Hence, the Principle of Simplicity tells us to prefer H1 to H4. If we reject the Principle of Simplicity, what grounds would we have for regarding H1 as *more likely true* than H4? None, apparently.

For our purposes, I think we can identify four main **facets of simplicity**.[10]

1. *The number of things postulated*. Here's an example, borrowed from Richard Swinburne: The French astronomer Leverrier postulated *one* planet to explain irregularities in the orbit of Uranus; he didn't postulate two planets, or three, and so on. (Of course, Leverrier's hypothesis was later confirmed—we call the planet Neptune.)

2. *The number of* kinds *of things postulated*. For example, a physical theory that postulates three kinds of subatomic particles, e.g.,

electrons, protons, and neutrons, is simpler than a theory that postulates, say, thirty-three different kinds of subatomic particles.

3. *The simplicity of the terms.* A term used in a hypothesis is complex to the extent that *it can be understood only by someone who understands some other term(s).* For example, my dictionary defines *proton* as "an elementary particle that is identical with the nucleus of the hydrogen atom, that along with neutrons is a constituent of all other atomic nuclei, that carries a positive charge numerically equal to the charge of an electron, and that has a mass of $1.673 \times 10^{-24}$ gram."[11] Obviously, one has to understand many other terms in order to understand *proton,* e.g., *elementary particle, nucleus, atom, positive charge, mass,* and $10^{-24}$. Thus, *proton* is a very complex term. The point is not that it is bad to use complex terms; rather, we must take such complexity into account when evaluating the simplicity of a hypothesis. By the use of technical definitions, we can (intentionally or inadvertently) hide complex ideas within a term, thus making a hypothesis appear simpler than it is.

4. *The number of statements within a hypothesis that receive little or no probabilistic support from other statements contained in the hypothesis.* This facet is grounded in the rules of probability, in particular, in what is called the *general conjunction rule.* Roughly speaking, this rule ensures that the more one says, the more one is likely to say something false. So when we add statements to a hypothesis, we generally lower its prior probability. More precisely, if A and B stand for any statements, the *general conjunction rule* says this: The probability of the conjunction "A and B" equals the probability that A is true *times* the probability that (B is true *if* A is true).[12]

Bear with me for a moment. I think it will be useful to work through a couple of examples illustrating the general conjunction rule. To this end, note that probabilities are expressed as numbers between zero and 1. Zero is the lowest degree of probability; 1 is the highest. Logicians assign contradictions a probability of 0, while simple necessary truths, such as "No circles are squares," are assigned a probability of 1. And in order to be *more probable than not,* a statement must have a probability higher than ½ or .5.

*Example 1*: Suppose I hold four cards in my hand: an ace, a king, a queen, and a jack. Assuming you select one card at a time, *at random*, what is the probability that you will select the ace on the first draw AND the jack on the second draw? (Assume you *retain* the first card you draw—you do not put it back in my hand before making your second draw.) Your chances of selecting the ace on the first draw are 1 out of 4, that is, ¼, or .25. Your chances of selecting the jack on the second draw (if you drew the ace on the first draw) are 1 out of 3 (only three cards are left), that is, $\frac{1}{3}$, or about .33. So the probability of "You select the ace on the first draw AND the jack on the second draw" $= \frac{1}{4} \times \frac{1}{3} = \frac{1}{12}$. *The lesson here is that adding statements to a hypothesis can lower its prior probability substantially.*

*Example 2:* What's the probability of selecting the ace on the first draw AND the jack on the second draw *if you do not retain the first card you draw but put it back into my hand?* (Again, assume you draw the cards at random—no tricks!) Note that in this case the first draw has no effect on the second. So the probability of selecting the ace on the first draw is $\frac{1}{4}$, and the probability of selecting the jack on the second draw (given that you drew the ace on the first but put it back in my hand) is also $\frac{1}{4}$. The probability of "You select the ace on the first draw AND the jack on the second" is then $\frac{1}{4} \times \frac{1}{4}$, or $\frac{1}{16}$.

Taken together the two examples underscore an important point: *When a statement is added to a hypothesis, the less support the statement receives from statements already in the hypothesis, the more the statement will lower the prior probability of the hypothesis.* This principle will come in handy as we examine arguments for Theism. Of course we cannot normally assign precise numerical values, as we can in the case of the cards, but the general principle will still be useful.

—Zach


Dear Zach,

Whew! I find it a bit ironic that your letter on simplicity is so complicated! I do have a few questions. Let me start with this: Are there any exceptions to the principle that *when we add statements to a hypothesis, we lower its prior probability?*

—Thomas


Dear Thomas,

Yes, there are a couple of special cases. First, suppose the statement added to the hypothesis follows *necessarily* from statements already in the hypothesis. Then the probability of the hypothesis remains the same when the statement is added, for the statement added was already implicit in the hypothesis. Here's a trivial example: If my hypothesis includes the statement that an object is a cube, I can add the statement that the object is not a sphere without altering the probability of the hypothesis.[13]

Second, suppose the statement added to the hypothesis has a probability of 1 *independent* of the statements already in the hypothesis. (Remember that 1 is the highest probability value.) Then if we add the statement to the hypothesis, the prior probability of the hypothesis remains unchanged. For example, we can add simple necessary truths (such as, "No circles are squares") to a hypothesis without changing its probability.[14]

—Zach

Dear Zachary,

I think I understand the technical points well enough. But now I have a more philosophical question. Given that simplicity has multiple facets, couldn't a hypothesis be simple in terms of one facet and complex in terms of another? If so, where does that leave us?

—Thomas

Dear Thomas,

Good question. Because simplicity has multiple facets, there are many cases in which we cannot say which hypothesis is simpler, *all things considered*. Perhaps one hypothesis is simpler with regard to facet 1, while a rival hypothesis is simpler with regard to facet 2, leaving us with no way to settle which is simpler, *all things considered*.

But when we can see that one hypothesis is simpler than another, good theorists prefer the simpler one, *other things being equal*, and the history of science bears this out. Scientists do not clutter their hypotheses with unnecessary complications. Leverrier could have postulated two, three, or four planets to explain the irregularities in the orbit of Uranus, but he needed to postulate only one, and so he stuck with that.

Of course, "other things being equal" is a crucial qualification. We reject overly simple hypotheses because they do not lead us to expect the phenomenon. Or we may reject them because they fit poorly with some background evidence. But when two hypotheses (a) do an equally good job of leading us to expect the phenomenon and (b) otherwise fit equally well with the background evidence, then we naturally tend to prefer the simpler one. And in such circumstances the simpler hypothesis is *more likely to be true*, according to the Principle of Simplicity.

—Zach

Dear Zach,

I think something more fundamental is bothering me now. I realize that we all naturally prefer relatively simple hypotheses. But what gives us the right to suppose that reality is simple? Consider modern physics, with its complicated theories about subatomic particles.

Just a "simple" question!

—Thomas

Dear Thomas,

Simple, indeed! Your question lures us into deep territory.

Let me start by noting that your comment about the complex nature of subatomic physics suggests a possible misunderstanding. Simplicity is always relative. If physicists could find simpler hypotheses that explained *all* the relevant phenomena, no doubt they would prefer those simpler hypotheses. But the simplest hypotheses *that explain the phenomena* are sometimes very complicated— presumably because reality *is* sometimes very complicated. The Principle of Simplicity does not tell us that theories should be simplistic! It just tells us to avoid *unnecessary* complications in our theorizing. (You can test a scientist's respect for simplicity by taking a well-confirmed theory, adding an unnecessary complication to it, and getting the scientist's reaction.)

But why suppose that the simpler of two hypotheses is more likely to be *true*, other things being equal? I do not think we can prove the Principle of Simplicity. If we tried, our "proof" would probably wind up presupposing the principle, and thus our "proof" would beg the question. But again and again we find ourselves presupposing the Principle of Simplicity. (That's why we are baffled whenever someone suggests a hypothesis containing obviously unnecessary complications.) So I suspect the Principle of Simplicity is a basic principle of thought. There are many such basic principles. For example, most philosophers accept certain "principles of credulity," such as, "If it seems to me that I perceive that something (such as a tree or a dog) is present, it *probably* is present." (Such a principle says, in effect, that I should give my sense experience "the benefit of the doubt," i.e., that I should trust my sense experience in the absence of some specific reason not to.)[15] Radical skeptics do not accept such principles of credulity and instead demand positive proof of the reliability of sense experience. It is one of the lessons of philosophy in the modern period that such proofs are pretty clearly beyond our reach—attempted proofs typically commit the fallacy of begging the question (i.e., assuming the point to be proved).[16]

The following example may be useful, not in proving the Principle of Simplicity, but at least in evoking the intuition that it is correct. Suppose we are plotting the course of an asteroid. And let's suppose (however unrealistically) that the data falls into the following pattern, with $x$ being the location of the asteroid at one time and $y$ being the asteroid's location an hour later.

$$x = 0 \quad 1 \quad 2 \quad 3 \quad 4$$
$$y = 0 \quad 2 \quad 4 \quad 6 \quad 8$$

Now we can picture our "data" on a graph:

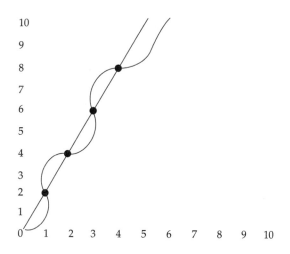

We can of course draw any number of lines through the points plotted on the graph. I've drawn two lines for illustration. The simplest line is a straight one that corresponds to the hypothesis $y = 2x$. The curved line fits perfectly with the data we have in hand, but it corresponds to a much more complicated formula.[17]

Now let's suppose that the simpler hypothesis, corresponding to the straight line, tells us that the asteroid will strike Cleveland, Ohio, while the other hypothesis, corresponding to the curved line, predicts that the asteroid will strike Columbus, Ohio. (Assume the asteroid will inflict great damage on a city but not on a wider area.) Further, suppose time is very limited and emergency medical supplies are limited, so we must focus our logistical efforts on one or the other of the cities, but not both. Shouldn't we focus our efforts on Cleveland, because that's where the asteroid will *probably* strike? So it seems to me. If you agree, then you see the plausibility of the Principle of Simplicity.

In any case, for the reasons given here, I think it is reasonable to include the Principle of Simplicity as part of the background evidence.

—Zach

Dear Zach,

The asteroid example is cute. I'm willing to adopt the Principle of Simplicity on a provisional basis. But if we accept the Principle of Simplicity, won't we have to assign Theism a lower prior probability than Naturalism? I think so, for at least four reasons.

First, Naturalism is simpler in terms of the first facet of simplicity, i.e., the number of things postulated, for Theists postulate an entity not found in the Naturalist's scheme, namely, God. But Naturalists don't postulate any entity whose existence is denied by Theists, for Theists fully accept the existence of the physical universe. Hence, Naturalism is simpler in terms of the first facet of simplicity.

Second, Naturalism is also simpler in terms of the second facet of simplicity, i.e., the number of *kinds* of things postulated. Two points here: (1) God is a *nonphysical person* or agent, and this is a *kind* of thing that does not appear in the Naturalist's scheme of things. As you mentioned earlier, even those Naturalists who accept the existence of nonphysical numbers or sets do not accept the existence of a nonphysical *agent or person*, who can cause events in the world. (2) Theists regard God as a *necessary* being, and that's another *kind* of thing that does not, or at least need not, appear in the Naturalists' scheme of things. (The second clause of Naturalism provides the *option* of postulating that physical reality exists of necessity, but I don't think many Naturalists go for that option.)

Third, Naturalism is simpler in terms of the third facet of simplicity, i.e., simplicity of terms. Naturalism employs no terms corresponding to *almighty* and *perfectly morally good*, and these terms are rather complicated. They are constructed out of simpler terms, such as *powerful* and *morally good*. They also raise questions such as, "Can God create a rock so big he cannot lift it?" and "Can any being be both perfectly loving and perfectly just—or do love and justice sometimes conflict?"

Finally, Naturalism is simpler in terms of the fourth facet of simplicity. Your version of Theism involves four independent claims, while your version of Naturalism involves only three claims.

All in all, if we accept the Principle of Simplicity, it seems to me that we have good reason to assign Theism a much lower prior probability than Naturalism.

—Thomas

Dear Thomas,

I agree that Naturalism (as I've stated it) is simpler than Theism. Therefore, unless other background evidence favors Theism, we must assign Naturalism a much higher prior probability than Theism. That seems right to me.

I should mention, however, that "Perfect Being" theologians and philosophers might disagree. These thinkers, who follow in the tradition of St. Anselm, would boil Theism down to something like, "There is exactly one being who is maximally perfect." They argue that a maximally perfect being must be morally perfect, omnipotent, omniscient, necessary, etc. Clearly, this way of formulating Theism contains fewer clauses or theses, and hence seems to be simpler in terms of the fourth facet of simplicity. Does Perfect Being theology provide us with a simpler version of Theism?[18]

I doubt it. Perfect Being theology changes nothing in regard to the first two facets of simplicity, for (1) it postulates an entity not postulated by Naturalism and (2) that entity belongs to a *kind* that does not appear in the Naturalist's scheme of things. Moreover, quite a lot is obviously packed into the term *maximally perfect being*. Such a being must have *all the great-making qualities that can be consistently combined* (from a logical viewpoint). Thus, *maximally perfect* is a rather complicated term. A great-making property is one "which it is intrinsically good to have, any property which endows its bearer with some measure of value, or greatness, or metaphysical stature, regardless of external circumstances."[19] So in order to understand *maximally perfect,* one must understand such terms as *intrinsically good* (i.e., good regardless of external circumstances), *greatness*, and *metaphysical stature*. And to understand *greatness,* one must presumably grasp the concept of having some good property (such as power, knowledge, or love) in the highest degree.

Also keep in mind that from "*x* is maximally perfect" we must be able to derive "*x* is maximally powerful, morally perfect, and necessarily existent." Logically speaking, then, Perfect Being theologians have to pack enough meaning into *maximally perfect* to yield these results. And not everyone thinks the Perfect Being theologians have done this. For example, would a maximally perfect being be one that is *morally* perfect, or would it somehow be beyond or outside of morality? Would a maximally perfect being be one that exists of necessity? Why is it "more perfect" to exist of necessity? The point here is that we may need to pack even more meaning into *maximally perfect* to ensure that it has the desired implications.

I submit that while Perfect Being theology *is* simpler in terms of facet 4, it achieves this simplicity at the expense of increased complexity of terms (facet 3). Hence, in the final analysis, I can't see that Perfect Being theology yields a simpler formulation of Theism.

I end where I began, agreeing with your claim that Naturalism is a significantly simpler hypothesis than Theism.

—Zach

Dear Zach,

I just read your most recent post. At first I was surprised that you would agree that Naturalism is significantly simpler than Theism. But on reflection, I guess you don't have much choice. The mere fact that there is an extensive literature debating the coherence of the concept of God shows that the Theistic hypothesis is enormously complex.

—Thomas


Dear Thomas,

I don't think it's fair to claim that the terms used in formulating a hypothesis are highly complex *simply on the grounds that* books have been written exploring questions about the meaning and logical relations of those terms. Philosophers have written books analyzing terms such as *physical object*. Does it follow that "Rocks are physical objects" is a highly complicated claim? Plenty of books have been written by philosophers exploring the meaning of moral words such as *ought, right*, and *duty*. Does it follow that "One ought not kill people at will" is a highly complicated hypothesis regarding morality?

Recall that a term is complex *in the relevant sense* to the extent that it can be understood only by someone who understands some other term(s). So, basically, we're asking, is the term primitive (not defined by means of other terms) or does it need to be defined using other terms? This is very different from exploring all the logical implications the term might have.

We also need to be a little more specific about the content of books discussing the coherence of the concept of God. Two points are especially important. First, many questions about the coherence of the Theistic hypothesis concern terms *not* included in my formulation thereof, such as *immutability, impassibility, pure actuality*, and *metaphysical simplicity*. (*Note:* Metaphysical simplicity—very important in medieval theology and still a key element in some theologies today—is a completely different concept than the concept of *theoretical* simplicity we are discussing. "God is metaphysically simple" means "God is not a composite entity, i.e., God has no parts.")

Second, discussions of the coherence of Theism do not always focus exclusively on the meaning of the terms internal to Theism. For example, such discussions may explore the logical relationships between the claim that God is all-knowing and the claim that humans sometimes act freely, or between the claim that God is good and the claim that there is evil and suffering in the world. Such discussions are apt to venture into issues well beyond the meaning of the terms involved in formulating Theism; indeed the discussion may be in part about the explanatory power of Theism—e.g., does it lead us to expect that humans never act freely?

By the way, philosophers have asked tough questions about internal tensions within the Naturalistic hypothesis, too. Michael Rea has noted that Naturalists seldom state their view explicitly—"few have bothered to spell out in clear and precise terms what exactly it means to be a Naturalist."[20] Rea goes on to argue that, given the various claims Naturalists make, it is difficult to state their view coherently. And Alvin Plantinga has argued that in a subtle way Naturalism is self-defeating (calls itself into question).[21]

To sum up, the fact that "books have been written" on the coherence of the concept of God seems to me *not* by itself a good reason to claim that Theism—in my formulation—is highly complex due to the terms involved.

—Zach

Dear Zach,

Could you say a bit more about Plantinga's claim that Naturalism is self-defeating? I'm interested in the suggestion that Naturalism somehow calls itself into question.

—Thomas

Dear Thomas,

Plantinga's argument is complicated and I can't do it justice in a short letter. At best I can only try to give you the basic idea. Here goes.

Our cognitive faculties (e.g., the five senses, reason, and memory) are **reliable** if they provide us with mostly true beliefs. Naturalists, like most philosophers, believe that the five senses, reason, memory, and introspection are reliable. (Philosophers who don't accept the reliability of these faculties are radical skeptics; and Naturalists are not radical skeptics, for Naturalists affirm science, common sense, and numerous philosophical claims.) Although our cognitive faculties are generally reliable, they can be unreliable or of doubtful reliability in certain circumstances. For example, alcoholics suffering from delirium tremens hallucinate pink rats and snakes. Notice that in this case, the cause of the experience (roughly, excessive consumption of alcohol over a long period of time) gives us a reason to doubt its reliability.

Plantinga's basic idea is that, from the standpoint of Naturalism, the origin of our cognitive faculties gives us a reason to doubt their reliability. Given Naturalism, our cognitive faculties evolved without God (or anyone else) overseeing their development. Only the "blind" forces of nature were at work, e.g., random genetic mutation and natural selection. Darwin himself wondered whether his theory of evolution undermined human knowing:

> With me the horrid doubt always arises whether the convictions of man's mind, which has been developed from the mind of the lower animals, are of any value or at all trustworthy. Would any one trust in the convictions of a monkey's mind, if there are any convictions in such a mind?[22]

From an evolutionary standpoint, the human brain and nervous system enable us to behave in ways that promote survival and reproduction. In other words, from the standpoint of evolution, it is *behavior* that matters, not beliefs. So it seems possible that humans might be successful at survival while having mostly false beliefs (and, hence, unreliable cognitive faculties).

Here's the question we have to ask: How likely is it that our human cognitive faculties are reliable, assuming that Naturalism is true (and that our cognitive faculties evolved without guidance from any intelligent being)? Plantinga argues that the probability is low or beyond knowing; and either way, Naturalism leads us to doubt the reliability of our cognitive faculties. But, as noted earlier, Naturalists themselves believe that our human cognitive faculties are reliable. Thus, Naturalism is self-defeating.

I've got to stop here for now. Let me emphasize that I'm not advancing or endorsing Plantinga's argument. I have merely been underscoring the point that philosophers raise questions about internal tensions within all sorts of views, Naturalism included.

—Zach

Dear Zach,

I understand that you are not advancing Plantinga's argument, but could you say a bit more about how it goes? I mean, look, if we had mostly false beliefs, we humans would never have survived. We'd have walked off cliffs or into the mouths of lions, we'd have eaten mud or sand, slept in streams or ponds, etc. So don't the mechanisms of evolution ensure the reliability of our cognitive faculties?

—Thomas

Dear Thomas,

Not according to Plantinga. One main reason is that human behavior is not caused simply by beliefs, but by a combination of belief and desire. And many different belief–desire combinations could result in the same behavior. Plantinga imagines a prehistoric hominid he calls "Paul." Paul is approached by a hungry tiger. Fleeing is presumably the behavior best suited to survival. But various belief–desire combinations could produce this behavior:

> Perhaps Paul very much *likes* the idea of being eaten, but whenever he sees a tiger, always runs off looking for a better prospect, because he thinks it unlikely that the tiger he sees will eat him. This will get his body parts in the right place so far as survival is concerned, without involving much by way of true belief. . . . Or perhaps he thinks the tiger is a large, friendly, cuddly pussycat and wants to pet it, but he also believes that the best way to pet it is to run away from it. Or perhaps he confuses running *toward* it with running *away* from it, believing of the action that is really running away from it, that it is running toward it; or perhaps he thinks the tiger is a regularly recurring illusion, and, hoping to keep his weight down, has formed the resolution to run a mile at top speed whenever presented with such an illusion; or perhaps he thinks he is about to take part in a sixteen-hundred-meter race, wants to win, and believes the appearance of the tiger is the starting signal.[23]

The point is that our beliefs could mostly be false yet still result in behaviors that promote survival. This being so, we lack good reason to suppose that the mechanisms of evolution would generate reliable cognitive faculties.

Plantinga suggests another way to see that our beliefs might be mostly false yet still adaptive from an evolutionary point of view. Suppose we believed that everything is conscious. Instead of believing simply "Here's a tree" or "There's a rock," our beliefs might be of the form "Here's a conscious being that's a tree" or "There's a conscious being that's a rock." Vast numbers of our beliefs would then be false but might still promote survival.

Let me add that some Naturalists think that beliefs do not even partially cause our actions. Rather, our movements and behavior are caused by brain processes, such as neuron firings (which are not regarded as beliefs). Views of this sort would seem to be particularly vulnerable to Plantinga's argument. Why should we suppose our beliefs are mostly true if the content of the beliefs is not even a causal factor in our behavior? Our beliefs could be wildly false, while our brain processes produce adaptive behaviors.

Of course, if a perfectly good God is guiding the evolutionary process, the picture changes dramatically, for such a God would presumably *not* set things up so that we were radically deceived about important matters. A perfectly good God would have our best interests in mind and so would have reason to provide us with reliable cognitive faculties.

—Zach

Zach,

Thanks for the short summary of Plantinga's argument. I'm not convinced, but I have a more concrete understanding of how internal tensions might *conceivably* arise within a Naturalistic view of the world.

But something is still bothering me. What could be more complicated than God? Isn't God supposedly beyond all human understanding? The deepest of deep mysteries? This being so, the Theistic hypothesis is bound to be extremely complicated, isn't it?

—Thomas

Dear Thomas,

Actually, I think you've now subtly changed the topic. The topic was *the degree of complexity of the terms* I used to formulate Theism. But you are no longer talking about my formulation of Theism, it seems to me; rather, you are talking about "the full reality of the divine nature" or something along those lines.

This illustrates why I think it's so important to have an explicit formulation of Theism. I have some idea how to argue for Theism *as I've formulated it*. I really have no idea how to argue for the existence of a God too complex for humans to understand. Consider the following.

First, if God does have mysterious aspects "too complex for humans to understand," those aspects are presumably of no use in arguments-to-the-best-explanation. One cannot explain some phenomenon via a hypothesis no human understands.

Second, different types of Theists would add different elements to Theism as I've formulated it. For example, classical Theists insist that God is *metaphysically* simple (without parts). They also insist that the being who is God is not only good but cannot fail to be good (under any possible circumstances). My formulation of Theism neither denies nor affirms these points; it just leaves them to be discussed some other time. I'm arguing for what might be called "Basic Theism," a view that can be elaborated in various ways—though I assume that the elaborations would have to be defended in some way, e.g., by appeal to argument, special revelation, or perhaps mystical experience.

Third, theologians commonly make a distinction between a partial and a complete (or exhaustive) understanding of God. For example, the typical view within the Christian theological tradition is that humans can have a partial understanding of God, but not a complete understanding. The partial understanding can be true, as far as it goes, even though it is incomplete. For example, it can be true that God loves human beings, even though there is much that humans do not understand about God.

Again, my main point is this: In assessing the complexity of Theism, it's very important that we stick to the terms I've explicitly employed. And one sign that the terms of Theism are not *highly* complex, I would suggest, is that most people can readily understand Theism. Suppose we just grant that the divine nature in its fullness is beyond our grasp. It obviously doesn't follow that Theism *as I've formulated it* is beyond our grasp. And yet Theism, as I've formulated it, is obviously a very significant metaphysical view, with important religious implications.

—Zach

Dear Zach,

OK, I see your point. But the fact remains that Theism is more complex than Naturalism with respect to *all four* facets of simplicity. And it seems to me that the first two facets (i.e., the number of entities postulated and the number of kinds of entities postulated) are especially significant. Thus, in comparison to Naturalism, isn't Theism similar to "Busby, *assisted by poltergeists*, stole the TV"?

—Thomas

Dear Thomas,

I don't think so. The comparison between Theism and "Busby, *assisted by poltergeists*, stole the TV" seems flawed in at least two ways.

First, in the case of the missing TV, the clause regarding poltergeists does not increase the *explanatory power* of the hypothesis. That is, "Busby stole the TV" does just as good a job of leading us to expect the phenomenon as does the more complicated hypothesis, "Busby, assisted by poltergeists, stole the TV." But many arguments for Theism claim, in effect, that Theism has greater explanatory power than Naturalism, i.e., that Theism does a better job of leading us to expect certain phenomena than does Naturalism. We have to look into this claim—it cannot simply be ignored. If Theism does a better job of leading us to expect certain phenomena than Naturalism does, your comparison isn't apt.

Second, I think there is some important background evidence that reasonably leads us to regard Theism as a hypothesis worthy of our consideration. Major religious traditions are based on Theism. These traditions have provided spiritual and moral guidance for vast numbers of people. And while these traditions may be very imperfect, surely the exemplary figures ("saints") in these traditions are very impressive and noble people. And the spiritual and moral teachings of these traditions, even if imperfect, are in many respects profound. Perhaps more importantly, within these traditions, many people claim to have experienced the presence of God. They claim, as it were, to have "sensed" the presence of a thoroughly good and overwhelmingly powerful Being.

I'm not claiming that this background evidence gives Theism a prior probability *equal* to that of Naturalism. I'm just claiming that it gives us a strong reason to take Theism quite seriously as a rival to Naturalism.

To sum up, it seems to me that there are major, relevant differences between Theism and "Busby, *assisted by poltergeists*, stole the TV." Your comparison really isn't on target.

—Zach

Dear Zach,

The first point in your last letter is well taken. *If* Theism has more explanatory power than Naturalism does with respect to some phenomena, *then* I agree that Theism is not in the same category as "Busby, assisted by poltergeists, stole the TV." (This may be a big "if," but I assume we'll get to discuss that issue soon.)

I'm not so sure about your second point, however. I can think of many reasons why religious traditions and religious experience are dubious as background evidence. If you look into the history of religious traditions, you see the usual human failings—power grabs, indifference to poverty and suffering, mean-spiritedness, hypocrisy—you name it. Some of the wickedest acts in history have been performed in the name of religion.

As for religious experience, it seems very subjective to me. People "experience" what they want to experience or what they've been told to experience. Some will look at a pattern in the clouds and say, "It's a sign from God." And every religion has its share of religious experience. Personally, I just don't see how an appeal to religious experience can be of much use to anyone who is looking for solid evidence for Theism.

In doubt,<br>Thomas

CHAPTER 2

# Religious Experience and Interpretation

Dear Thomas,

Thanks for your recent post on religious traditions and religious experience.

Agreed: Many horrible things have been done in the name of religion. Once you get large numbers of people living within a religious tradition—or claiming to do so, such things are likely to occur sooner or later, aren't they? But I don't see that this lamentable fact disproves the official teachings of the traditions.

The official teachings of Judaism, Christianity, and Islam are surely in many ways noble, profound, and insightful. Many would testify that the spiritual teachings of these traditions have had a tremendous impact on them, inspiring them, strengthening them, and guiding them through times of difficulty.

I want to focus on the fact that many of the exemplary leaders within these religious traditions claim to have had a kind of direct awareness of God's presence. These exemplary leaders, it seems to me, are not people we can easily write off as weak, silly, and/or superstitious. From a spiritual and moral perspective, they stand head and shoulders over most of the human race. So I don't think we should simply dismiss religious experience out of hand.

Your friend,
Zach

Dear Zach,

Do you endorse the following argument: "Some people claim to have experienced the presence of God. Hence God exists"?

—Thomas

Dear Thomas,

No, I have a more modest and nuanced claim to defend: Theism deserves to be taken seriously as a metaphysical hypothesis *partly because* of the reports of people who've had experiences of *what they took to be* a divine presence.

Recall our recent discussion of explanations for "the missing TV." One hypothesis was that a certain person named Busby stole the TV. Another was that Busby, *assisted by poltergeists*, stole the TV. You suggested that Theism is like the latter hypothesis; I objected to the comparison on two grounds:

1. Unlike the "poltergeist-assisted theft" hypothesis, Theism arguably has more *explanatory power* than its main rivals with regard to certain phenomena.

2. No one (as far as I know) claims to have had experiences of poltergeists *assisting thieves*, but many people have had mystical experiences they take to be experiences of God.

You seem to doubt that point 2 is very significant. While I don't think that religious experience settles the issue of God's existence, I want to suggest that religious experience is important background evidence that gives Theism a higher prior probability than it would otherwise have. In any case, I think a discussion of religious experience would be useful in several ways.

First, a religion is a way of life, not just a set of beliefs. And a consideration of religious experience reminds us of that. In short, an examination of religious experience may help to take Theism out of the realm of abstraction.

Second, if there is a God, then I assume that a religious life will properly take the form of devotion to God. And religious experience can give us some insight into the ways in which deeply religious people relate to God and feel about God.

Finally, many people view religious experience as an important ground for their religious beliefs, and, this being so, we surely ought to consider whether there is any merit to this point of view.

—Zach

Dear Zach,

If you really think a discussion of religious experience will be of use, I'm willing to hear what you've got to say. Maybe you could begin by telling me what sorts of religious experiences you have in mind.

—Thomas


Dear Thomas,

Why don't we start with some actual reports of religious experience? There are many varieties of religious experience, but the most interesting form of religious experience for our purposes is the direct awareness of a divine presence, i.e., of an overwhelmingly powerful, thoroughly good *Thou*. Here are some examples.

1. I was in perfect health: We were on our sixth day of tramping, and in good training. . . . I can best describe the condition in which I was by calling it a state of equilibrium. When all at once I experienced a feeling of being raised above myself. I felt the presence of God—I tell of the thing just as I was conscious of it—as if his goodness and his power were penetrating me altogether. The throb of emotion was so violent that I could barely tell the boys to pass on and not wait for me. I then sat down on a stone. . . . I thanked God that in the course of my life he had taught me to know him. . . . Then, slowly, the ecstasy left my heart; that is, I felt that God had withdrawn the communion which he had granted, and I was able to walk on, but slowly, so strongly was I still possessed by the interior emotion.[1]

2. There was not a mere consciousness of something there, but fused in the central happiness of it, a startling awareness of some ineffable good. Not vague either, not like the emotional effect of some poem, or scene, or blossom, or music, but the sure knowledge of the close presence of a sort of mighty person, and after it went, the memory persisted as the one perception of reality. Everything else might be a dream but not that.[2]

3. I know an officer on our police force who has told me that many times when off duty and on his way home in the evening, there comes to him such a vivid and vital realization of his oneness with this Infinite Power, and this Spirit of Infinite Peace so takes hold of and so fills him, that it seems as if his feet could hardly keep to the pavement, so buoyant and so exhilarated does he become by reason of this inflowing tide.[3]

4. Then, just as I was exhausted and despairing—I had the most wonderful sense of the presence of God. He was in a particular place in the room about five feet from me—I didn't look up, but kept my head in my hands and my eyes shut. It was a feeling of

an all-embracing love which called forth every ounce of love I had in me. It was the tenderest love I have ever encountered.[4]

5. Although the room was dark and I was alone, I had an overwhelming feeling that I was not alone. Someone was there with me. So near that this presence seemed to completely enfold me. I was not afraid but very awed. It was a comforting presence, and almost as suddenly as I had time to realize this, it quickly departed, and I knew I was alone again.[5]

6. I was walking along a long, lonely country road by myself, worried sick and in near despair. Then came the experience. It lasted about 20 minutes—I sensed a presence on my right, keeping level with me as I went along. A mental message was conveyed to my mind, the sense of it being: "Don't worry; it will all turn out all right." It was not the message that counted so much as the overwhelming sense of infinite understanding, compassion, and sympathy.[6]

7. Particularly in the countryside, I am overwhelmed by the feeling that something all-powerful and merciful and sympathetic is very close, so close that communication by prayer is imperative—I want to speak and can speak to that something and it understands my needs and desires.[7]

8. Then, in a very gentle and gradual way, not with a shock at all, it began to dawn on me that I was not alone in the room. Someone else was there, located fairly precisely about two yards to my right front. Yet there was no sort of sensory hallucination. I neither saw him nor heard him in any sense of the word "see" and "hear," but there he was; I had no doubt about it. He seemed to be very good and very wise, full of sympathetic understanding, and most kindly disposed towards me.[8]

9. The English mystic Walter Hilton said: How that presence is felt, it may be better known by experience than by any writing, for it is the life and the love, the might and the light, the joy and the rest of a chosen soul. . . . He [God] cometh privily sometimes when thou art least aware of Him, but thou shalt well know Him; . . . for wonderfully He stirreth and mightily He turneth thy heart into beholding of His goodness, and doth thine heart melt delectably as wax against the fire into softness of His love.[9]

10. St. Teresa of Avila wrote: In the beginning . . . I was ignorant of one thing—I did not know that God is in all things: and when He seemed to me to be so near, I thought it impossible. [But] Not to believe that He was present was not in my power; for it seemed to me, as it were, evident that I felt there His very presence. . . . A most learned man, of the Order of the glorious Patriarch St. Dominic, delivered me from this doubt; for he told me that He was present: . . . this was a great comfort to me.[10]

11. Simone Weil had an experience she described as follows: In a moment of intense suffering, when I was forcing myself to feel love, but without desiring to give a name to that love, I felt, without being in any way prepared for it (for I had never read the mystical writers) a presence more personal, more certain, more real than that of any human being, though inaccessible to the senses and the imagination.[11] (Commenting on her numerous experiences of this kind, Weil remarks: In my arguments about the insolubility of the problem of God I had never foreseen the possibility of that, of a real contact, person to person, here below, between a human being and God. I had vaguely heard tell of things of this kind, but I had never believed in them.[12])

12. The French Carmelite Brother Lawrence once remarked that "he felt much closer to God in his day-to-day activities than most people ever believed to be possible. The worst trial he could imagine was losing his sense of God's presence, which had been with him for so long a time."[13]

Such examples could be multiplied indefinitely. What we have here, it seems to me, is not a mere outpouring of emotion, but fairly clear descriptions of a direct awareness of a divine presence. Let's call this sort of experience *Theistic mystical experience*, to distinguish it from other kinds of religious experience, such as a feeling of oneness with the universe or an intense feeling of peace and joy or a religious vision that involves sensory imagery (e.g., a deity sitting on a throne).

—Zach

Dear Zachary,

The quotations are interesting. Taken together, they make quite an impression. And I don't doubt that these people had some sort of profound experience. But we can't just accept the reports at face value, can we?

—Thomas

Dear Thomas,

Before we ask how we should respond to reports of religious experience, I think it would be helpful for us to think in a more general way about two issues. First, how should we respond to our own experiences? Second, how should we respond to testimony, i.e., to what other people tell us?

The word *experience* is used very loosely in ordinary English. For example, someone might say, "In my experience, dogs are dangerous." This use of the word indicates a lesson or generalization drawn from particular cases, and it can appear in religious contexts too, e.g., "In my experience, prayer helps me live more fully." For present purposes, I want to avoid this use of the term. I want to focus on experience in the sense of *direct awareness*, as when one is looking at a tree or touching a desk. And I want to suggest that the following principle applies to experience understood as direct awareness:

> *Principle of Credulity*: It is rational to accept what experience indicates unless special reasons apply.[14]

I realize that "unless special reasons apply" is vague, so let me explain what I have in mind. Suppose it seems to you that you are looking at a tree. Your visual experience indicates that there is a tree in front of you. Is it rational for you to believe that there is a tree in front of you? Under normal circumstances, I assume, the answer is yes. But let's consider two unusual circumstances.

First, suppose you have been walking in the desert for days, without water. You are badly dehydrated and feverish, nearing the point of collapse. You have a visual experience that seems to be of palm trees in the distance, surrounding a pool of water. In such a case you would have good reason to doubt that you had really seen a tree. You are very likely hallucinating.

Second, suppose it seems to you that you see a tree jogging. Of course, you have excellent reasons to believe that trees do not jog; they just don't have the right physical equipment for jogging. So you would have good reason not to accept the proposition that you see a tree jogging. (*Note*: You can't actually *see* something unless it exists; a visual experience that does not correspond to reality is an illusion or a hallucination.)

In the first case, even though the visual experience of palm-trees-surrounding-a-pool is not one you would question under normal circumstances, in the special circumstances described, you would have reason to doubt that your visual faculties are working properly. In the second case, you have good reason *apart from the circumstances in question* to think that the apparent object of your experience, a jogging tree, is not really present.

In effect, the Principle of Credulity tells us to give "the benefit of the doubt" to our experience (in the sense of direct awareness). We accept what experience tells us in the absence of special reasons not to. Does this seem reasonable?

—Zach


Dear Zach,

It seems reasonable. But I suspect that many philosophers would question your Principle of Credulity. How would you respond to them?

—Thomas

Dear Thomas,

Most philosophers probably accept something along the lines of my Principle of Credulity—implicitly if not explicitly. The alternative is in fact a pretty radical type of skepticism.

Instead of giving experience the benefit of the doubt, radical philosophical skeptics demand proof that it's **reliable** (i.e., that it yields truth for the most part). For example, a radical philosophical skeptic may point out that an all-powerful demon could cause you to have hallucinations at any time. Maybe what you call your ordinary experience is just a series of hallucinations caused by an all-powerful demon!

But the demands of the radical skeptics cannot be satisfied. For example, attempts to prove that sense experience is reliable inevitably beg the question (i.e., assume the point to be proved). To illustrate: Suppose I try to prove that I see a tree by touching it. This "proof" assumes that my tactile experience (touching) is reliable. But tactile experience is just another form of sense experience. How do I know my tactile experience is reliable?

I can ask *you* if you see the tree, but will that help? No, for this attempted "proof" assumes I know, e.g., (a) that you exist, (b) whether you state (or otherwise indicate) that you see a tree, and (c) whether you are sincere. How would I know these things? Clearly my knowledge would depend on my sense experience, and so this attempted proof goes nowhere.[15]

Unless we operate with something like the Principle of Credulity, we fall into radical philosophical skepticism. So, unless I hear objections from you, I'm going to take the Principle of Credulity for granted.

—Zach

Dear Zach,

Does what you're saying boil down to this: "We have to have *faith* in our cognitive faculties—vision, hearing, touch, memory, etc. We really can't know that they are reliable"? If so, maybe the skeptics are on the right track: We know nothing or virtually nothing.

—Thomas

Dear Thomas,

In my opinion, any reasonable philosophy has to enable us to judge that many things are known—or at least justifiably believed—and many others aren't.

Take a mundane example. Suppose I'm standing at an intersection, preparing to cross the street. I look both ways. I *seem* to see a truck advancing rapidly toward me from the right. And suppose I have no good reason to reject what my visual experience indicates. (As far as I know, my eyes are healthy, there is ample light, I have not taken any mind-altering drugs, and so on.) Am I *equally* justified in believing *either* of the following statements?

1. There is a truck coming down the street.
2. There is no truck coming down the street.

Any philosophy that answers yes seems to me a failure. Such a philosophy isn't reasonable, and I doubt that anyone can really live in accordance with it. (Anyone who tried probably wouldn't live long!)

I accept the Principle of Credulity because to reject it is to fall into the kind of disastrous philosophy I've just described. That seems to me reason enough to accept it.

—Zach

Dear Zach,

I see your point. And I certainly don't wish to endorse radical skepticism. So I accept the Principle of Credulity, at least as applied to sense experience. But we cannot simply assume that it also applies to religious experience, can we?

—Thomas

Dear Thomas,

I think we ought to apply the Principle of Credulity to any form of experience (in the sense of "apparent direct awareness"). Having seen that we cannot prove the reliability of sense experience—that we must give sense experience "the benefit of the doubt," how can we reasonably demand proofs for the reliability of other types of experience? To do so is to operate with an unjustified double standard, it seems to me.[16]

I'm not suggesting that people should uncritically accept the content of any strange experience that comes their way. As we have seen, there can be good reasons *not to accept* what sense experience seems to indicate; and the same goes for religious experience.

Let me add that I think the Principle of Credulity is a special case of a more general principle. In philosophy we always have the question, "Where do we start in our thinking?" We have to start somewhere, of course. It seems we cannot give arguments for everything.[17] Where do our "first premises" (the ones we don't argue for) come from? What justifies them? I believe that we tacitly accept what might be called the Starting Principle:

*Starting Principle*: It is rational to accept what seems to be so unless special reasons apply.

Please keep in mind that this principle is not intended to apply to inferences and generalizations. It applies to experience (direct awareness), as we've already seen. But I think it has much broader applications. For example, it applies to memory. Last summer, while hiking by myself, I saw a deer. I remember that. I have no way of proving that I saw that deer, and I certainly don't see the deer at the moment. But I have no reason to reject what my memory tells me in regard to this deer sighting, so I accept what my memory indicates.

I think the Starting Principle also applies to introspection, which enables us to know our own conscious mental states. Just now I feel a little sad (I don't know why). I have no good reason to doubt that I feel a little sad, so I believe I do feel a little sad. And that seems entirely reasonable to me.

The Starting Principle also applies, in my opinion, to what is sometimes called *rational intuition*. For example, it seems to me that $1 + 2 = 3$ and that no triangle is a circle. It seems to me that these things *must* be true, and their negations *cannot* be true. Moreover, in the absence of reasons to doubt these apparent rational intuitions, I'm reasonable in accepting them.

In this connection, let me note something odd about the radical skeptics. They are often skeptical about experience but not skeptical about introspection and rational intuition. For example, they usually assume that they can know various things about their own conscious mental states. Radical skeptics don't usually doubt that they have visual experiences of the sort we associate with seeing trees; rather, they doubt that these experiences reliably inform them about the reality *external* to their minds. Similarly, radical skeptics seem to think they can grasp simple logical principles (presumably, by rational intuition). So oddly—and I think inconsistently, radical skeptics apparently accept the Starting Principle (or something like it) where some cognitive faculties are concerned while rejecting it for others.

To return to my main point: Yes, I think the Principle of Credulity should be applied to religious experience. If we refuse to apply it and demand some sort of proof for the reliability of religious experience, then I think we are arbitrarily demanding that religious experience should meet a standard that even sense experience cannot meet.

—Zach

Dear Zach,

Very well. The Principle of Credulity should be applied to religious experience. I'll go along with that. But *at best* this would allow the mystics themselves to accept what their religious experiences indicate. The Principle of Credulity in no way tells the rest of us to accept what the mystics report, right?

—Thomas

Dear Thomas,

Right. But a principle analogous to the Principle of Credulity applies to testimony, i.e., to what other people tell us.

*Principle of Testimony*: It is rational to accept what others tell us unless special reasons apply.[18]

Most of what we know is known through testimony. We assume something like the Principle of Testimony when we consult a reference book, use a map, go to the doctor, ask someone their name, ask for directions, and so on. It's instructive, I think, to consider the case of a scientist, say, a chemist. Most of what a chemist knows about chemistry is learned from reading textbooks and journals—that is, learned via testimony. No chemist has time to redo all (or even most) of the experiments that have brought the science of chemistry to its present state.

Of course, we are all very aware of "special reasons" that rightly lead us *not* to accept what someone tells us. One person's report may conflict logically with another's. We may have good reason to doubt the sincerity of the reporter (or "testifier"); e.g., he's lied to us before. We may have good reason to doubt that the reporter is truly in possession of the information he or she is reporting; e.g., she is making pronouncements about technical matters in which she has no expertise.

Let me make two further observations about testimony. First, notice that we do not normally have proof that our source has access to the relevant facts or information. For example, when I use a reference work, such as an encyclopedia, I give the authors and/or editors the benefit of the doubt. I seldom do any kind of thorough checking up on how they know what they assert. And in fact, for practical reasons, it would be impossible for me to do detailed checks on all my sources. If I want to have a wide knowledge of the world, I have to place a significant degree of trust in other people.

Second, even a sincere person with genuine expertise can be mistaken. Reference works, physicians, maps, etc., are not infallible. So we cannot reasonably reject testimony simply on the grounds that it might be false. Of course it *might* be false. All of our sources of information are fallible.

Is the Principle of Testimony acceptable to you?

—Zach

Dear Zach,

I'm willing to accept the Principle of Testimony, but I'm getting a little concerned about where this is all heading. Suppose a mystic has an *apparent* experience of God. She can then apply the Principle of Credulity. In the absence of special reasons to reject what her experience indicates, she is rational in believing that she has experienced God. But what about those of us who have not had any religious experiences? This is where the Principle of Testimony will come into play. Those of us without religious experiences of our own have the sincere assertions of the mystics to go on. But does this give us good reason to believe that God exists? I doubt it. Questions abound.

—Thomas

Dear Thomas,

I agree—questions abound. But again let me assure you that the conclusion I'm heading for is relatively modest. I think we can probably best approach these issues indirectly. Let me try out some philosophical parables on you, OK?

> *The First Parable of the Courier.* A courier with a vitally important and urgent message set forth on a journey through uninhabited and mountainous lands. Because winter was fast approaching, he knew he would die in the mountains if he failed to find a pass through to his destination. He met an old scout who claimed he had once crossed the mountains. The old scout told the courier how to find a pass through the mountains. The courier believed the old scout, took his advice, and set out toward the mountains.
>
> *The Second Parable of the Courier.* A courier with a vitally important and urgent message set forth on a journey through uninhabited and mountainous lands. Because winter was fast approaching, he knew he would die in the mountains if he failed to find a pass through to his destination. He met two scouts, each of whom claimed he had once crossed the mountains. But the scouts disagreed about the location of the pass and how to find it. Each warned that following the advice of the other would lead to death in the mountains. The courier, confused by the disagreement between the scouts, concluded that their advice was unreliable. He decided to ignore the scouts completely and so set out to find his own way through the mountains.
>
> *The Third Parable of the Courier.* A courier with a vitally important and urgent message set forth on a journey through un-

inhabited and mountainous lands. Because winter was fast approaching, he knew he would die in the mountains if he failed to find a pass through to his destination. He met two scouts, each of whom claimed he had once crossed the mountains. But the scouts disagreed about the location of the pass and how to find it. Each warned that following the advice of the other would lead to death in the mountains. The courier took some time to discuss these matters with the scouts. Each of them seemed sincere and experienced. The courier felt it would be folly for him to disregard the advice of the scouts and to set out on his own. But whose advice should he take? After much discussion and reflection, he found himself inclined to think that one of the scouts was somewhat more credible than the other. So he took that scout's advice and set out on his way.

Can we agree that the courier acts wisely in the first and third parables but unwisely in the second parable?

—Zach

Dear Zach,

Yes, that seems right. But what do these parables prove?

—Thomas

Dear Thomas,

The first parable simply illustrates that accepting testimony from people who've had unusual experiences (that one has not had) can be entirely rational. I don't think that's a very controversial point, but it's definitely something I'm assuming, and I wanted to make it explicit.

The second and third parables concern the more complex situation in which one has some reason to doubt testimony. How should one respond? Well, obviously, if the reason to doubt is conclusive, one should disregard the testimony as unreliable. But the parables draw attention to the fact that "reasons to doubt" come in degrees and may not be conclusive. In these types of cases, it seems we have to make a qualified appeal to the Principle of Testimony. As the second parable illustrates, rejecting the testimony completely in this sort of case is not wise, not rational. One or both of the scouts may be mistaken, but they surely know more about the mountains than the courier does. Their advice is more likely to be right than his guesses, which are not based on any experience of the trail ahead.

Now, I'm not going to claim that there are no reasons to doubt the reports of religious experience. But are these reasons conclusive? Or do they instead leave us with testimonial evidence we should not simply reject as worthless?

—Zach

Dear Zach,

So the question is whether we have a conclusive reason to doubt either the reliability of religious experience itself or the reliability of the reports of (testimony concerning) religious experience. Well, there are plenty of reasons we need to consider, or so it seems to me. Here's a list.

1. Mystics are undoubtedly interpreting their experience. We don't know exactly what their experiences are really like. Indeed, the mystics themselves may be unable to distinguish their experiences from theological interpretations thereof.

2. It's not clear how it would be possible for finite human beings to experience the presence of a being who is supposedly *infinite* in power, knowledge, goodness, etc. God is simply too vast to be an object of human experience.

3. Most people don't have the sorts of vivid religious experiences that you've appealed to.

4. Sense experience can be tested, but religious experience cannot. For example, if you think you see a tree in front of you, you can walk forward and touch the tree to test your visual experience. There are no such tests for religious experience.

5. Religious experience may be caused by psychological or physiological factors. For example, Freud thought religious experience was caused by psychological factors.

6. There are many different religious experiences, and they cannot all be reliable. Some reports contradict others.

Taken together, this is an impressive list of reasons for rejecting religious experience as unreliable. That's what I think, anyway.

—Thomas

Dear Thomas,

Whew! That's quite a list. A good list too. But the question is whether these reasons add up to a conclusive or decisive reason to reject Theistic mystical experience as unreliable. I think they don't, but the only way to argue for that is to discuss the items on the list, one at a time.[19]

Let's take it from the top: What makes you think that the mystics interpret their experiences?

—Zach

Dear Zach,

All perceiving necessarily involves interpretation. Consciously or unconsciously, we *see things as* this or that; nothing is simply presented to us in our experience. The famous duck-rabbit drawing supports this thesis.

When you first look at the drawing, what do you see? A duck? A rabbit? (You can see this as a drawing of a rabbit looking to your left or as a duck with its bill pointed skyward.) Whatever you see initially—duck or rabbit—you are engaged in interpretation.

Obviously, the same goes for religious experience. The mystics probably have some sort of feeling or emotion that they interpret theologically.

—Thomas

Dear Thomas,

Let's call the claim that all perceiving necessarily involves interpretation, *the thesis of total interpretation*. It's a thesis that many people find plausible nowadays.

But notice that the thesis of total interpretation applies just as much to sense experience as it does to mystical religious experience. So if this thesis does not lead us to reject sense experience as unreliable, it shouldn't lead us to reject religious experience as unreliable.

On the other hand, if we claim that religious experiences are interpreted but sense experience is not, then we are operating with an unjustified double standard. We certainly need an argument to show that religious experiences are subject to interpretation but sense experience is not.

For what it's worth, I don't deny that humans interpret their experiences, but a key question is whether, through perception, we are presented with *something* independent of any interpretive judgment.

I'm inclined to think we are, and here's why. Ask yourself: What's the difference between thinking about a tree (e.g., mentally describing a tree to yourself) and actually seeing one? When you see a tree, something is presented to you in your experience—something you don't control, something that's stubborn and won't go away, something you cannot simply reinterpret. Even in the duck-rabbit case, notice that you are presented with something: at minimum, an irregular, unbroken line.[20]

Also, I think we distort many of the reports of religious experience if we insist on regarding them as cases in which people had strong feelings or emotions that were then interpreted in accordance with the subjects' theological beliefs. Go back and look at the quotations I sent you. They read, for all the world, as if the subjects found themselves simply presented with a very powerful, thoroughly good presence.

—Zach

Dear Zach,

I'm mulling over the points in your last letter. I do see that my appeal to the thesis of total interpretation raises important questions. But how would it even be *possible* for finite human beings to have a direct awareness of God? For example, isn't an experience of an *almighty* being simply beyond the human capacity?

—Thomas

Dear Thomas,

The possible content of experience cannot (reasonably) be legislated from an armchair. We have to look and see, i.e., consider the actual reports of a wide range of experiences. When we do that, the evidence indicates that a great many people have had experiences that *seemed to them* to be of an infinitely powerful, thoroughly good presence.

—Zach

Dear Zach,

I agree that we cannot legislate from an armchair what sorts of experiences humans are capable of. But still, if someone comes to me and says he had a direct experience or perception of God, I wonder how that could be. I mean, we know that visual experience involves the eyes, the optic nerve, and so on. What organs and mechanisms are involved in the case of Theistic mystical experience?

—Thomas

Dear Thomas,

I don't know. But I think William Alston has an interesting response to your question:

> It must be admitted that we have no idea as to the "mechanism" of this mode of awareness, if, indeed, there is any such thing. Perhaps God doesn't work through natural, much less physical, means to make Himself perceptible by us. Perhaps He supernaturally brings about the requisite experience, as Catholic mystical theology has always held. If God exists, . . . this is a possibility that cannot be ignored. But the main point here is that the credentials of this alleged mode of perception do not depend on our understanding of how it is effected. After all, people were amply justified in supposing themselves to see physical objects in their environment long before anyone had any adequate idea of the mechanisms involved.[21]

I might add that young children are fully justified in believing all sorts of things through their sense experience, even though they may have no understanding of the mechanisms involved. The point, of course, is that ignorance of the processes or mechanisms involved in an experience is not a good reason to regard it as unreliable.

—Zach

Dear Zach,

Thanks for sending along the quotation from Alston. He makes a very interesting point. A solid point, I think.

But I wonder how one could even know that one had had an experience *of God*. What does an almighty, perfectly good Being "look like"? How would you know it was *God* who had appeared to you?

—Thomas

Dear Thomas,

What does God "look like"? Of course, if you are asking for visual imagery, it is not there in the reports I sent to you. Visual imagery is sometimes present in religious experiences. But given that God is nonphysical, I take it that God does not literally have a certain shape or color.[22]

The descriptions I sent to you provide typical accounts of nonsensory Theistic experiences. What's presented to the subjects, if we take their own reports seriously, is an infinitely powerful, thoroughly good *Thou*. The subjects have a strong impression of the presence of an invisible Person or Mind. Perhaps your question, or at least a key part of it, is this: "How can one be directly aware of *power* or *goodness*? Don't these properties have to be *inferred*?"

Consider that, in ordinary sense experience, we are often presented with objects as having powers or *dispositions*, i.e., capacities or tendencies to behave in certain ways. For instance, suppose I see a red flower. In a normal case, if I report seeing a red flower, I don't mean simply that I saw a flower that *looked or appeared* red to me at the time (as a white flower might *look* red in certain lighting). In reporting that I saw a red flower, I am normally reporting that I had a visual experience of a physical object having certain powers or dispositions, i.e., that under normal lighting, normal perceivers (in general) would also see something red if they looked at the flower. *In other words, in very ordinary experiences, we are commonly presented not merely with the "surface properties" of objects but with their powers, dispositions, or capacities.* And of course, *being very powerful* (or even almighty) is a power or capacity. So, at least in principle, a direct awareness of an entity as very powerful—or even almighty—seems to be possible.[23]

Also consider that, in perceiving something, we often perceive only a rather limited number of its features. I casually remark, "I saw my friend Jessica, yesterday." Actually, I was presented with the left side of her face as she walked past my office window. But I certainly haven't misreported my experience in saying, "I saw my friend Jessica, yesterday." The report is accurate as long as what was presented to me is a reliable guide to Jessica's presence. (Keep in mind that a reliable guide need not be infallible.) The upshot is that one can have a reliable experience of God without experiencing all of God's features (though of course the experience must include reliable indicators of a divine presence, such as infinite power and goodness).[24]

Finally, consider that our own subjective, emotional reactions figure into our recognition of certain types of features. Sometimes upon meeting a person we regard him as less than trustworthy primarily because he invokes in us a feeling of uneasiness. In this type of case, our subjective, emotional reactions serve (in combination with presentations made through sense experience) as indicators of certain types of qualities, and these indicators are very important in dealing with social realities. While these indicators are fallible, we would be foolish to ignore them.

Now, in the Theistic mystical experiences we've examined, the subjects were presented with a personal presence, and they had an immediate impression of its infinite power and goodness. Their subjective, emotional reactions were of profound awe, of feeling very "small" or finite, of being loved, of extraordinary peace, and so on. All in all, I think that's what one might expect an experience of God to be like.

—Zach

Dear Zach,

Your last letter reminded me of a strange dream I had once when I was a kid. It was near Halloween, and that probably explains why I had the dream—actually, it was a nightmare. (We had been reading ghost stories.) Anyway, there was an *invisible* malicious THING in my room. IT was located in one corner of the room, and I could feel IT beaming hatred at me. Within the dream, a terrible sense of dread came over me. I woke up scared half to death.

Of course, there was no evil presence in my room. I was just dreaming. But your letter made me realize that I actually have some idea, from my own experience, of what it might be like to have a direct awareness of *an invisible person with moral qualities*. So, on reflection, it's not such a huge step to suppose that a human being can have an experience that *seems* to be of God. I mean, the mystics might be describing their experiences correctly and fairly, even if their experiences are no more reliable than my nightmare.

But I still suspect there's plenty of room for interpretation to come into the picture, where religious experience is concerned.

—Thomas

Dear Thomas,

You are right to press the issue of interpretation further. My earlier comments were primarily meant to call into question the common suggestion that religious experience is basically just a "feeling" (e.g., of warmth or excitement) that devout people interpret theologically; and others have the same experience but do not interpret it theologically.

Clearly, religious experiences are often described in terms quite specific to one religion—e.g., as experiences of Christ, Krishna, or Allah. This certainly raises a question about the extent to which background theological beliefs may enter the picture. I have to admit that when I read experience reports containing elaborate theological content, e.g., detailed accounts of the Holy Trinity, I feel that I'm reading highly interpreted accounts. We have to distinguish *careful* reports of religious experience (by which I mean reports that plausibly describe just what the subject was presented with) from highly interpreted reports.

But the same thing comes up with accounts of sense experience. Listen to two people describing a traffic accident. One person chooses her words carefully, sticking to a sensible account that plausibly indicates what she was presented with. Another person who saw the same accident may give a loose account, full of what are plainly judgments that go well beyond what he could possibly have been presented with. We don't throw out all accounts of an accident simply because some of them are careless and chock-full of dubious inferences or interpretations. Right?

I suggest that we can handle the issue of interpretation via the following principles. First, work with a first-person report of the experience (as opposed to a secondhand account). Second, the more tradition-specific the terminology of the report, the more likely it contains interpretation or inference (going beyond what was actually *presented* in the experience). For example, "I had a vision of the Holy Trinity," with its use of technical terminology from Christian theology, is much more tradition specific than "I was aware of the presence of an overwhelmingly powerful, thoroughly good being." Third, to what extent is the experience described in terms employed across cultures (making allowances for translation from one language to another)? Even if an experience report contains some tradition-specific elements, it may (in effect) provide wording that allows us to give a summary that is free or nearly free of tradition-specific elements. For example, suppose the word *Allah* is used but other aspects of the report indicate that the experience was of an infinitely powerful and merciful being. Terms equivalent to *merciful*, *powerful*, and *unlimited* or *infinite* appear in all (or virtually all) cultures. So an experience report of a being who is merciful and of infinite power does not *by itself* ground a charge that the report contains interpretation or inference.

If you take these principles and look back at the list of experience reports I sent to you recently, I think you'll agree that most of them contain little to justify the charge that they contain interpretation or inference—or if they do, no more than careful reports of sense experience do. The accounts strike us as responsible attempts to describe what the subject was *presented with*. Again, this doesn't prove the experiences were reliable (e.g., they might be hallucinations of some sort), but I think it does mean that we cannot write the experiences off as theological interpretations of some experience whose *genuine content* can be given in nontheological terms, such as "I felt a sense of oneness with the universe" or "I was overcome by an intense feeling of well-being."

—Zach

Dear Zach,

You're last letter was interesting but I don't have time for a proper reply. I'll be out of town for the next couple of weeks and won't be able to write until I get back.

Your friend,
Thomas

# CHAPTER 3

# Is Religious Experience Reliable?

Dear Zach,

I'm back in town now and eager to continue our discussion. Our correspondence on the issue of interpretation has helped me a lot. But I still have many doubts about the reliability of religious experience—and of Theistic mystical experience in particular.

Looking back at our correspondence, here's a list of issues you've not yet addressed.

1. Most people don't have the sorts of vivid religious experiences that you've appealed to.
2. Sense experience can be tested, but religious experience cannot. For example, if you think you see a tree in front of you, you can walk forward and touch the tree to test your visual experience. There are no such tests for religious experience.
3. Religious experience may be caused by psychological or physiological factors. For example, Freud thought religious experience was caused by psychological factors.
4. There are many different religious experiences, and they cannot all be reliable. Some experience reports contradict others.

That list still looks impressive to me. You have your work cut out for you!

—Thomas

Dear Thomas,

I'll try to give very brief replies to your first two questions in this letter. And if my replies are too brief, feel free to follow up as needed.

*Question 1.* An experience can be reliable even if only a very small percentage of people have it. Take the example of a superb tracker. He or she can see things that the vast majority of people cannot, e.g., bear tracks partially obscured by rain. Or again, take the example of a musically gifted person who can hear very subtle harmonies or disharmonies that most people cannot hear at all. In this connection it's worth noting that religious traditions suggest that spiritual or moral preparation may be a prerequisite for religious experience, e.g., "Blessed are the pure in heart, for they shall see God." (How many people can claim to have *this* preparation? Not many, I should think.)[1]

*Question 2.* No doubt we all trust sense experience, in part because it does allow us to make many predictions that check out (in terms of further sense experiences). *But we cannot simply assume that all reliable forms of experience are highly similar to sense experience.* Consider introspection. I "look within" and realize that I'm feeling a bit sad or anxious or excited. Other people cannot directly access these feelings of mine to assure me they're present. How can I test the reliability of introspection? Any test is likely to be circular—perhaps I simply "look within" again and find that same feeling. On the other hand, maybe I don't find that same feeling, maybe I now feel differently—or so introspection tells me. As far as I can tell, I don't really need independent tests for my introspective experiences. I just apply the Starting Principle ("It is rational to accept what seems to be so unless special reasons apply"); and I have *no good reason* to doubt that my introspective experiences usually deliver truth. So it's not clear that experiences are reliable only if they are testable—or only if they are testable in the way sense experiences are.

Nevertheless, there *is* a kind of test for Theistic mystical experience. In fact, mystical writers and spiritual directors have shown a lot of interest in distinguishing genuine experiences of God from illusory ones. The basic idea is that if the subject has experienced God's presence, certain results will follow. These include interior peace, trust in God, patience with trials, sincerity, self-forgetful charity, and not being concerned with useless matters. Criteria for identifying false or illusory religious experiences include anxiety, presumption or despair, impatience with trials, duplicity, and being concerned with useless matters.[2]

—Zach

Dear Zach,

To be honest, I don't find the so-called tests for Theistic mystical experience very impressive. The tests are religious in nature, so don't they beg the question?

—Thomas

Dear Thomas,

The tests for sense experience all rely on sense experience; in that way they are all circular. For example, one tests visual experience by means of tactile experience. But we still see value in those tests, right? So if we do not value the tests for Theistic mystical experience *simply because they are religious in nature,* aren't we operating with an unjustified double standard? So it seems to me.

Surely it is reasonable to suppose that if someone has experienced the presence of God, certain beneficial results are likely to follow. A "close encounter" with perfect goodness would presumably be a kind of moral and spiritual wake-up call.

In addition, I think the tests for religious experience give us a reason to approach the Theistic mystics with respect. Such characteristics as interior peace, patience with trials, sincerity, self-forgetful charity, and not being concerned with useless matters are admirable. To put it mildly, these aren't the characteristics of flakes and con artists.

Finally, *and most importantly,* remember—as the case of introspection indicates—a type of experience can be reliable without being testable in the way sense experience is.

—Zach

Dear Zach,

Fair enough. Let's just suppose that the Theistic mystics do often have admirable qualities and that this is due at least in part to their religious experiences. Still, couldn't religious experiences in general, and Theistic mystical experiences in particular, be caused entirely by natural factors, e.g., psychological or neurological ones?

For example, Freud thought that mystical experiences were generated by psychological need. As children we learn to go to our parents for help when we face problems too big for us to solve. As we get older, we encounter problems too big for our parents to solve, but the pattern of going to authority figures is deeply entrenched, so some people long desperately for an authority figure who can solve the problems of death, sin, injustice, and so on. The longing is so strong in some that they have hallucinations of a Heavenly Father.

In short, *whether or not God exists*, some people would have Theistic mystical experiences. So how can such experiences tell us anything about the existence of God?

—Thomas

Dear Thomas,

Regarding Freud, possibilities don't make probabilities. Freud's hypotheses are imaginative and intriguing, but they certainly are not *established* scientific theories. Here are some further points to bear in mind with regard to Freud's views.

First, it's not easy to get solid evidence concerning the presence and strength of the unconscious desires in question. And even if they are present, are they strong enough to cause hallucinations? How could that be shown? It's not shown by the mere fact that Theistic mystical experience occurs—unless we assume that God doesn't exist. But of course that assumption begs the question.

Second, Theistic mystical experiences often contain elements apt to run counter to wish fulfillment, such as awe, conviction of sin, and the feeling of being utterly subordinate.

Third, suppose—for the sake of the argument—that one must have a deep desire for God's presence in order to have a Theistic mystical experience. That might well be true. But it does not follow that such experiences are unreliable.

Finally, if God does exist, it wouldn't be at all surprising to find that humans have psychological mechanisms that prompt them to turn to God for help.

—Zach

Dear Zach,

I'm sure you will admit that mentally ill people sometimes have unreliable religious experiences. I read about a man who claimed that God appeared to him and commanded him to kill all persons of a certain race. Surely you'll agree that that particular religious experience was not of the reliable sort. Most likely it was due to psychological or neurological causes. So we know that some religious experiences have naturalistic causes. How, in practice, do we distinguish a reliable religious experience from a "religious hallucination" caused by purely natural factors? *If we have no practical way to distinguish reliable religious experiences from unreliable ones, then don't we have good reason to doubt the reliability of all religious experiences?*

—Thomas

Dear Thomas,

About the man who allegedly had an experience in which God commanded him to commit genocide: I agree, of course, that the experience was not of the reliable type. And, yes, I would assume it was caused by purely naturalistic factors—assuming the man didn't simply make it up.

I don't claim to have a complete account of how to distinguish reliable religious experiences from unreliable ones, but perhaps I can offer some instructive examples.

1. Some religious experiences conflict with sense experience. For example, some mystics claim to have experiences indicating that change is unreal or that time is an illusion. But our sense experience constantly indicates that things do change over time. Of course, mystics sometimes claim that their mystical experiences override or correct sense experience. But that seems backwards to me. While I resist a dismissive attitude toward religious experience, I think we have to regard sense experience as a paradigm of reliable experience. In my view, any religious experience that conflicts with sensory experience should be considered unreliable.

2. The reports of some religious experiences are very obscure. We don't really understand the content of the experience, so we can hardly judge it as reliable.

3. The reports of some religious experiences contain contradictions. In this case, the report is like eyewitness testimony that contains contradictions. Minor contradictions may not lead us to reject the testimony completely, but they indicate that we cannot accept it as true on all counts. Major contradictions rightly lead us to regard the witness as unreliable.

4. If the subject is known to be insane, of weak moral character, or wicked, then we have good reason to doubt the accuracy of report.

5. If the subject claims to have experienced God as morally evil, then I think we should regard the experience as unreliable. And here's why. An evil God would be untrustworthy and would deliberately promote harm. And if there were a morally evil but almighty Deity, then a morally evil entity would control the universe, including those aspects of the universe through which humans came into existence. Thus, if there were an evil God, our cognitive faculties would be formed by it either directly or via processes under its control. In such a case, would our cognitive faculties be reliable? Well, consider the following analogy. Suppose you were locked in a room by yourself. Statements written on note cards are slipped into the room every few minutes. The sentences are about matters concerning which you have no prior information; moreover, you have no independent way to check or corroborate the statements. You believe (never mind why) that the source of the written statements is an evil Deity. Now, if you

really believe this, should you judge that the information you are receiving is reliable, i.e., true for the most part? Of course not. Under such circumstances you would be very foolish to conclude that the information was reliable. You would rightly judge that given the source, the information is not to be trusted.

Now, suppose someone—call him Fred—has a mystical experience and as a result believes that an evil but almighty God exists. Fred's situation is analogous to yours in the "locked room" case—except that Fred's belief has larger ripple effects. An evil Deity might well take pains to ensure that Fred's cognitive faculties are unreliable. And Fred would be foolish to assume that his cognitive faculties are reliable if they are formed by an evil Deity (either directly or indirectly through processes it controls). Indeed, Fred would rightly judge that the reliability of his cognitive faculties is highly doubtful. But if there is a question mark over all his cognitive faculties, the reliability of his mystical experience is also in doubt. In this way, Fred's mystical experience *as of* an evil God is self-defeating (i.e., it calls itself into doubt).[3]

Now, does any of this help with your example of someone claiming that God told him to commit genocide? Point 5 is relevant if we can assume the following:

  A. Any Deity who commands an evil act is evil.
  B. Genocide is evil.

Given these assumptions, you've described an experience of an evil God, and, for reasons I've just given, I think such experiences are self-defeating.

—Zach


Dear Zach,

Your list of ways to detect unreliable religious experiences is interesting and helpful. The first four items make good sense to me, but I'm not sure I buy the fifth—your claim that experiences of an evil God are self-defeating. Even if God is evil, we can be sure our cognitive faculties are reliable, because they enable us to get around in the world, to obtain what we need to stay alive, etc. Right?

—Thomas


Dear Thomas,

You're claim is plausible but (in my opinion) mistaken. Here's one way to see that: Some philosophers, such as T. H. Huxley, have suggested that the human mind is an epiphenomenon (a mere by-product of purely physical processes). From this point of view, one's mental states, e.g., desires, feelings, and beliefs, do not cause one's actions. In fact, mental states don't cause anything at all. One's actions are caused by processes in one's brain, e.g., neurons firing. (Of course the brain processes are linked to the rest of one's body via the nervous system.) These brain processes also cause one's mental states (beliefs, desires, etc.), according to epiphenomenalism, but the mental states themselves do not cause one's behavior.

Now, if epiphenomenalism were true, our beliefs could mostly be wildly false and yet they would have no negative effect on our behavior (because they would have no effect at all). Brain processes (not mental processes) would cause us to behave in ways that tend to promote survival. And an almighty but evil God could presumably construct creatures in such a way as to make epiphenomenalism true. Moreover, such a God might want to make epiphenomenalism true, either as a cruel joke or simply because that's "one interesting way to construct a creature." And if epiphenomenalism were true, then our capacity to get around and survive would give us *no assurance whatever* that our cognitive faculties are reliable. So if we are under the thumb of an evil God, then, for all we know, our cognitive faculties are unreliable.[4]

—Zach

Dear Zach,

I'm still not convinced. Suppose I have a nightmarish mystical experience and as a result I come to *believe* that there is an almighty but evil God. It's a scary thought, but how would I react? Would I stop believing what my eyes and ears tell me? Would I stop using logic? Would I stop relying on my memory? No, I'm quite sure I wouldn't. And frankly, I think continuing to rely on my cognitive faculties would be the smart move. It would be more sensible than falling into radical skepticism. So I don't think an experience of an evil God would seriously call my whole belief system into question.[5]

—Thomas

Dear Thomas,

I partly agree. No doubt you would in fact go on relying on your cognitive faculties; and in *one* sense that would be the reasonable (or "sensible") thing to do. From a pragmatic or practical point of view, you wouldn't really have much of an alternative. For example, it might well be psychologically impossible for you to become a radical skeptic, ceasing to believe that there are other people, trees, dogs, etc.

But does the fact that you would go on assuming the reliability of your cognitive faculties show that there is no good reason to doubt their reliability? Consider the following case. Jill is 23 years old and believes she will probably live for many years. But then her doctors tell her that she has a fatal disease and will probably die within six weeks: Ninety percent of those who get the disease die within six weeks. She gets a second and third opinion, but all the doctors agree that she has the fatal disease and will probably die within six weeks. No one knows why 10 percent of those who get the disease are able to survive it. So, based on what the doctors have told Jill, it seems she has only one chance in ten of living more than six weeks. But suppose Jill is a rather optimistic person—she continues to believe that she will probably live for many years.[6]

Is Jill irrational? Her response to the bad news seems natural and *may* be healthy. An optimistic outlook is generally very important in resisting diseases. So, perhaps, in this type of case, her cognitive faculties are working in a healthy way (functioning properly) in yielding an optimistic belief—at least temporarily. Let's assume that the optimistic belief is rational, *in the sense of being in her best interests*. But if so, then this case indicates that our cognitive faculties—even when they are functioning properly—don't *always* operate in such a way as to produce truth. When one's chances of survival are poor, one may be better off not believing that—*at least for a while*. But in this type of situation, human nature seems to be constituted so as to favor *survival* over accepting *truth*.

So, although Jill's belief may be rational in a *practical* sense (it's in her best interests), we can see that it is poorly grounded. If she were concerned *only* with getting the truth, she would not believe that she will probably live for many years. In other words, what the doctors have told Jill undermines her belief, in the sense of calling its *truth* into question.

The same goes for believing that an evil God exists. Yes, if you had that belief, you might very well go on trusting your cognitive faculties, and that might even be a healthy reaction, but *your belief in the existence of the evil God would in fact call the reliability of all your cognitive faculties into question, thus placing a question mark over all your beliefs*. In such a situation, to the extent that what you want is truth, you are in big trouble—for all you know, most of your beliefs are false. Thus, a mystical experience of an evil Deity is indeed self-defeating.

—Zach

Dear Zach,

Now I see your point. But suppose you're right. Suppose mystical experiences *as of* an evil Deity are self-defeating. And suppose this means we should reject (as unreliable) the experience of the man who claimed that God appeared to him and told him to commit genocide. Question: Doesn't this immediately create a problem for Jews and Christians? According to the Old Testament (e.g., 1 Samuel 15:1–3), didn't God command the Israelites to kill all the Canaanites (i.e., commit genocide)?

—Thomas

Dear Thomas,

Oh, boy! The passage you cite—and there are some others like it—is indeed problematic. Does the following principle seem correct to you?

> If we already have good evidence for the perfect goodness of God and good evidence that God commands X, then we have good evidence that X is morally right.

It seems correct to me. But the "if clause" here is not an easy one to satisfy. And until we have satisfied it for X = genocide, we rightly assume that genocide is wrong. After all, if genocide isn't wrong, what is? So, whatever our final understanding of those puzzling Old Testament passages may be, *in the context of a discussion of God's existence*, I still think it makes sense to assume both of the following:

A. Any Deity who commands an evil act is evil.
B. Genocide is evil.

If there are *in the end* good reasons to reject either A or B, they are not available to us at the moment, given the assumptions we have to make *for the purposes of discussing whether an almighty and perfectly good God exists*.

Well, that's my basic response. I don't wish to get bogged down in discussions of problematic Biblical passages. But let me follow up with three comments.

First, suppose my next-door neighbor claims that God appeared to him and told him to commit genocide. I would certainly regard my neighbor's religious experience as unreliable. And I'm confident that most people, including most Jews and Christians, would have the same reaction if their neighbors made similar claims.

Second, many religious believers take God's goodness for granted. The church or the Bible says that God is good, and that satisfies them. If we ask for arguments in support of the reliability of these sources, most believers struggle to answer. Or they answer (in effect) that the Bible is inspired by God. But of course we can't know that the Bible is inspired by God if we don't know there is a God. These believers often fail to realize that it is not a trivial task to provide evidence for God's goodness.

Third, I'm trying to defend Theism, not everything contained in the Theistic traditions. The Bible contains many puzzling passages, but one can reasonably be a Theist even if one does not see how all of them can be true.

—Zach

Dear Zach,

At risk of shocking you, allow me to announce that I don't disagree with anything in your last letter!

So at this point I accept all five of your proposed ways of identifying unreliable religious experiences. I understand that you are not claiming that the list is complete, but I regard it as a good start. You've convinced me of this much: One can accept some types of religious experience as reliable without falling into an "anything goes" attitude in this area.

But now I want to get back to the issue of Naturalistic causes. Have you read Newberg et al., *Why God Won't Go Away*?[7] These researchers have identified mechanisms in the brain that provide a Naturalistic explanation for religious experiences in general.

Neuroscientists know which part of the brain keeps one oriented in physical space. This part of the brain works constantly with input from the senses to help one draw a sharp distinction between one's body (self) and the rest of the physical world. Now, in certain circumstances, input from the senses to the orientation area is sharply decreased. In such circumstances, the orientation area of the brain is "blinded," that is, deprived of input from the senses. (Researchers have found that such a state of the brain is correlated with certain states of mind that can be induced by meditation.) When the orientation area of one's brain is deprived of input from the senses, *it is unable to find any boundary between one's body (self) and the world*. The self would then appear endless or identical with the world.

Of course, it is very common for religious mystics to have experiences in which they are "at one" with the universe, or in which the subject–object distinction breaks down. From the standpoint of neuroscience, this is not at all surprising if the orientation area of the brain is deprived of sensory input.

Another mechanism involves interaction between the right-orientation area of the brain and the attention area. This type of interaction can occur when the subject is focused exclusively on a single mental image. Take the example of a mental image of Christ; in intense meditation, the right-orientation area has

nothing to work with but the input streaming in from the attention area. It has no choice, therefore, but to create a spatial reality out of nothing but the attention area's single-minded contemplation of Christ. As the process continues, as all irrelevant neural input is stripped away and the mind becomes more focused, the image of Jesus "enlarges" until it becomes perceived by the mind as the whole depth and breadth of reality.[8]

It seems to me that this gives us a neuroscientific explanation of virtually any mystical experience. And let me add that these mechanisms aren't wild guesses. They are known to be present. And while the application to mystical experience may not yet be fully confirmed, it is backed up to some extent by empirical research.

—Thomas

Dear Thomas,

Thanks for bringing *Why God Won't Go Away* to my attention. It's very informative as regards neuroscience and I found it fascinating, but I don't see that it provides us with a good reason to doubt the reliability of Theistic mystical experience.

It is true, as you point out, that a great many mystics report experiences of becoming one with the universe, reality, or God. Where "becoming one" is to be understood in a strong sense, so that the subject merges with the object ("the subject–object distinction breaks down"), the brain mechanisms you've described plausibly account for the experience.

But the claim that the subject–object distinction breaks down is highly problematic. Surely there can be no experience without an "experiencer" (i.e., a subject). So if someone claims to have had an experience in which the subject–object distinction broke down, we rightly question the reliability of the experience. Certain brain mechanisms may well fully account for such puzzling experiences.

You might want to review the list of Theistic mystical experiences I sent you earlier. Those experiences differ in at least three important ways from the experiences highlighted in *Why God Won't Go Away*. First, in the Theistic mystical experiences, the subjects feel a strong sense of closeness to God, but they never identify themselves with God. They never state or imply that the subject–object distinction has broken down. And several of the accounts make it *explicit* that the subject retained a clear distinction, not only between him- or herself and God, but between him- or herself and the physical surroundings.

Second, note too that, in the Theistic mystical experiences, the subjects are not focusing on *any* sensory image (such as an image of Christ); they are directly aware of a personal presence that they do not *literally* see, touch, smell, hear, or taste.

Third, the Theistic mystical experiences involve *communion* between persons, what Martin Buber called an I–Thou relationship. The subject is not focused on a static image—there is an exchange of love, sympathy, comfort, and/or encouragement. Sometimes a specific message is received ("It'll turn out all right.").

To sum up, Theistic mystical experience seems to differ significantly from the experiences highlighted in *Why God Won't Go Away*. And the brain mechanisms described in that book do not, as far as I can tell, lead us to expect Theistic mystical experience.

One last point: Remember that brain processes cause *sense* experiences too—but the brain processes aren't the whole story. Using the Principle of Credulity, I reasonably take it that my sense experiences reveal a physical reality *distinct* from me. Similarly, the Theistic mystics take it that their mystical experiences reveal a divine reality *distinct* from themselves. And as far as I can see, neuroscience does not show the mystics to be unreasonable in doing so.

—Zach

Dear Zach,

Thanks for your recent letter on neuroscience and religious experience. I may have jumped to conclusions concerning the implications of some of the research. I suspect you are right to suggest that neuroscience provides a plausible explanation of some types of mystical experiences but not others. And maybe you are right to claim that neuroscience gives us no good reason to doubt Theistic mystical experience in particular.

But you have yet to deal with the toughest problem of all: the fact that the reports of experiences within one religious tradition often conflict with those in other religious traditions. It's as if we are jurors in a court of law and each eyewitness contradicts the previous eyewitness. We jurors don't know whom to trust.

—Thomas

Dear Thomas,

I think we need to do some careful sorting out of the reports of religious experience. First, many such reports are *different* from the reports of Theistic mystical experience but *logically consistent* with them. Here are some examples.

- A report of a vision of the Blessed Virgin Mary does not conflict logically with the reports of Theistic mystical experience. Both reports *could* be true, logically speaking. (I realize that the tradition-specific elements in a vision of the Blessed Virgin Mary may raise questions in your mind, but that's another issue entirely.)

- Suppose someone reports an experience of a presence that is good but *limited in power*. Here again there is no clear logical conflict. From a Theistic standpoint, such an experience might be an experience of an angel. (I'm not here defending such experiences as reliable. I'm just noting the absence of logical conflict.)

- Suppose someone reports an experience of oneness with the universe. Such vague terminology *might* merely indicate that there is *some sort* of underlying unity among all things, and this vague claim is not inconsistent with Theism, as far as I can tell.

Second, cases of conflict will involve reports of experiences of God (or ultimate reality) in which the descriptions of God (or ultimate reality) explicitly or implicitly contradict the reports of the Theistic mystics. Here are what I take to be the main sorts of conflict cases.

- Suppose someone reports an experience of God as almighty but evil or "beyond good and evil."

- Suppose someone reports an experience of ultimate reality as absolutely "one," i.e., as containing no distinctions or differences. For example, in one of the forms of Hinduism, Advaita Vedanta, mystics characteristically experience Brahman (reality) as *undifferentiated being*. These experiences are taken to indicate that all apparent differences are unreal (including the difference between you and me, between you and this letter, and between you and Brahman).

- Suppose two mystics report an experience in which God (almighty and thoroughly good) appears and conveys a message but the message one mystic reports ("Humans may eat meat") conflicts logically with the message the other mystic reports ("Humans may not eat meat").

To sum up, the reports of many kinds of religious experience are logically consistent with the reports of Theistic mystical experience; the reports of some kinds of religious experience are clearly in logical conflict with the reports of Theistic mystical experience; and logical conflicts can occur between two or more reports *within* the realm of Theistic mystical experience.

—Zach

Dear Zach,

OK. You admit there are conflict cases. Shall we take them up in order? Of course, I already know what you think about experiences of an almighty, evil Deity. But what about one who is "beyond good and evil"?

—Thomas

Dear Thomas,

What exactly does it mean to be "beyond good and evil"? An almighty Deity is either concerned about human welfare or not concerned. Suppose the Deity is totally unconcerned about human welfare. Two problems arise.

First, if an almighty Deity is totally unconcerned with human welfare, then it seems to be morally flawed, for an almighty Deity would be in a position to prevent or alleviate human suffering. If an almighty Deity is simply unconcerned with human suffering, it lacks love or benevolence. And to lack these traits is a moral defect. Right? But, then, the experience report of an almighty God "beyond good and evil" is inaccurate.

Second, go back to the "locked room" case. You are receiving messages on slips of paper every few minutes. You have no independent means of checking the messages for accuracy, etc. But this time you believe that the source of the messages is a Deity who is "beyond good and evil" and *totally unconcerned with human welfare (including your own welfare)*. Should you regard the messages as true for the most part? Obviously not. You would be very foolish to assume the messages were true for the most part. You would rightly judge that, given the source, the "information" is not to be trusted.

Now, suppose someone—call her Jo—has a mystical experience and as a result believes that there exists an almighty Deity who is "beyond good and evil" and totally unconcerned with human welfare (including her own welfare). Jo's situation is analogous to yours in the locked-room case—except that her belief has larger ripple effects. Jo would be foolish to assume that her cognitive faculties are reliable if they are formed (directly or indirectly) by such a Deity. Rather, Jo would rightly judge that the reliability of her cognitive faculties is in doubt. But if there is a question mark over all her cognitive faculties, the reliability of her mystical experience is also in doubt. In this way, Jo's mystical experience *as of* a God "beyond good and evil" is self-defeating. And of course, this won't be true simply of *Jo's* mystical experience but of any mystical experience that is relevantly similar.

On the other hand, suppose there's an almighty Deity who is "beyond good and evil" but concerned *to some degree* with human welfare. Here again, the experience report seems to me inaccurate. If the being is highly concerned with human welfare, then it seems to have a degree of benevolence, which is a moral virtue. If the Deity is concerned with our welfare but only a little bit, it is surely morally deficient. If the Deity is concerned to some *significant* degree with our welfare (but not highly concerned), it is like a human with a rather weak (or poorly formed) moral character. In that case again I fail to see how it can correctly be described as "beyond good and evil." It is morally mediocre.

Furthermore, the less concerned the Deity is with our welfare, the more any experiences of the Deity are apt to be self-defeating. After all, the less the Deity cares about our welfare, the more reason we have to doubt the reliability of our cognitive faculties, which are formed by the Deity (either directly or indirectly via processes under the Deity's control). To see this, put yourself back in the "locked room": You are now receiving messages from a Deity whom you believe to be concerned with human welfare but only in the way a morally mediocre person is concerned with human welfare. Could you count on such a Deity to provide you with true messages for the most part? I don't think you can confidently answer yes. You just wouldn't know what to expect.

To sum up, alleged experiences of an almighty Deity who is "beyond good and evil" are highly problematic. The experience reports are of questionable accuracy, for such a Deity appears to have moral qualities. And if those moral qualities are negative (e.g., the Deity doesn't care about human welfare or behaves like a human with a poorly formed moral character), the experiences seem to be self-defeating.

—Zach

Dear Zach,

So far you've focused on alleged experiences of a personal Deity. But what about mystical experiences that indicate the ultimate "oneness" of things? I'm particularly intrigued by mystical experiences in which all apparent differences are revealed as unreal. Here's an example from the Sufi mystic, Gulshan-Raz.

> Every man whose heart is no longer shaken by any doubt knows with certainty that there is no being save only One. . . . In his divine majesty the *me*, the *we*, the *thou* are not found, for in the One there can be no distinction. Every being who is annulled and entirely separated from himself hears resound outside of him this voice and this echo: *I am God:* he has an eternal way of existing and is no longer subject to death.[9]

I find this sort of experience fascinating. It presents us with a picture of reality completely at odds with the typical Western view. And here is an experience of a reality that is *truly beyond good and evil.*

—Thomas

Dear Thomas,

You may have seen this classic passage from *The Upanishads*:

> As pure water poured into pure water remains the same, thus, O Gautama, is the Self of a thinker who knows. Water in water, fire in fire, ether in ether, no one can distinguish them; likewise a man whose mind has entered into the Self.[10]

The Advaita Vendanta school of Hinduism takes this passage to indicate that "reality is one" (nondual), in the strong sense that *there are no real distinctions* (e.g., no real distinction between one human and another, between oneself and the universe, or between one physical object and another). Obviously, such experiences would be at odds with traditional Theism, which insists on a distinction between creatures and the Creator and on real distinctions between created individuals.

But the claim that reality is distinction-less-ness conflicts with sense experience. Sense experience tells us that you are distinct from a rock, that you are distinct from your dog, and that you are distinct from me. When mystical experiences conflict with sense experience, don't we have to regard the mystical experiences as unreliable?

—Zach

Dear Zach,

The Hindu mystics don't reject sense experience. They say it belongs to *maya*, the world of illusion. Mystical experience gives a deeper insight into the nature of reality.

—Thomas

Dear Thomas,

You speak as if Hindu theology and philosophy *in general* regard the world of differences as an illusion. This is not so. Advaita Vedanta is the best-known school of Hinduism *outside of India*, and this school does teach that there are no real distinctions. But the majority of Hindus do not follow Advaita Vedanta. For example, many Hindus are closer to the tradition of the medieval philosophers Ramanuja and Mahdva. These philosophers affirm that distinctions are real.[11] Incidentally, they also view God as in many respects similar to the God of Christians, Jews, and Muslims: personal, almighty, all-knowing, eternal, and good.

If we say that sense experience is reliable within *maya*, the world of illusion, we are making a distinction between *maya* and reality. Is this a real distinction, a real difference? It would seem so. But then what has become of the claim that all distinctions or differences are unreal? The teachings of Advaita Vedanta appear to be self-contradictory—a point not lost on Ramanuja.[12]

But again, for me, the idea that sense experience is illusory in some way, so that it must be corrected by mystical experience, seems highly problematic. Sense experience is a *paradigm* of reliable experience. I have defended Theistic mystical experience from various criticisms, but I've never suggested that it is on a par with sense experience. And while I reject empiricism—the idea that *only* sense experience is reliable—I see no respectable grounds for regarding mystical experiences as *more reliable* than sense experience. Where sense experience and mystical experience conflict, I think we must give precedence to sense experience.

—Zach

Dear Zach,

I must agree that sense experience is a paradigm of reliable experience. So I do share your skepticism about mystical experiences that purport to reveal things contrary to what our sense experience tells us.

But even if we set these types of experiences aside, you have to face the fact that there are many logical conflicts between the teachings of the world religions. So the content of *any* religious experience is bound to conflict with the content of some other religious experience, right? And doesn't this give us reason to doubt the reliability of all religious experiences?

—Thomas

Dear Thomas,

I think we need to think this through very carefully. First, we have to make a distinction between the total set of teachings (doctrines) of a religion and the portion of those teachings that is grounded in religious experience. For instance, the Christian religion involves a number of historical claims, e.g., that Jesus died on a cross. This historical claim is based not on religious experience, but on accounts in the Gospels—which Christians regard as based on eyewitness accounts. So, in spite of their various doctrinal differences, it *might* be that the typical religious or mystical experiences of Christians, Jews, and Muslims are similar and generally consistent. We have to look closely at the content of the *experiences* rather than at creeds or other general doctrinal summaries.

Second, when inconsistencies between experience reports occur, they often involve tradition-specific terminology. This raises the question whether the inconsistencies result from inference or interpretation. The core content of the experiences may be consistent.

Third, remember that there is plenty of disagreement within sense experience. Think of eyewitness accounts of an accident or robbery in a court of law—eyewitnesses often disagree on some points; we don't necessarily throw out their entire testimony. So we shouldn't reject all mystical experience simply because we find some significant disagreement between mystics. If we do reject all mystical experience in this manner, we're operating with an unjustified double standard. Or so it seems to me.

—Zach

Dear Zach,

Agreed: Not every doctrinal conflict is based on something revealed in a religious experience. But some are. Mohammed reported mystical experiences in which he received revelations from God (via the angel Gabriel, as I recall). Some of those revelations contradict Christian teaching. For example, "Say: He is God alone: / God the Eternal! / He begetteth not, and He is not begotten" (Koran 112).[13] That clearly contradicts the Christian doctrine that Jesus Christ is the only begotten Son of God.

—Thomas

Dear Thomas,

We certainly cannot accept as veridical every reported mystical experience, even if the purported object is God. That would lead to contradictions, as in the case of conflicting alleged revelations.

But clear cases of this type seem to be the exception, not the rule. Perhaps the typical Theistic mystical experience is of God performing acts such as comforting, encouraging, and strengthening the subject. And these types of experiences occur within many religious traditions. Also, keep in mind that the reports of *sense* experiences come into logical conflict fairly regularly. It doesn't follow that we should reject sense experience in general as unreliable. Similarly, we should not reject mystical Theistic experiences *in general* simply on the grounds that they sometimes give rise to conflicting experience reports.

Also, as I mentioned previously, I think many of the conflicts between reports of Theistic mystical experience involve tradition-specific elements. That's certainly true of the case you've quoted from the Koran. In these types of cases, I believe there are legitimate questions about the degree to which the experience report contains inference or interpretation. Hence, while it is clear that the experience reports are in logical conflict, it is open to question whether the experience has been described accurately.

Where does this leave us? For reasons I've just given, the conflicts between reports of Theistic mystical experience do not give us a good reason to reject Theistic mystical experience *in general* as unreliable. Also, Theistic mystical experience seems to stand up better under scrutiny than those forms of mystical experience whose content is clearly inconsistent with it, such as the experience of radical "oneness" or the experience of an evil God. So the alleged problem of conflicting mystical experiences does not give us a good reason to reject Theistic mystical experience. Not as far as I can see, anyway.

Throughout our discussion of Theistic mystical experience we've seen that many of the objections to it are based on confusions and/or arbitrary double standards. Furthermore, we've seen that the spiritual fruits of Theistic mystical experience rightly command respect. All in all, *I don't think we've seen any good reason to flatly reject Theistic mystical experience as unreliable.*

—Zach

Dear Zach,

I got into a discussion with some people at work today. I mentioned that you and I are discussing religious experience. One of my coworkers immediately launched into a short lecture! He said that alleged mystical experiences of God are in the same category as alleged sightings of Sasquatch or of extraterrestrials. He gave these reasons for regarding sightings of Sasquatch (and of extraterrestrials) as unreliable.

First, in general, we have to be wary of the human fascination with strange and amazing things. There's a part of us all that wants to believe that such things occur. (It's what leads many people to pay money for tabloids with ridiculous headlines, such as, "Woman Pregnant by Intergalactic Traveler.") When this fascination with the strange and amazing is mixed with religious sentiment, it can give rise to superstition. And historically, it often has.

Second, there's the matter of indirect evidence. If Sasquatch exists, there should be evidence in the forests, just as there is for other kinds of animals—tracks, droppings, lairs, and so on. If Sasquatch were not a mere legend, there would be strong evidence of this type by now. Similarly, if the accounts of extraterrestrials were true, there would be strong indirect evidence as called for by the accounts, such as footprints or tracks made by landing vehicles. Somehow, evidence of this type always turns out to be phony or highly ambiguous.

Third, with all the high-powered observation equipment scientists have these days, visiting extraterrestrials or Sasquatch would not go undetected.

Honestly, I was a bit taken aback by this lecture, which was delivered with great feeling and confidence. I couldn't help but wonder how you would respond to it.

—Thomas

Dear Thomas,

A nice three-point lecture! I would respond as follows.

The first reason does apply in the case of Theistic mystical experience. All or most of us are in some way fascinated by the possibility of a mystical experience that directly reveals something important, something that we as humans yearn to know. However, while the first reason merits consideration, surely it is not strong enough by itself to indicate that Theistic mystical experience is unreliable. After all, we know that very strange and improbable things do sometimes occur.

The second reason takes us back to the issue of tests for Theistic mystical experience. And there are two things to keep in mind: (1) As the case of introspection shows, we cannot assume that all reliable forms of experience are subject to the kinds of tests sense experience is subject to. (2) Moreover, as we've seen, there is a kind of test for Theistic mystical experience: We would expect people who've had a direct awareness of God to show signs of having experienced a presence both infinite in power and perfectly good: a new set of priorities, greater love for others, trust in God, increased inner peace, etc. This sort of test may not settle things, but surely it has some value.

The third reason is, I believe, very important in the case of Sasquatch (and of extraterrestrials) but not relevant to Theistic mystical experience. There simply is no relevant "God-detection" equipment.

So the analogy with alleged sightings of Sasquatch (and of extraterrestrials) doesn't seem very close or helpful to me. I think my "Third Parable of the Courier" is a better analogy. Remember how it goes?

> *The Third Parable of the Courier.* A courier with a vitally important and urgent message set forth on a journey through uninhabited and mountainous lands. Because winter was fast approaching, he knew he would die in the mountains if he failed to find a pass through to his destination. He met two scouts, each of whom claimed he had once crossed the mountains. But the scouts disagreed about the location of the pass and how to find it. Each warned that following the

advice of the other would lead to death in the mountains. The courier took some time to discuss these matters with the scouts. Each of them seemed sincere and experienced. The courier felt it would be folly for him to disregard the advice of the scouts and to set out on his own. But whose advice should he take? After much discussion and reflection, he found himself inclined to think that one of the scouts was somewhat more credible than the other. So he took that scout's advice and set out on his way.

The courier had some reason to doubt the testimony of the two scouts (in regard to the location of the mountain pass) but not a good enough reason to write their testimony off as worthless. The courier rightly regards the claims of the scouts as significant evidence, though not sufficient to justify belief. Similarly, I think that the testimony of the Theistic mystics is significant evidence for the existence of God but does not by itself justify the belief that God exists.

—Zach

Dear Zach,

I suppose I might agree that the testimony of Theistic mystics is reasonably regarded as evidence for God's existence. But how significant is that evidence? Is there any way to specify that?

—Thomas

Dear Thomas,

It seems to me that the degree of significance depends on the strength of the reasons for doubting the testimony of the mystics. There is of course no "strength-o-meter" that can specify such strength in precisely quantifiable units. But I don't think this means that our answer must be hopelessly vague or subjective.

One thing we can do is appeal to analogies. Your coworker offered the "Sasquatch" analogy. I've offered the Third Parable of the Courier. It seems to me that my courier analogy is much nearer the mark than the Sasquatch analogy. If that's right, the testimony of the Theistic mystics gives us good reason to take the Theistic hypothesis quite seriously. The mystics' testimony does not by itself justify the belief that God exists, but it provides more than just a tiny bit of support. The degree of support is significant—just as the courier finds the testimony of the scouts significant (and so not easily dismissed)—though insufficient to support belief.

Perhaps we can best try to specify the degree of support by reflecting on some of Theism's disadvantages relative to Naturalism. I noted earlier that Theism is more complicated than Naturalism in four ways (corresponding to the four facets of simplicity):

1. It postulates an entity (God) that Naturalism does not postulate.
2. It postulates a *kind* of entity that Naturalism does not postulate (specifically, a necessarily existing, nonphysical person).
3. It employs somewhat more complex terms (e.g., *almighty*).
4. It contains more claims.

I think that Theistic mystical experience helps to offset points 1 and 2 by taking Theism out of the realm of *mere* speculation. Put simply, postulating God is not like postulating quarks; no one claims to have seen (or otherwise directly experienced) quarks. All our information about quarks is obtained indirectly, by inference.[14] But many claim to have had a direct experience of God—and if I'm right, there is no conclusive reason to reject these experiences as unreliable.

I suggest that the testimony of the Theistic mystics makes up for *at least one* of the ways in which Theism is more complex than Naturalism. *If the testimony of the mystics doesn't count for at least this much, it seems to me that we've relegated it to insignificance.* And I think that would be a mistake. Indeed, I'm inclined to think that the testimony of the mystics largely makes up for Theism's greater complexity in regard to *both* of the first two facets of simplicity. But I'll rest content with the more modest claim: The testimony of the Theistic mystics makes up for *at least one* of the ways in which Theism is more complicated than Naturalism.

Let me know what you think.

—Zach

# CHAPTER 4

# A Cosmological Argument

Dear Zach,

I'm still pondering your last letter on religious experience. Frankly, I'm not sure what to think at this point, and I suspect it will be a while before I do. (Sometimes it's like that for me.) But I'd still like to discuss some arguments for the existence of God. And I'm willing to accept your conclusions about religious experience *for the sake of the argument*. Can we proceed on that basis?

—Thomas

Dear Thomas,

Of course. Why don't we consider a cosmological argument? Roughly speaking, a *cosmological argument* moves from the existence of the cosmos or universe to the existence of God. But the cosmological argument comes in many forms, and I'd like to present a version that starts with the fact that there are many *contingent* beings.

As usual, I'll need to clarify some key concepts before I can actually state the argument. We'll need a clear understanding of the concept of a contingent being and of the contrasting concept of a necessary being. And I think we can best clarify these concepts by first considering the related concepts of contingent and necessary truths.

Let's begin with the concept of a necessary truth. Here are some examples of **necessary truths**—truths that cannot be false under any possible circumstances:

1. Either frogs exist or it is not the case that frogs exist.
2. All married men are married.

3. All husbands are married.

4. One plus one equals two.

5. If Mary is older than Al, then Al is younger than Mary.

6. Nothing is red all over and green all over at the same time.

7. Whatever has color has size.

These examples fall into certain significant categories. Items 1 and 2 are true by virtue of their logical form. For example, if we let "A" stand for "Frogs exist," then item 1 is of the form "Either A or not A"; and from the standpoint of classical logic, all propositions having this form must be true. If we let "A" stand for "married" and "B" for "men," then item 2 has the form "All things that are A and B are A." Again, every proposition having this logical form must be true.

Item 3 can be transformed into one that is true by virtue of its logical form by replacing synonyms with synonyms, specifically, by replacing *husbands* with *married men*. Philosophers use the term **analytic** to refer to any statement that is either (a) true by virtue of its logical form or (b) transformable into one that is true by virtue of its logical form by replacing synonyms with synonyms.[1]

Item 4 is a mathematical truth. Since it does not seem possible for mathematical truths to be false, philosophers commonly regard mathematical truths as necessary.

Items 5 through 7 are more difficult to classify. They do not seem to be analytic. Philosophers use the word **synthetic** to refer to propositions or statements that are not analytic. Although items 5, 6, and 7 seem to be synthetic, it also seems impossible for them to be false under any circumstances. Accordingly, many philosophers regard them as synthetic but necessary.

With these comments about necessary truths in hand, it's easy to define *contingent truth*. A contingent truth is any truth that is not necessary; that is, a **contingent truth** is one that could have been false under different circumstances. Examples include:

8. Socrates was a married man.

9. There are 50 states in the United States of America.

10. Frogs exist.

Though these propositions are true, it is easy to see that they could have been false under different circumstances. Regarding item 8, Socrates was in fact married to Xanthippe, but he might have chosen not to marry at all. Regarding item 9, becoming a state in the United States depends on a vote by Congress, and so any one of the states currently in the union might have been turned down, in which case there would be forty-nine states in the United States of America rather than fifty. Regarding item 10, according to evolutionary theory, frogs evolved from simpler forms of life, and so there was a time when there were no frogs. Had the Earth been destroyed by a large asteroid prior to the evolution of frogs, there presumably would never have been any frogs at all.

Does the distinction between necessary and contingent truths seem clear to you?

—Zach

Dear Zach,

I'm not sure I believe that there are any necessary truths. For example, "All husbands are married" seems to be true by definition; that is, it's just true because English speakers define *husband* in a certain way. But words can change meaning over time, and, as a matter of historical fact, they often do. So "All husbands are married" is currently true, but it might not be true a few hundred years from now. What if, over time, *husbands* comes to mean *rich elderly men*; then "All husbands are married" would no longer be true, right? And if this is possible, then "All husbands are married" is not a *necessary* truth.

—Thomas

Dear Thomas,

I think we need to make a distinction between sentences and propositions. Consider these sentences:

1. Grass is green.

2. Das Gras ist grün.

Sentence 2 translates sentence 1 into German. So these sentences can be used to express the same truth (or falsehood). That is to say, these sentences can be used to express the same proposition. A **proposition** is a truth or falsehood that may (or may not) be expressed in a sentence. Whereas a sentence belongs to a particular language, such as English or German, a proposition does not.

The meaning of words—and hence of sentences—can change over time, no doubt about that. It does not follow that the propositions they express change in truth value (from true to false, or vice versa). For example, the following sentence expresses a geometrical truth:

3. No circles are rectangles.

If you understand *circle*, *rectangle*, *No*, and *are* in the conventional way, you understand that this sentence expresses a true proposition—indeed, a necessarily true proposition. But over time, *circle* might change in meaning so that it comes to mean what we now mean by the word *square*. In that case sentence 3 would express a false proposition. But this wouldn't change the geometrical truth currently expressed by sentence 3. We would simply have to find a different sentence to express that truth.

Make sense?

—Zach

Dear Zach,

OK, I think I understand the distinction between sentences and propositions. Would the following be necessary truths?

A. All uncles are men.
B. All dogs are animals.
C. Every event has a cause.
D. No human can run a mile in 1 minute.

I'm pretty sure A and B are necessary—I'm less sure about C and D.

—Thomas

Dear Thomas,

Yes, A and B are necessary truths. If something is not a man, then it won't count as an uncle. And if something is not an animal, then it clearly cannot be a dog.

I don't think C is necessary. "Every *effect* has a cause" is a necessary truth. (Nothing counts as an effect unless it has a cause.) But it seems to me that an event could in principle occur uncaused; e.g., a tiny physical particle might spontaneously move without being caused to do so. I'm not at the moment making a claim about how our universe actually works; I'm just saying that there could be a universe (or reality) like that.[2] (I think an almighty God could create a physical universe that operated in that way, with some events occurring by chance.) So I don't think C is necessarily true. But that's just my own metaphysical intuition—certainly not something I regard as obviously true.

This reminds me, however, of an important clarification I should make. *For all we know*, some events do not have causes. But our lack of knowledge here does not prove that "Every event has a cause" is a contingent truth. To see this, just consider that some mathematical truths are not known at all, for example:

*Goldbach's Conjecture*: Every even number greater than 2 is equal to the sum of two prime numbers.

Goldbach's Conjecture has never been proven and neither has its negation (i.e., "Not every even number greater than 2 is equal to the sum of two primes"). Yet, since we are dealing here with mathematics, either Goldbach's Conjecture or its negation is presumably a necessary truth. (We just don't know which it is.) Therefore, we must be on guard against reasoning like this: "For all we know, proposition P is false, so P is not a necessary truth." For all we know, Goldbach's Conjecture is false, but nevertheless it may turn out to be a necessary truth. If some mathematician proves Goldbach's Conjecture (or its negation), that would settle the matter.

Is D—"No human can run a mile in 1 minute"—necessary? I assume it is physically impossible for a human to run that fast. Natural causes (codified in laws of nature) cannot produce that result: Human nerves, bones, and muscles just aren't up to running that fast. But supernatural causes are metaphysically possible, in my view. So, perhaps with divine assistance (e.g., strengthening bones and muscles), a human could run a mile in a minute, in which case D is not a necessary truth.

—Zach

Dear Zach,

If God can cause exceptions to "No human can run a mile in 1 minute," why can't God cause exceptions to any generalization, including "All squares are rectangles" or "All dogs are animals"? It seems to me that if an almighty God exists, then there are no necessary truths. There is a circumstance in which any generalization is false, namely, the circumstance in which God causes an exception to it.

—Thomas

Dear Thomas,

Most philosophers and theologians recognize a distinction between what is *physically* impossible and what is *metaphysically* (or logically) impossible. Something is **physically impossible** if natural causes cannot produce it, but a physical impossibility might occur if supernatural causes are operative (e.g., God works a miracle). However, if there are necessary truths, then any event, situation, or object that would render them false is **metaphysically impossible**. Such things simply cannot happen (or exist), period.

Consider an example. It is physically impossible for a human to fly (unaided by technology), but presumably God could cause a human to soar through the air. However, suppose I claim that a human is flying while (simultaneously) *not* flying (using the word *flying* in the same sense in both instances); *that's* a metaphysical impossibility. (It conflicts with a necessary truth along these lines: No one can have a property and lack that property at the same time.) Or suppose I claim that a biologist discovered a colorless green frog; again, that's a metaphysical impossibility. (It conflicts with the necessary truth that everything green has a color.) Because metaphysical impossibilities conflict with necessary truths, they are absolutely impossible—not possible under any circumstances whatsoever. According to most theologians (at least since the time of Aquinas), even an almighty being cannot bring about metaphysical (or logical) impossibilities.

Incidentally, most religious believers implicitly recognize the distinction I've just made. For example, in discussions of the problem of evil, believers will often appeal to human free will to explain the presence of evil in the world. But why doesn't God cause people to choose *freely* only the good? Answer: The "choices" wouldn't be free if fully caused by God. In other words, it is a necessary truth that no coerced act is free. The appeal to free will (to explain the presence of evil) makes no sense if we suppose that a human act can be both fully caused by God and yet free. So religious believers (at least implicitly) recognize that even an almighty being cannot bring about metaphysical (or logical) impossibilities.

—Zach

Dear Zach,

OK, I'm willing to accept the distinction between necessary and contingent truths. I think I get the basic idea. But would you agree that in some cases it is difficult to be sure whether a given truth is necessary or contingent?

—Thomas

Dear Thomas,

Yes, and that's how it is with many, perhaps even most, philosophical concepts. A philosophical concept may be very useful even though its application is not clear in some (or even many) cases.

Let me now link our discussion of necessary and contingent truths to the concepts of necessary and contingent beings. A **contingent being** is an entity that actually exists but might not have existed. A vast number of entities seem to be contingent. For example, humans in general would seem to be contingent beings. (If my parents had never met, I presumably would never have come into existence at all. And had one of my parents died at an early age, I assume they would never even have met one another, since they did not meet at all until they were young adults.) Furthermore, most things we know of come into existence at some point. And unless the processes that bring such things into existence are metaphysically necessary, those processes might not have occurred, and so, presumably, the entities in question might not have existed.

Just as a contingent truth is true but might have been false, so a contingent being is one that does exist but might not have. And suppose we claim, with regard to any contingent being, that it exists, e.g., "I (Zach) exist" or "You (Thomas) exist." Such propositions are contingent truths, not necessary ones. More generally, we can state the relationship between contingent beings and contingent truths as follows: *A being is contingent if (and only if) every proposition affirming its existence is a contingent truth.*

The opposite of a contingent being is a necessary being. A **necessary being** is one that could not fail to exist under any possible circumstances. *A being is necessary if (and only if) at least one proposition affirming its existence is a necessary truth.*[3] It's a matter of controversy among philosophers whether there are any necessary beings. Of course, Theists typically claim that God is a necessary being. So examining the cosmological argument will move us into this area of controversy.

—Zach

Dear Zach,

It has been some time since I read David Hume's *Dialogues Concerning Natural Religion*, but your last letter jogged my memory. I seem to recall that Hume argued along these lines:[4]

> If there is a necessary being—call it *Yahweh*, then "Yahweh exists" is a necessary truth. But a truth is necessary only if (a) its denial (or negation) is a contradiction or (b) a contradiction can be derived logically from its denial. For example, "All husbands are married" is a necessary truth, and its denial, "Not all husbands are married," logically implies "At least one husband is not married," which in turn implies "At least one married man is not married" (which is a contradiction). But consider existential statements, such as "Santa exists." The denial of "Santa exists" is of course "Santa does not exist"—which is clearly not a contradiction. And there is no way, logically speaking, to derive a contradiction from it. The same goes for "Zeus exists" and "Baal exists." "Zeus does not exist" is not a contradiction and neither is "Baal does not exist"; nor can we logically derive contradictions from these statements. And presumably, "Yahweh does not exist" is no different. Hence, "Yahweh exists" is not a necessary truth. And therefore, Yahweh is not a necessary being.

That's a plausible argument, isn't it?

—Thomas

Dear Thomas,

Your summary of Hume's argument is very nice! And, yes, I admit that the argument is plausible. But I think there's a snag in the reasoning.

The negation of any necessary truth is a **necessary falsehood**, i.e., a proposition that cannot be true in any possible circumstances. (Examples: "Green is not a color," "1 + 1 = 11," and "Circular squares exist.") But it is now widely recognized among philosophers that not every necessary falsehood is a logical contradiction, of the form "A and not A." For example, Saul Kripke has convinced many philosophers that identity statements, such as "Water is $H_2O$," are necessary truths. If something is water, it must be $H_2O$; if it is not $H_2O$, then it cannot be water. Suppose we visited another planet and found something that looked, smelled, and tasted like water but wasn't $H_2O$. Would we claim that it was water? Surely not. (We might call it "fool's water" on analogy with "fool's gold," but surely we would deny that it is water. If fool's gold isn't gold, then "fool's water" isn't water!) But if "Water is $H_2O$" is necessarily true, then "Water is not $H_2O$" is necessarily false. (In general, the negation of a necessary truth is a necessary falsehood.) And although "Water is not $H_2O$" is necessarily false, it is not a contradiction—not of the form "A and not A." Nor can one show that "Water is not $H_2O$" is necessarily false by deriving a contradiction from it. So Hume's argument rests on a false assumption about necessary truths.[5]

Kripke's examples are especially interesting, because if he's right, some necessary truths cannot be known *a priori*. A statement is **knowable *a priori*** if either (a) it is self-evident or (b) it can be logically derived from self-evident statements. A statement is **self-evident** if it can be known simply by understanding the concepts involved. Typical examples of *a priori* statements include:

1. Every wife is married.

2. Whatever has color has size.

3. $31 \times 13 = 403$.

Items 1 and 2 are self-evident. In order to know item 1, we don't need to do an empirical study, e.g., by interviewing a large sample of wives to determine the percentage that are married. We understand that a wife is a married woman, so we immediately see that item 1 is true—indeed, necessarily true. Regarding item 2, if we understand the concept of color, we see that whatever has color must be spread out in space—at least a little bit, and hence it must have some size, even if it's quite small. Item 3 is not self-evident (at least not for most of us), but it can be derived from self-evident statements, specifically, the statements we employ as we work out the multiplication (e.g., $3 \times 1 = 3$, $3 \times 3 = 9$, $1 \times 31 = 31$, and so on). So item 3 is also knowable *a priori*.

Clearly, "Water is $H_2O$" is not knowable *a priori*. It had to be discovered through scientific research—empirical investigation. You can't see that it's true simply by sitting in your armchair and reflecting on the concept of water. Yet, if Kripke is right, and I think he is, "Water is $H_2O$" is a necessary truth.[6]

Note that item 2 also runs contrary to Hume's assumption that, if a truth is necessary, we can always show this by deriving a contradiction from its denial (negation). The denial of item 2 is "Something has color but not size," which is not self-contradictory. It's *not false by virtue of its logical form,* as is, say, "Something has *size* but doesn't have *size*." Moreover, there doesn't seem to be any way, logically speaking, to derive a contradiction from "Something has color but not size." *Hume is assuming that all necessary truths are analytic. The problem is that some necessary truths are pretty clearly synthetic.* For this reason, Hume's famous argument fails.

—Zach

Dear Zach,

Your last letter was interesting and helpful. Honestly, I hadn't realized that Hume's views about necessity were so vulnerable to objections.

After reading your letter, I got out my old copy of Hume's *Dialogues.* In spite of all you've said, Hume seems right when he says, "Whatever we can conceive as existent, we also conceive as nonexistent."[7] We can conceive that unicorns exist, but we can also conceive that they don't, so they don't exist of necessity. We can conceive that Baal exists, but we can also conceive that Baal does not exist, so Baal doesn't exist of necessity. Similarly, we can conceive that God exists, but we can also conceive that God doesn't exist; therefore, God does not exist of necessity.

—Thomas

Dear Thomas,

I think Hume's assumption that *whatever is conceivable is possible* is also quite dubious.

What is it for something to be conceivable? Presumably, I conceive of something by grasping the concepts and propositions involved. Go back to Goldbach's Conjecture. Can we conceive that it is true? Well, we can understand the concepts involved, and we can understand what Goldbach's Conjecture means. But we don't know whether it's true. And if it is not true, it is necessarily false (the same goes for any math statement). So, even though we may think we can "conceive" that Goldbach's Conjecture is true, for all we know it is necessarily false.

What is it for something to be possible, in this context? There are two very different meanings that we must not confuse: (1) In the relevant sense, a statement is **possibly true** if it is not necessarily false. Examples: "I am wearing a tin foil hat" (I'm not, but I could be). "Columbus is the capital of Ohio" (it is, and whatever is actually true is not necessarily false, and so is possibly true). Here the possibilities are metaphysical in nature. (2) But sometimes when we say something is "possibly true" we mean that it is true *for all we know*, that is, that the information we have on hand does not rule it out. Philosophers call this **epistemic possibility**. (Epistemology is the part of philosophy that deals with questions about *knowledge*.) Goldbach's Conjecture is possible in this sense; *for all we know*, it's true. But this does not prove that Goldbach's Conjecture is possible in the metaphysical sense. The failure to distinguish carefully between these two kinds of possibility can easily lead to philosophical disaster.

Now, here's a little thought experiment. Travel back in time before the discovery that water is $H_2O$. Back then, I think, people might well have found it "conceivable" that water is not $H_2O$. And in one sense they would have been right, for one cannot discover that *water is $H_2O$* simply by grasping the concepts involved. If all one has to go on is a grasp of the relevant concepts, then, *for all one knows*, water is not $H_2O$. But as we've seen, it would be a huge logical mistake to move from "For all I know, water is not $H_2O$" to "It is *metaphysically* possible that water is not $H_2O$." (That's like arguing, "For all I know Goldbach's Conjecture is false, so it's metaphysically possible that Goldbach's Conjecture is false." But for all we know, Goldbach's Conjecture is true, and if it's true, it's necessarily true, in which case it *cannot* be false, metaphysically speaking.)

I hope it is clear, at this point, that something might be conceivable, or at least seem conceivable, without being metaphysically possible. In some cases, human powers of conception are adequate to the task, as in the case of "Circular squares exist." (Simply grasping the concepts enables us to see that the statement must be false.) But in other cases our conceptual grip on an issue just does not get us deep enough into the nature of things, and then the appeal to conceivability will be inadequate.

Hume thought he could conceive of the nonexistence of God. That's understandable, *in a sense*. It seems conceivable that there is no entity that is almighty, perfectly morally good, etc. And many would add that atheism (i.e., God does not exist) is *epistemically* possible, true "for all they know." But as we've just seen, such claims in no way show that atheism is *metaphysically* possible.

—Zach

Dear Zach,

I do see that *being metaphysically possible* and *being epistemically possible* are two very different things. But I'm still a little uneasy about the notion of a necessary being. Is God the only alleged example of a necessary being?

—Thomas

Dear Thomas,

No, many philosophers think that certain abstract entities, such as numbers, are necessary beings. Recall that, in general, mathematical truths are necessary truths. For example:

A. There is an even number between 7 and 9.

But if A is a necessary truth, then the number 8 is apparently a necessary being. For if A is true, then there must be a number 8, and A is *necessarily* true.

—Zach

Dear Zach,

Hmmm. To be honest, I've never thought about the existence of numbers. But if there were no physical objects, would there be any numbers? I doubt it. And surely it is possible that there are no physical objects—at any rate, Theists would have to accept this, since they believe God freely created physical reality.

—Thomas

Dear Thomas,

If there were no physical objects, then the number of physical objects would be zero, right? The number would be zero and not 1, not 2, not 22, and so on. Or so it seems to me. Thus, if we could rid the world of physical objects, I don't think we would thereby rid it of numbers.

Let me add that I don't think it's plausible to suggest that numbers are physical objects. If the number 8 is a physical object, which one is it? Any answer one could give seems plainly wrong.

—Zach

Dear Zach,

Maybe the numbers exist only in our minds. Maybe numbers are just thoughts.

—Thomas

Dear Thomas,

I don't buy the idea that numbers exist only in our minds. If a nuclear war eliminated all human life, there would still be various things in existence, presumably, and certain facts would still hold, e.g., that there are *more than three* planets in the solar system. Right?

—Zach

Dear Zach,

Interesting. Well, maybe numbers do exist of necessity. But can Theists accept that? If the number 8 exists of necessity, it can't fail to exist under any circumstances. And doesn't it follow that the existence of the number 8 is outside of God's control? And isn't that contrary to what Theists hold about God as Creator and Sovereign?

—Thomas

Dear Thomas,

The relationship between God and what philosophers call *abstract entities* (such as numbers and sets) belongs to a highly speculative area of philosophical theology. Various positions are compatible with traditional Theism.

Theists insist that God created the physical universe ("the heavens and the Earth") and all that is contained therein. God is the creator of all the quarks, atoms, stars, planets, and galaxies. God is the creator of all forms of life, from single-celled animals to human beings. If there are any finite unembodied spirits, i.e., angels, God created them also. To summarize this in philosophical terms, we can say simply that *God is the creator of all the contingent beings.*

But God did not create himself. Nor did God create any part or aspect of himself, e.g., his eternality or omnipotence. Did God create the numbers? Well, there are reasons from within the Theistic traditions for answering no. When ordinary believers say that God created something, they normally mean that God brought it into existence at some point in time—the entity in question was not always in existence. But from the standpoint of traditional Theism, it appears that numbers have always been in existence. Here's why: Jews, Christians, and Muslims are monotheists; they insist that there is exactly one God—i.e., there always has been and always will be just one God. (It's not as if, say, polytheism was once true, but then all of the gods except one died off!) And of course, from the standpoint of traditional Theism, God has always *known* that there is exactly one God. But assuming "There is exactly one God" is a meaningful statement, it has always implied that "There are not two gods," "There are not seventeen gods," and so on. And God has always known all these things. So, from a theistic perspective, it appears that the numbers are eternal.

Now, being eternal is not the same thing as being necessary. Some philosophers (e.g., Aquinas) have suggested that God might create some things eternally. That is, some things might be dependent on God for their existence, and yet they might always have existed because God has always been freely creating and sustaining them. The argument in the previous paragraph does nothing to eliminate this apparent possibility. But if the numbers are eternal yet created, then God could "uncreate" them, i.e., annihilate them. Were that to happen, then there would be no fact of the matter about how many gods there are—there wouldn't be one God, there wouldn't be zero gods, there wouldn't be fourteen gods, and so on. But that seems metaphysically impossible. If there is a God, then there has to be some number of Gods—one or two or twenty-nine—some specific number. Anyway, that's what I think.

I believe that numbers are necessary beings. And I don't see this as a Theistic "heresy." Notice that numbers are causally inert; they are not agents. A number cannot make a decision. A number cannot form a purpose. A number cannot move a physical object by bumping into it. Numbers don't have electrical charges. Numbers cannot rise up and lead a rebellion against God. And so on. In short, even if numbers exist of necessity, they do not threaten God's sovereignty.

But it's instructive to think about the existence of numbers. It at least gives us some examples of entities that *seem* to exist of necessity.

—Zach

Dear Zach,

At this point, I'm willing to admit that, for all I know, some things are necessary beings. And I gather that your cosmological argument attempts to explain the presence of contingent beings by appeal to a necessary being, namely, God. But, to be honest, I don't feel a desperate need to explain the presence of contingent beings. Should I? And I find myself wondering if scientists would care about this issue. I rather doubt that they would.

—Thomas

Dear Thomas,

One of the all-time great philosophical questions is "Why is there something rather than nothing?" The cosmological argument attempts to answer this question.

Many of the greatest philosophical minds have wondered at the fact of existence. Might there have been nothing at all? Why is there anything in existence? Such questions are clearly fundamental, and they arise from the childlike sort of wonder that fuels philosophy.

By the way, some scientists do show a keen interest in the question "Why is there something rather than nothing?" For example, some physicists have speculated that "the physical universe blossomed forth spontaneously out of nothing, driven by the laws of physics."[8] Whether this highly speculative suggestion counts as "scientific" may be doubtful, but my point is simply that some scientists are clearly intrigued by ultimate questions of being.

Of course, the fact that we can ask a question is no guarantee that we can answer it. And a phenomenon might turn out to be what philosophers call a **brute fact**, i.e., a fact that cannot be explained. But as thinkers we naturally would like to explain as much as we can. And why insist that something is a brute fact in advance of considering any possible explanations for it? If something can be explained, then, by definition, it's not a brute fact. So if plausible explanations are available (or can be constructed) for phenomenon X, then we have plausible grounds for denying that X is a brute fact! In short, you find out what can be explained by *trying* hard to explain things, not by being incurious.

One more thing: Theism and Naturalism are fundamental metaphysical views or hypotheses. As such, they are meant to help us obtain *the deepest and most comprehensive* understanding of the whole of life and reality. No fundamental metaphysical view gains ground by admitting it lacks the resources to explain something. Take any phenomenon, X: If metaphysical position A can explain X and metaphysical position B cannot, then B is losing ground to A (at least to some extent). Philosophically speaking, we want the view that gives us the best explanation of as much of reality as possible.

—Zach

Dear Zach,

All right, I'm philosophical enough to find "Why is there something rather than nothing?" an intriguing question. But then why isn't the phenomenon "Something exists"? Why focus on *contingent* beings?

—Thomas

Dear Thomas,

Let me come at your question a bit indirectly. First, if a being is not contingent, then it is one that *must* exist. In other words, a non-contingent being is a necessary being. Second, as we've seen, both Theism and Naturalism postulate entities. And Theism postulates a necessary being, God. Recall our formulation of Theism.

> **Theism**: (1) There is exactly one entity that is (2) perfectly morally good and (3) almighty and that (4) exists of necessity.

Now, why does this necessary being exist? Well, according to the Theist, nothing brought God into existence. God's existence is not dependent on that of any other being. Theists will simply observe that, *by its very nature, a necessary being is one that cannot fail to exist under any circumstances.* If someone wants to know why God exists, that sums up the answer. (The more detailed response would parallel our discussion of necessary and contingent truths, sentences and propositions, epistemic and metaphysical possibilities, etc.)

Given my formulation, Naturalists *may* postulate a necessary being (or necessary beings) or they may postulate *only* contingent beings:

> **Naturalism**: (1) There is a self-organizing physical reality (i.e., there is a physical reality whose nature is not imposed by a god or by any other force or agent), (2) physical reality exists either necessarily, eternally, or by chance, and (3) leaving aside possible special cases (e.g., sets or numbers), all entities are physical entities.

Now, to answer your question "Why focus on contingent beings (as the phenomenon) in formulating a cosmological argument?" In a nutshell, both Theists and Naturalists *can* postulate a necessary being; and if they do, they will say that by its very nature it cannot fail to exist. And whatever one side says about the nature of necessary beings, the other side can presumably say too. Contingent beings, however, do exist *but might not have existed*. Logically speaking, there are various possible explanations of the presence of contingent beings. And here Theistic and Naturalistic explanations will diverge. The Cosmological Argument is an attempt to show that, as regards the presence of contingent beings, Theism has more explanatory power than Naturalism.

—Zach

Dear Zach,

OK, I now see why we're focusing on contingent beings. How does the argument go?

—Thomas


Dear Thomas,

Theism postulates a necessary being who is almighty and so has the power to bring the contingent beings of our acquaintance into existence. Also, Theism postulates an almighty *person* and hence an entity who can make choices. The choices or volitions of God can thus explain the presence of contingent beings in the world, *assuming God has reason to create anything at all.* Any being God freely chooses to create, he might also freely choose not to create, and hence any being God freely chooses to create is a contingent being.

But does God have reason to create anything at all? Yes. A perfectly morally good being would be a loving being, hence generous. A loving and generous being would have reason to create entities with which to share good things. So God would have reason to create conscious beings who can enjoy good things as well as reason to create the good things for conscious beings to enjoy. It seems especially clear that God would have reason to create intelligent conscious creatures along with things for them to enjoy, such as beauty, interesting activities, pleasures, and satisfying personal relationships.

I don't think we can say *precisely* how probable or likely the presence of contingent beings would be, if God exists, but their presence surely is not very surprising on the assumption of Theism. We can at least say that much.

Does Naturalism lead us to expect the presence of contingent beings? First we have to ask whether Naturalism regards *all* of physical reality as contingent. If so, then Naturalism simply postulates the presence of contingent beings as a brute fact—unexplained and inexplicable. We cannot *explain* the very presence of contingent beings in the world simply by *postulating* contingent beings. Thus, to "get into the game" here, Naturalism will need to say that some aspect of physical reality exists of necessity. In this connection, Hume remarks:

> Why may not the material universe be the necessarily existent Being? . . . We dare not affirm that we know all the qualities of matter; and, for aught we can determine, it may contain some qualities which, were they known, would make its nonexistence appear as great a contradiction [metaphysical impossibility] as that twice two is five.[9]

Of course, this is not something Naturalists typically say, and saying it would complicate their hypothesis. Which aspects of physical reality are necessary and why should we think this? According to contemporary physics, even the smallest subatomic particles have not always existed but came into being early in the expansion of the cosmos. And remember, a necessary being cannot fail to exist under any circumstances and so will be without beginning.

Nevertheless, suppose the Naturalist simply builds into his hypothesis that some part or aspect of physical reality exists of necessity. Given this specification, does Naturalism lead us to expect the presence of contingent beings? I think the answer is clearly no. Naturalism tells us that physical reality is self-organizing. Simply adding that some part of physical reality is necessary leaves us with no idea how the necessary part accounts for or causes the presence of contingent beings.

At this point we can state an initial version of the cosmological argument:

**Premise 1**. The prior probability of Theism is lower than that of Naturalism (due to Naturalism's greater simplicity) but high enough to make the theistic hypothesis well worth considering.

**Premise 2**. Theism leads us to expect the phenomenon, namely, the presence of contingent beings, but Naturalism does not. (*Note*: As we've seen, God would have good reason to create contingent beings. Naturalists who think that all of physical reality is contingent do not give us a hypothesis that leads us to expect contingent beings; rather, these Naturalists simply postulate the presence of contingent beings *as a brute fact*. And if Naturalists state merely that some part of physical reality is necessary—without explaining how the necessary part accounts for the presence of contingent beings, then the presence of contingent beings is still left as a brute fact.)

**Conclusion**: Theism explains the presence of contingent beings better than Naturalism does—hence, this phenomenon is evidence in favor of Theism over Naturalism.

It might be useful to compare this argument to an outline of an "argument for quarks":

**Premise 1**. The existence of quarks has a low prior probability but not so low as to justify our dismissing it outright. (Recall that quarks cannot be directly observed.)

**Premise 2**. Physical theories involving quarks do a very good job of leading us to expect a wide range of physical phenomena, far better than the available alternatives.

**Conclusion**: Physical theories involving quarks explain the relevant phenomena much better than the alternatives do (and so the phenomena support theories involving quarks over the alternatives).

Let me know what you think.

—Zach

Dear Zach,

According to your first premise, Naturalism has a higher prior probability than Theism. So, even if Theism has more explanatory power with respect to the presence of contingent beings, that explanatory power might be offset by Naturalism's advantage in prior probability.

—Thomas

Dear Thomas,

You're right. How can we explore this issue? I think we can best explore it by considering what Naturalists would have to add to their hypothesis in order to explain the presence of contingent beings. Naturalists must postulate a necessary being *and* they must postulate one that somehow accounts for contingent beings. Something along the following lines will do the trick, I think. The italics highlight the new or altered elements.

**Necessity Naturalism**: (1) There is a self-organizing physical reality, *(2) some part (or aspect) of physical reality exists of necessity, (3) the necessary part (or aspect) of physical reality generates additional parts or aspects of physical reality in a contingent manner (not of necessity)*, and (4) leaving aside possible special cases (e.g., sets or numbers), all entities are physical entities.

I call this *Necessity Naturalism*, to distinguish it from our initial formulation of Naturalism, which we may now refer to as *Basic Naturalism*.

I need to clarify clause 3 of Necessity Naturalism in two ways. First, why use the phrase *in a contingent manner*? Why couldn't the necessary part of physical reality generate the rest *of necessity*? Because then there would be no contingent beings. If a necessarily existing entity $X$ *necessarily* generates entity $Y$, then $Y$ is necessary too. Second, Naturalists might want to be more specific about the "contingent manner." For example, physicists tell us that certain processes in nature occur randomly. Atoms in radioactive elements decay at random. And in a quantum vacuum, fluctuations occur at random. Such random processes are probabilistic or statistical in nature; that is, over a certain period of time the events will *probably* occur (as opposed to necessarily occur). So Naturalists might want to replace *in a contingent manner* with something more specific, such as *in a random manner*. But as far as I can tell, nothing in our discussion will hang on this.[10]

Thanks to clauses 2 and 3, Necessity Naturalism leads us to expect the presence of contingent beings. Indeed, as far as I can see, in regard to the presence of contingent beings, Necessity Naturalism has as much explanatory power as Theism does. But notice that Necessity Naturalism is more complicated than Basic Naturalism. Basic Naturalism, you'll recall, is simpler than Theism, in four ways.

A. It postulates fewer entities (specifically, it postulates no entity corresponding to God in the Theist's scheme).
B. It postulates fewer *kinds* of entities (specifically, it does not postulate a necessarily existing, nonphysical person).
C. It employs less complex terms (specifically, it has no terms corresponding to *almighty* and *perfectly morally good*).
D. It contains fewer claims (specifically, three as opposed to Theism's four).

The picture alters substantially if we move to Necessity Naturalism. Regarding item D: Recall the fourth facet of simplicity. As we add statements to a hypothesis, we lower its prior probability, especially when what we add receives little or no support from statements already contained in the hypothesis. And, as far as I can see, the various claims within Necessity Naturalism provide little or no support for one another. Moreover, Necessity Naturalism, like Theism, contains four claims. So, where Necessity Naturalism is concerned, we can cross off point D.

Regarding B: Necessity Naturalism, like Theism, postulates something that exists of necessity (and is hence eternal). That partly cancels point B. But there is more. This necessary being has a specific structure. It is a physical entity that generates other physical entities in a contingent (nonnecessary) manner. And where Theists appeal to divine choices or volitions, Naturalists will presumably opt for some sort of nonpersonal mechanism that produces entities in a contingent fashion. Let us call this sort of necessary being a *contingent-being generator*. Now, this idea of a necessarily existing impersonal physical being that contingently generates other physical beings is obviously rather complex. Note also that since there is no way to detect necessary existence by observation, we cannot detect the presence of the contingent-being generator through observation. The upshot is this: Necessity Naturalism postulates a *kind* of entity not postulated by Theism: a necessarily existing, impersonal contingent-being generator. And a key aspect of this entity is *unobservable*, namely, its necessity. Hence, where Necessity Naturalism is concerned, we can cross off point B.

Regarding A: Necessity Naturalism does not postulate fewer entities than Theism. Theism postulates God, and Necessity Naturalism does not; but Necessity Naturalism postulates a necessarily existing, impersonal contingent-being generator, and Theism does not. So the two views do not differ with regard to the first facet of simplicity, and we can cross off point A.

Regarding C: While it remains true that Theism contains somewhat more complex terms than Necessity Naturalism, we must remember the result of our discussion of Theistic mystical experience. There I argued that Theistic mystical experience makes up for (or offsets) *at least one* of the ways in which Naturalism is simpler than Theism. Given this result, Necessity Naturalism and Theism appear to be equal in prior probability. At any rate, I see no basis for assigning Theism a lower prior probability than Necessity Naturalism.

Let me add a point of clarification here. People often think of God as by definition mysterious and beyond all human understanding. *Please remember that we are discussing Theism as I've formulated it, not a hypothesis that includes everything people often claim about God.* And the hypothesis I've formulated is not all that difficult to understand. I think the average high school student can probably understand it pretty well.

Theism and Necessity Naturalism also appear to be about equal in explanatory power *as regards the presence of contingent beings*. Theism explains their presence via divine volition; Necessity Naturalism explains their presence via an impersonal mechanism, the contingent-being generator. Accordingly, our cosmological argument apparently results in a "tie" between Theism and Necessity Naturalism.

If correct, this is a very significant result. Naturalists face a dilemma: They can stick with Basic Naturalism or adopt a more complicated view, such as Necessity Naturalism. Either way, a problem arises: (1) Basic Naturalism, we agreed, is much simpler than Theism, and so Basic Naturalism has a much higher prior probability. But our consideration of the cosmological argument indicates that Basic Naturalism is in fact too simple: It is unable to account for the presence of contingent beings. (2) When we complicate the naturalistic hypothesis so that it can account for contingent beings, the playing field immediately becomes level: We have two major metaphysical positions that seem indistinguishable with regard to prior probability and explanatory power *as regards the presence of contingent beings.*

Let me know what you think.

—Zach

Dear Zach,

Let me see if I have this straight. According to you, your cosmological argument does not show that God exists, but it does lead us to modify the Naturalistic hypothesis (so that it can explain the presence of contingent beings). The modified version, Necessity Naturalism, has the same prior probability as Theism—assuming Theism gets a bit of a boost from Theistic mystical experience. And with regard to the presence of contingent beings, Necessity Naturalism apparently has the same degree of explanatory power as Theism.

So Naturalists face a dilemma. If they stick with Basic Naturalism, their hypothesis has a higher prior probability than Theism but is then too simple to explain certain phenomena, in particular, the presence of contingent beings. On the other hand, if Naturalists adopt Necessity Naturalism, their hypothesis can explain the presence of contingent beings, but the advantage in prior probability is lost.

Maybe the Naturalist should just revert to Basic Naturalism and write off contingent beings as a loss?

—Thomas

Dear Thomas,

I'm afraid that sort of move comes at a cost. I've heard Theists claim that this or that phenomenon—for example, animal pain—is unimportant and they don't really need to try to explain it. Funny how that never seems convincing to non-Theists!

Naturalists can stick with Basic Naturalism if they so desire. But the cost is the failure to explain the presence of contingent beings. How great is that cost? The best way to ascertain the cost is to do what we have just done: Determine what needs to be added to Naturalism to enable it to explain the presence of contingent beings.

Naturalists *do* face a dilemma: Either (A) admit they cannot explain the presence of contingent beings or (B) complicate their view by adopting Necessity Naturalism. As we've seen, (B) leads to a "tie" with Theism. But so does (A): Basic Naturalism has far less explanatory power than Theism with regard to the phenomenon of contingent beings. And the best way to measure the difference in explanatory power is to see what would have to be added to

Basic Naturalism to remedy the deficiency. Our discussion of Necessity Naturalism provides the answer.

—Zach

Dear Zach,

I'm pondering your claim that there is a dilemma here for Naturalists—very interesting. But while I ponder this, I want to go back and examine some assumptions that I probably should have questioned before, OK?

For example, even if the notion of a necessary being makes sense, do we really need it to explain the presence of contingent beings? Hume suggested the possibility of an infinite (i.e., beginningless) series or succession of contingent beings:

> In such a . . . succession of objects, each part is caused by that which preceded it and causes that which succeeds it. Where then is the difficulty? But the *whole*, you say, wants a cause. I answer that the uniting of parts into a whole, like the uniting of several distinct countries into one kingdom, . . . is performed merely by an arbitrary act of the mind and has no influence on the nature of things. Did I show you the particular causes of each individual in a collection of twenty particles of matter, I should think it very unreasonable should you afterwards ask me what was the cause of the whole twenty. This is sufficiently explained in explaining the cause of the parts.[11]

In short, if each being in the series of contingent beings has a cause (namely, the immediately preceding member of the series), the series itself is fully explained. How would you respond to Hume?

—Thomas

Dear Thomas,

Consider an illustration. Suppose that the series of contingent beings were merely a series of self-propagating robots, each one bringing the next into existence. No matter how far back in time you go, there was just one of these robots functioning. Each robot functions for, say, ten years, then, in the last few minutes of functioning, propagates a new robot. (Just as the new robot starts to function, the old one ceases to function and disintegrates.) Now, in this scheme, we have a cause for the existence and functioning of each of the robots. But we have not identified a cause of the robot series as a whole. For example, what causes (or caused) the series to be one of *robots* rather than one of rocks, roses, rats, or reindeer? What is the cause of there being any *robots* at all? That question has not been answered.[12]

In the same way, even if we know that each contingent being is caused to exist by some other contingent being, we still do not have an explanation for the fact that there are contingent beings. There might have been nothing at all or only necessary beings.

—Zach

Dear Zach,

You may be right. But if we are thinking of contingent beings, not as individuals, but as a group or aggregate, I'm worried that some sort of fallacy has gone undetected.

Suppose someone reasons as follows: "Each part of the airplane is very light. So, the airplane itself is very light." Clearly, this is an invalid inference. Enough light parts, when joined together, constitute a large, heavy object.

Yet, you seem to be assuming that the group or aggregate of contingent beings is itself a contingent being. On what grounds? Simply that each part of the aggregate is contingent? If so, I fear your argument may contain some sort of part–whole fallacy.

—Thomas

Dear Thomas,

Your airplane example is a good example of the *fallacy of composition*. We cannot *in general* assume that if the parts of a whole have a certain property, then the whole has that same property. But not every inference from the nature of the parts to the nature of the whole is invalid. For example, "Each part of the machine weighs over one ounce and the machine has six parts. So the machine weighs over one ounce." That's a valid inference. In assessing part-to-whole reasoning, we have to examine the details, especially the property involved. (In this case, the property is *weighing over one ounce*.)

Let's approach this a bit indirectly. As we've already seen, there is a relationship between contingent beings and contingent truths: A being is contingent if (and only if) every proposition affirming its existence is a contingent truth. Now, suppose we make a conjunction out of contingent truths (i.e., join them with "and"): "I exist *and* you exist *and* my brother exists *and* your sister exists." Will the statement as a whole be a contingent truth? Yes, and logicians are fully in agreement on that. It doesn't matter how many contingent truths are put together to form a conjunction: The resulting conjunction, no matter how long, will be a contingent truth. You simply can't get a necessary truth by conjoining contingent truths.

It seems to me equally obvious that you cannot get a necessary being by placing contingent beings together into an aggregate. Suppose we make a pile of beings. Each being we place in the pile has this property: It can fail to exist at any time. Now, can the pile itself fail to exist at any time? Yes, obviously, it would fail to exist at time $T$ if each being composing it failed to exist at $T$.

As far as I can see, then, there is no fallacy of composition in the cosmological argument I've proposed.

—Zach

Dear Zach,

Forgive me if I seem to be playing devil's advocate, but I want to be sure I understand these issues. What about the idea that every being is necessary? Maybe each thing is brought into existence by logical necessity, ultimately stemming from some necessary fact. Maybe every feature of the world is necessary. How can we claim to know otherwise?

—Thomas

Dear Thomas,

The idea that *every feature of the world is necessary* is very implausible. And so is the idea that *every being is necessary*.

First, these ideas are in conflict with modern science. According to science, many natural laws are statistical in nature. Statistical laws are probabilistic: Given the initial conditions, the results are probable, not necessary, and more than one result can occur. For instance, according to modern physics, the laws governing subatomic particles (e.g., electrons and protons) are statistical.

Second, if the processes of the world are logically necessary and can be traced back to some ultimate necessary fact, then every event is determined in the strongest possible sense. Why accept that? Virtually everyone has deep-lying metaphysical intuitions to the contrary. For example, I've got a red shirt on, but it certainly seems to me that I *could have* put a white shirt on instead. I think we ought to accept such metaphysical intuitions in the absence of *very strong* arguments to the contrary.[13]

Make sense?

—Zach

Dear Zachary,

Yes, it does. I'm satisfied that there are contingent beings and that not everything happens of necessity.

But it seems to me that Theists cannot explain every contingent fact. How about God's decision to create? God could have chosen not to create anything, right? So "God chose to create $X$" is a contingent fact. And unless Theists want to postulate a "God-behind-God," who caused God to choose to create $X$, God's choices will have to go unexplained. Hence, no view can explain all contingent facts. That being so, what good is it to explain the presence of contingent beings at all?

—Thomas

Dear Thomas,

I agree that Theists cannot explain every contingent *fact*. And your example of God's choices or volitions is a shrewd one. God doesn't *have* to create, so if God chooses to create, the fact that he so chooses is contingent; i.e., it did occur but it might not have occurred.

Please note, however, that the phenomenon we are trying to explain is not "All contingent facts." We are trying to explain the presence of contingent *beings* in the world. And we can draw an important distinction between facts and beings. Here are some statements of contingent *fact*:

a. I am smiling.
b. I decided to write you a letter today.
c. I think Bill Murray is funny.

A fact—at least as I'm using the term here—involves (1) a being and (2) some property of that being. For instance, example a in the being in question is me, and the property is the property of smiling. Example c involves two beings, Bill Murray and me, and a complex relation between the two. On the other hand, examples of contingent beings include: me, you, my desk, your dog, the Empire State Building, and so on. All of these beings have properties, of course, but the phenomenon we are trying to explain is simply the *existence* of those beings. That's different from trying to explain why these beings have all the properties they have.[14]

Please note that I have never suggested that *every contingent fact has an explanation*. This claim is a version of what philosophers call the **Principle of Sufficient Reason**. That principle is very controversial. It has often been employed in cosmological arguments, but it is not used (and not presupposed) in the argument-to-the-best-explanation we've been considering.[15]

Your example of God's volitions is a good one to keep in mind when thinking about the Principle of Sufficient Reason. Is there an explanation for the fact that God chose this or that? Well, God will presumably have *reasons* for the choices he makes, but the reasons may not fully explain the choice in a given case, because God may have had equally good reasons to choose otherwise. For example, suppose God is confronted with the choice of granting a prayer request, and suppose God happens to know that good will result if he grants the request but that an equal good will result if he denies it. His reasons for granting the prayer are counterbalanced by his reasons for denying it. Suppose God grants the prayer request. What explains that fact? All we can say is that God made a choice. Nothing, it seems to me, can usefully be added. Such is the nature of free choice.

But Theism can explain the presence of contingent *beings* in the world. And, as we have seen, so can a suitably modified form of Naturalism, namely, Necessity Naturalism.

—Zach

Dear Zachary,

I'm feeling a bit confused. Where does the cosmological argument leave us?

—Thomas

Dear Thomas,

I think our discussion of the cosmological argument has clarified some very important points.

First, Theism has more explanatory power than Basic Naturalism, as regards the presence of contingent beings. Basic Naturalism, though nicely streamlined, is too simple to provide an explanation of the presence of contingent beings. Something more complicated, such as Necessity Naturalism, is needed if Naturalists are to explain the presence of contingent beings.

Second, if Naturalists complicate their hypothesis in order to respond to the cosmological argument, then, as far as I can see, there is no reason to assign Theism a lower prior probability than Naturalism. As far as I can tell, Theism and Necessity Naturalism have about the same prior probability—if we grant that Theistic mystical experience provides a modest degree of support for Theism (as discussed previously).

Every move one makes in philosophy comes at a cost. And to sum up, the Naturalist can respond to the cosmological argument, but the response comes at the cost of lowering the prior probability of Naturalism significantly. It will be very important to keep this in mind as we look at further arguments for Theism.

—Zach

Dear Zach,

Wouldn't alternative God hypotheses explain the presence of contingent beings just as well as Theism (as you've defined it)? For example:

**Polytheism**: (1) There are many entities who are (2) perfectly morally good and (3) almighty (taken together) and who (4) exist of necessity.

Let me know what you think.

—Thomas

Dear Thomas,

You raise a very important point. A phenomenon does not provide support for just *one* hypothesis. It may provide support for many. But if we are going to consider alternative theological hypotheses, we have to evaluate them via two basic questions (as we would any other hypothesis):

1. What is their *prior* probability relative to Theism?
2. What is their *explanatory power* relative to Theism? Do they do as good a job of leading us to expect the phenomenon (i.e., the presence of contingent beings) as Theism does?

Question 1 is key in the case of Polytheism. Applying the first facet of simplicity (number of entities postulated), Polytheism is plainly more complicated than Theism, and hence it will have a lower prior probability than Theism. So, even if Theism and Polytheism have the same explanatory power with respect to contingent beings, Theism is the better hypothesis.

—Zach

Dear Zach,

Let's consider some other theological alternatives. How about this?

**Transcendent Theism**: (1) There is exactly one entity who is (2) beyond good and evil and (3) almighty and who (4) exists of necessity.

I call this *Transcendent Theism* because in this way of thinking God transcends morality altogether.

—Thomas

Dear Thomas,

There are several problems with your proposed Transcendent Theism.

(1) A morally perfect (hence loving and generous) God has reason to create conscious beings with whom to share good things. In a nutshell, that's why Theism explains the presence of contingent beings well. But what reason would a Deity beyond good and evil have? That's unclear. Perhaps you could dream up a motive, but you would need to add that to the hypothesis, thus complicating it and lowering its prior probability.

(2) Is the God of Transcendent Theism a person, i.e., a being who can know things and *make choices*? If not, I fail to see how Transcendent Theism explains the presence of any contingent beings. If so, then I fail to see how the God of Transcendent Theism can be "beyond good and evil." Is this almighty person indifferent to the suffering of its creatures? If so, then it is unloving and hence morally flawed. On the other hand, if it cares about the suffering of its creatures, then it would seem to have some degree of moral goodness. In short, the very idea of a personal being who is beyond good and evil seems problematic.

(3) On the most natural interpretation, a God "beyond good and evil" is indifferent to our best interests. But then—as we've noted previously—we are in trouble as knowers. Recall the "locked room" case? If you are in a locked room receiving info written on slips of paper and you have no way of checking up on the info, can you rightly assume the info is reliable, *given that the source is an entity who is indifferent to your best interests*? Surely not. And if there is an almighty Deity who is indifferent to our best interests, then our supposed "knowledge" depends on cognitive faculties formed by (or under the supervision of) that Deity. And we cannot count on a God indifferent to our best interests to provide us with *reliable* cognitive faculties. So, on the most natural interpretation, Transcendent Theism calls all human knowing into question, and thus it is a self-defeating hypothesis.

—Zach

Dear Zach,

OK, Transcendent Theism does seem to be highly problematic. What about the idea that there is a God who is limited in power? For example:

**Finite Theism**: (1) There is exactly one entity who is (2) perfectly morally good and (3) powerful enough to create contingent beings (but not almighty) and who (4) exists of necessity.

What do you think?

—Thomas

Dear Thomas,

Your *Finite Theism* is vague about how much power the Deity has. In this view, God might have enough power to create a few contingent beings, but does God have enough power to create all those contingent beings that comprise the actual physical universe? This is a serious question. To illustrate, process philosophers and theologians postulate a Deity who is limited in power in order to explain the presence of suffering in the world. But if God is too weak to eliminate suffering, then why should we suppose that God has enough power to create the physical universe?[16]

We can of course *stipulate* that God has exactly enough power to create and sustain all the contingent beings (and no more power than that), but that's a bit strange. Suppose we replace your third clause of Finite Theism with this:

   (3+) just powerful enough to create and sustain all the contingent beings in our universe

*Prior to considering the phenomenon*, how likely is it that the Deity has exactly enough power to produce the phenomenon and no more? Well, apart from considering the phenomenon, we would have *no reason at all* to make (3+) our hypothesis. So a hypothesis that includes (3+) will have an *extremely* low prior probability. Moreover, with the modified clause (3+), Finite Theism becomes very contrived and arbitrary. *A satisfying hypothesis needs to describe the features of the object postulated independent of any reference to the phenomenon.* And that's what our original formulation of Theism does.

And remember that Theistic mystical experience provides background evidence in support of the postulate of an almighty Deity, whereas no mystics report the presence of a Deity with *just enough* power to create and sustain all the contingent beings.

—Zach

Dear Zach,

One last try? Consider this:

**Imperfect Deity hypothesis**: (1) There is exactly one entity who is (2) morally imperfect and (3) almighty and who (4) exists of necessity.

A morally imperfect Deity would be a mixture of good and evil. Such a Deity might even be mostly good and might be generous enough to want to create conscious beings and share good things with them, but with moral lapses or blind spots regarding the suffering of creatures. Also, the Imperfect Deity hypothesis might do a better job of explaining the suffering in the world than Theism can.

—Thomas

Dear Thomas,

Your Imperfect Deity hypothesis merits serious consideration. However, as your own comments indicate, "moral imperfection" might be realized in a variety of ways. For example, a morally imperfect being might be very good (with occasional moral lapses), it might be mostly evil but occasionally "nice," or it might be a roughly even mix of good and evil. These cases are obviously very different. Let's consider them each briefly.

1. The mostly evil Deity would, as we've seen previously, lead to serious doubts about the reliability of our cognitive faculties. Such a Deity might very well want us to be systematically mistaken about most of the things that matter to us most. And an almighty being could easily secure this result. So, a "mostly-evil Deity" hypothesis is self-defeating—accepting it would give us a reason to doubt it (along with everything else we believe)!

2. A half-good and half-evil Deity seems to me to lead to the same problem. Such a Deity would be highly untrustworthy and might very well not care enough about us to give us reliable cognitive faculties. (Put yourself back in the locked room, receiving info you can't check up on. If you know the source of the info is half good and half evil, would you expect the info to be for the most part true? I don't think we can plausibly answer yes.)

3. A mostly good (but imperfect) Deity would presumably be somewhat generous (or perhaps intermittently generous), so it would have good reasons to bring intelligent conscious creatures into existence and to share good things with them. Thus, a "mostly good" Deity hypothesis would lead us to expect the presence of contingent beings. Also, assuming that having the truth is generally in our best interest, a "mostly good" Deity would *probably* try to ensure that our cognitive faculties are reliable; hence this hypothesis does not seem to be self-defeating.

So, the "mostly good" Deity hypothesis seems to have about the same explanatory power as Theism, as regards the presence of contingent beings. How does its prior probability compare to that of Theism? If we include Theistic mystical experience in the background evidence, as I think we should, then the "mostly good" Deity hypothesis does not fit very well with background evidence, for the Theistic mystics characteristically report experience of a *thor-*

*oughly* good and almighty Deity. For this reason, I believe Theism has a bit of an edge in prior probability.

Of course, philosophers such as David Hume have claimed that the Imperfect Deity hypothesis explains the presence of suffering and evil better than Theism does. We'll have to consider this claim when we discuss the problem of evil. And when we discuss the moral argument for the existence of God, we will have to consider whether the Imperfect Deity hypothesis explains certain features of the moral realm as well as Theism does.

But remember that my primary interest is in Theism and Naturalism. And Naturalists cannot accept the Imperfect Deity hypothesis. Indeed, if the Cosmological Argument provides good evidence for a "mostly good" Deity, it provides an important challenge to Naturalistic hypotheses.

Your friend,
Zach

# CHAPTER 5

# A Design Argument

Dear Zachary,

Reviewing our last exchange of letters, I see the overall situation as follows: Naturalists can respond to the cosmological argument, but only by complicating their position. This more complicated version of Naturalism, Necessity Naturalism, seems to have about the same prior probability as Theism. So far, then, Theism and Necessity Naturalism seem to be "tied."

Where do we go from here?

Your friend,
Thomas

Dear Thomas,

Shall we look at an argument from design?

Scientists tell us that if certain fundamental features of the physical universe had been only slightly different, it would not support life. To use the current idiom, the universe is "fine-tuned" for life. Some examples will help to clarify the meaning of this expression.

- If the initial force of the big bang explosion had been slightly stronger or weaker—by as little as one part in $10^{60}$, then life would be impossible. If the "bang" had been slightly weaker, the universe would have collapsed back on itself almost immediately. If the "bang" had been slightly stronger, the cosmic material would have been blown apart and isolated; stars and galaxies would have failed to form.[1] And, to the best of our knowledge, life depends on energy derived from stars such as our Sun.

- There is an "almost unbelievable delicacy in the balance between gravity and electromagnetism within a star. Calculations show that changes in the strength of either force by only one part in $10^{40}$ would spell catastrophe for stars like the Sun."[2]

- If the weak nuclear force (which governs radioactive decay) had been slightly stronger or weaker, heavy elements could not have formed. And heavy elements such as carbon are presumably necessary for life—there can be no life at all if there are only gases such as hydrogen and helium.[3]

- If the strong nuclear force (which binds together such particles as protons and neutrons) had been just 2 percent stronger (relative to the other forces), all hydrogen would have been converted into helium (hence there would be no hydrogen for stars to burn). If the strong nuclear force had been 5 percent weaker, there would be nothing but hydrogen. Either way, life would presumably be impossible.

- If the electromagnetic force were 4 percent weaker, there would be no hydrogen.[4] But hydrogen fuels the stars, including of course the Sun. If the electromagnetic force were a little stronger, there would be no planets.[5] Either way, life would presumably be impossible.

Over twenty such physical parameters must have values that fall within highly restricted ranges in order for life to be present.[6]

To get a feel for what "fine-tuned" means, it might be helpful to imagine that you receive a "Creation Machine" for Christmas. The Creation Machine has over twenty dials on it. You set the dials and push the start button to create a universe. One of the dials is labeled "Force of Gravity." The dial has $10^{40}$ marks around it. Now, $10^{40}$ is a big number:

$$10^{40} = 10,000,000,000,000,000,000,000,000,000,000,000,000,000$$

If you set the "Force of Gravity" dial but are off by one mark, you will get a universe that does not contain life. Similar remarks could be made about each of the dials.

To the best of our knowledge, each of the various physical parameters (force of gravity, strong nuclear force, mass of the electron, etc.) could have been different from what it is. The question naturally arises, what explains the fact that these parameters have values that support life? What accounts for the fact that the universe is "fine-tuned" for life?

—Zach

Dear Zach,

Well, yes, the facts about "fine-tuning" are amazing. But they plainly invite further scientific investigation, and I have little doubt that science will eventually explain them.

—Thomas

Dear Thomas,

I hadn't meant to suggest that, from the standpoint of science, the facts about fine-tuning must forever be regarded as nothing more than an amazing coincidence. For example, physicists have discovered that the weak force and the electromagnetic force "are naturally *united* by their quantum field-theoretic description even though their manifestations seem to be utterly distinct in the world around us."[7] In other words, the weak and electromagnetic forces have a common origin in the so-called electroweak force and thus, in spite of appearances, are not ultimately independent of one other. Furthermore, superstring theory, which is currently being developed by physicists, may someday reveal that many of the facts about fine-tuning are linked.

But by the nature of the case, there can be no scientific explanation for the *ultimate* (most fundamental) structures of the physical universe. Any scientific laws or principles corresponding to such structures would presumably be fundamental or ultimate ones. Put it this way: Suppose physicists completed all their work, discovered everything that humans can know about the operation of the physical world. There would presumably be some "most basic" laws of physics. *Physicists could discover these laws but could not explain why they are present, for there would be no "more basic" laws or principles to revert to.* With this in mind, here's the phenomenon the design argument attempts to explain.

> *Phenomenon*: The ultimate (most basic) structures of the physical universe support life—intelligent, conscious life; and given that slight changes in the most basic structures would alter the facts about fine-tuning, slight changes in these structures would destroy their capacity to support life.

The current scientific descriptions of fine-tuning are presumably not descriptions of the *most basic* structures of our universe. (Physicists haven't finished their work and perhaps they never will.) But whatever the *most basic* structures of our universe are, they plainly support intelligent, conscious life—and *since scientists could not, by the nature of the case, discover more basic structures than the most basic ones, science could not explain these most basic structures; science could only describe them.*

—Zach

Dear Zach,

I doubt if most scientists would be interested in explaining the phenomenon you describe. If it can't be explained scientifically, who says it needs to be explained at all? If there is a rock-bottom level in scientific explanation, perhaps that's where human inquiry rightly comes to an end.

—Thomas

Dear Thomas,

I don't think you're speaking for science. Rather, you are expressing a philosophical position I call *scientism*, roughly the view that the only explanations worth having are scientific ones.

There are many important things that science, by the nature of the case, cannot explain.[8] First, science cannot validate the scientific method (i.e., explain why we are justified in following that method). Very roughly, the scientific method involves identifying observable facts to be explained, proposing hypotheses, and testing the hypotheses *empirically*. Science simply employs this method; it does not justify the method. Any justification thereof must be *philosophical* in nature.

Second, science cannot justify certain presuppositions of the scientific method, e.g., the principle of the uniformity of nature (roughly, that laws of nature hold in all times and places, including places too distant for humans to observe and times prior to the existence of humans). Another example: the presupposition that sense experience is reliable. Any justification of such presuppositions would have to be philosophical rather than scientific.

Third, science cannot account for the very presence of physical reality. Some physicists suggest that our universe resulted from random fluctuations in a quantum vacuum. But of course this explanation, even if correct, presumes the existence of a quantum vacuum, which itself belongs to physical reality.

Fourth, if there is an ultimate purpose for human existence or for the existence of the universe, this is not something scientists typically regard as a matter for *scientific* research.

Fifth, science cannot explain various apparent moral facts, e.g., that certain acts are right or wrong, that certain character traits are virtues or vices, or that people are morally responsible under certain circumstances. Of course, scientists can study human *beliefs* about morality or human behavior (including what sorts of acts people in a given culture praise or condemn others for doing). But rightness and wrongness do not seem to be directly observable properties. Suppose Mr. A strikes Mr. B, is the wrongness of the act directly observable? In fact, Mr. A may be defending himself from Mr. B's attack, in which case Mr. A's action is presumably not wrong at all; so it seems we cannot *directly observe* wrongness.

Some people are not interested in anything science cannot (in principle) explain. But this in no way makes them more "scientific" than anyone else. If they hold the view that *only scientific explanations are worth having*, they are taking a philosophical position, one that they would have difficulty defending. Why are scientific explanations the only one's worth having? Science cannot answer that question! The only possible answers are *philosophical* in nature. In other words, to explain why scientific explanations are the only ones worth having, one would have to offer a nonscientific explanation!

—Zach

Dear Zach,

I hadn't meant to advocate scientism. But I'm still not sure that the phenomenon you've described—"The ultimate structures of the physical universe support intelligent, conscious life"—stands in need of explanation. How do you know that this fact is not a brute, inexplicable fact? After all, not everything can be explained.

—Thomas

Dear Thomas,

I agree: Not everything can be explained. *Whatever* view we take, there will be some ultimate hypothesis—the claim that some entity has *such-and-such* features, and for this we will have no explanation.

But we are looking for an ultimate metaphysical postulate that will explain *as much as possible*. We want to go as deep as we can. Why *are* things as they are?

We don't know what the ultimate or most basic structures of the physical universe are. But we do know that, whatever they are, they support life—intelligent conscious life. And we know that *extremely* slight alterations in the structure of our universe would make life impossible. That's something to wonder about, isn't it? It surely isn't silly or irrational to want an explanation of the fact that the basic structures of the physical universe support life.

Is our life-supporting universe simply a brute fact? Perhaps the best way to find out is to look at the proposed explanations. If there are plausible explanations, then why insist that the life-supporting universe is simply a brute fact? Off hand, I can't think of any good reason.

—Zach

Dear Zach,

Many, many features of the physical world are improbable. Consider the precise location of all the air molecules in your room (taken as a group) at this moment. What are the chances that these molecules would be in precisely the location they are in? According to physicists, the laws governing the behavior of physical particles are statistical in nature. Roughly speaking, this means that the laws allow for more than one result given the initial conditions; e.g., one second from now, *this* particular air molecule will most probably be in location $X$, but there is a lesser probability that it will be in location $Y$. With this in mind, the probability that the air molecules in your room (taken as a group) are in the precise location they are in at this moment must be *extremely* low. Nevertheless, we don't need to invoke God to explain the location of the air molecules in your room—it's just a coincidence. And maybe our fine-tuned universe is just a coincidence too.

—Thomas

Dear Thomas,

"It's just a coincidence" is one possible explanation of our fine-tuned universe, but we have to consider whether it's the best explanation. As I see it, the main, rival explanations of our life-supporting universe are as follows.[9]

1. *Coincidence*: Our universe might have had many different basic structures, the vast majority of which would not be life-supporting. The actual structure of the physical universe is simply a coincidence.

2. *Physical necessity*: The ultimate physical structures *can be* of only one form, and that is the form our universe takes.

3. *Percentage of possible universes*: Some large percentage of the total number of *possible* physical universes is life-supporting (i.e., the basic structures in those possible universes would support life if the universes were actual). Hence, any actual universe has a good chance of being life-supporting.

4. *The many-universes hypothesis*: Some (rather special) part of physical reality generates multiple universes. Call this part of physical reality the *universe generator*. The universe generator generates *many* universes, with their basic physical structures (laws, constants, and initial conditions) varying at random. And since there have been or are many actual universes, it is not surprising that at least one supports life.

5. *Theism*: The universe supports life because life fulfills certain divine purposes (or at least is a means to their fulfillment).

Naturalists are free to adopt explanations 1 through 4.

—Zach

Dear Zach,

That's an interesting list of possible views, but it still seems to me that the best move for the Naturalist is simply to appeal to coincidence.

—Thomas

Dear Thomas,

Given your recent note, I think we need to discuss some preliminary matters before exploring the list of explanations of fine-tuning. Let's go back to our most recent formulation of Naturalism:

> **Necessity Naturalism**: (1) There is a self-organizing physical reality, (2) some part of physical reality exists of necessity, (3) the necessary part of physical reality generates additional parts of physical reality in a contingent manner (not of necessity), and (4) leaving aside possible special cases (e.g., sets or numbers), all entities are physical entities.

Does this version of Naturalism, taken *as is*, lead us to expect a life-supporting universe? No. There is no relevant logical or probabilistic link between *being self-organizing* and *being life-supporting*. Many physicists assume that physical reality could take a multitude of forms, most of which would *not* support life. (To put this in terms of the Creation Machine, many physicists assume that the dials could be turned to *many* different settings and that most of these settings correspond to universes that would not support life.) Hence, the hypothesis that physical reality is self-organizing does not *by itself* lead us to expect a universe whose basic structures support life.

Nor does the situation improve if we add the assumption that part of physical reality exists of necessity and generates contingent beings. A contingent being is merely one that does exist but might not have existed, such as a pebble, a planet, or an atom of hydrogen. And there is no relevant logical or probabilistic connection between *being contingent* and *being life-supporting*.

So, from the standpoint of Necessity Naturalism, there is no reason to expect a life-supporting universe. It remains a brute fact.

—Zach

Dear Zach,

Wait a minute! Think of the configuration of rocks on a mountainside after an avalanche has occurred. Label all the rocks with numbers, 1, 2, 3, etc., and write out a description of the location of all the rocks. Why are these rocks, taken as a group, in exactly the location they are in? The answer is "It's just a coincidence." Some things are highly improbable, but the best explanation is still an appeal to coincidence. Right?

—Thomas

Dear Thomas,

There are several things to keep in mind regarding your avalanche example. First, we have experience with avalanches. We (humans) have often observed them. We know the apparently random distributions of rocks that result from avalanches. Experience gives us a good idea of the sort of distribution of rocks to *expect* after an avalanche. *But we have not observed multiple universes, with differing fundamental physics, come into being. And whatever is known of the initial stages of our own universe is known entirely through extrapolation.* So we are in no position to say what sort of universe is apt to occur by coincidence.

Second, although the distribution of rocks resulting from an avalanche may appear to be random, rocks are subject to laws of nature. (More accurately, rocks move in patterned ways that scientists can formulate as laws of nature.) Assuming the laws of physics are true, many distributions of the rocks are improbable in the extreme; e.g., after the avalanche is over, the rocks won't be found floating ten feet above the ground; they will be scattered down the side of the mountain below the point at which the avalanche began. But we are trying to explain, in part, *the very presence of laws of nature that can support life*. So to say that a life-supporting universe is "just a coincidence" is to say, in part, that the fundamental structures of the physical universe, including the *most basic* laws of nature, are as they are by coincidence—sheer luck on a cosmic scale. And what sort of *fundamental* laws do we get when they are formed purely by chance? No one knows.

Third, and related to my first two points, the behavior of rocks in an avalanche is a phenomenon science can explain. But, as I've noted previously, since we are trying to explain the most fundamental structures of the physical universe, a scientific answer is by the nature of the case unavailable.

Fourth, rocks scattered down the side of a mountain are one thing, a life-supporting universe is another. Life in general, but especially conscious, intelligent life, is an extraordinary phenomenon, one that commonly evokes a sense of wonder. It is also something an intelligent being might well be interested in producing. And of course a life-supporting universe is a means of producing life.

To sum up, the analogy between "This pattern of rocks occurred by coincidence" and "Our life-supporting universe occurred by coincidence" breaks down completely under scrutiny. Any similarities pale by comparison to the important, relevant dissimilarities. Under these circumstances, I find the appeal to coincidence strained and unsatisfying.

—Zach

Dear Zach,

At this point I'm willing to concede that an unadorned appeal to coincidence is not a very plausible explanation of the fact that the physical universe is life-supporting. But is an appeal to theology any better?

—Thomas

Dear Thomas,

Let me outline a design argument for the existence of God. Recall our formulation of Theism:

**Theism**: (1) There is exactly one entity that is (2) perfectly morally good and (3) almighty and that (4) exists of necessity.

As we've noted previously, a perfectly morally good being would be loving, and a loving being would be generous. A generous being would have reason to create entities with whom to share *good* things, that is, things that *merit* a response of wonder, admiration, and/or delight. (I believe this sense of *good* is a very important one, commonly employed in our most basic judgments of value.) So God would have reason to create conscious beings who can enjoy good things as well as reason to create the good things for conscious beings to enjoy. It seems especially clear that a loving God would have reason to create *intelligent* conscious creatures along with things for them to enjoy, such as beauty, interesting and significant activities, physical and mental pleasures, and satisfying personal relationships—for these are all of great value.

Now, "intelligent conscious creatures" wouldn't have to be physical or embodied creatures. They could be angels, for example. A generous God would have reason to create both embodied and unembodied intelligent conscious creatures, since both could enjoy God's blessings. Of course it doesn't necessarily follow that God would create both—one can have a good reason to do something but decide not to do it. Nevertheless, it wouldn't be surprising if God created one or the other (or both) of these kinds of intelligent creatures. Furthermore, given that God is generous, it would be quite surprising if he didn't create *any* intelligent beings to share good things with.

Would God have specific reasons to create *embodied* living things? Yes. First, physical life is a *good thing*, in the sense that it merits a response of wonder, admiration, and/or delight. Of the wonders we humans know about, plants and animals are surely very high on the list. The world would be a much poorer place without them. And if the simpler forms of physical life are good, the more complex forms, including the more intelligent types of animals, are of even greater value. Thus, God would have reason to create intelligent, physical life.

Second, a fine-tuned universe is a means to creating and sustaining embodied life. *Perhaps* God could create embodied life *ex nihilo*. But a fine-tuned universe is at least one way to bring embodied life into existence and sustain it.

Third, as already noted, God would have reason to create intelligent living things *capable of interesting and significant action*. And physical reality provides an appropriately stable setting for such action. To illustrate, even the simplest human acts depend on laws of nature: You ask to borrow a pencil and I hand it to you—I'm counting on the pencil not to evaporate, suddenly explode, or turn into jelly. Perhaps we can conceive of a stable environment that is not governed by laws of nature, but that doesn't change the fact that a natural-law-governed environment is a suitable stage for action. So if God has reason to create intelligent physical life capable of interesting and significant action, God has reason to create a physical setting governed by laws of nature. And our fine-tuned universe is precisely such a setting.

We can now combine the second and third points: A fine-tuned universe is *both* a means for producing (and sustaining) intelligent agents *and* a suitable stage for their actions. Therefore, since God has reason to create intelligent embodied life capable of interesting and significant action, God has reason to create a fine-tuned universe too.

Fourth, if God creates life by means of a fine-tuned universe, then the creation of life carries with it at least two additional goods: (1) the aesthetic excellence of the physical universe. From the grandeur of the galaxies to the exquisite finery of a tiny flower, the universe is shot through with beauty. And this beauty is a good that can be shared with intelligent conscious creatures. (2) The marvelous intricacy of the universe as a "mechanical" (i.e., nonteleological) system: I don't see how anyone can read a book on physics without coming away with a feeling that, if the universe is the product of design, it's a pure "marvel of engineering."

Now, even if God has good reasons to create a life-supporting physical reality, we can't specify exactly how probable it is that God would act on those reasons, but we can say that a life-supporting universe is *unsurprising* if there is a God who has good reasons to create such a universe. With this in mind, we can sum up a design argument as follows.

**Premise 1**. Theism and Necessity Naturalism have the same prior probability. (More precisely, there is no good reason to assign Theism a lower prior probability than Necessity Naturalism—that was the upshot of our discussion of the Cosmological Argument.)

**Premise 2**. On the assumption that Necessity Naturalism is true, there is no reason to expect a universe that supports life. But on the assumption that Theism is true, God would have good reasons to create a life-supporting universe, and so a life-supporting universe is not at all surprising (though it is not guaranteed).

**Conclusion**: Theism explains the presence of our life-supporting universe better than Necessity Naturalism does—hence, our life-supporting universe provides evidence in favor of Theism over Necessity Naturalism.

What do you think?

—Zach

Dear Zach,

Even if your argument works, it works only against Necessity Naturalism. Surely Naturalists can produce a revised hypothesis with more explanatory power. How about the idea that the ultimate structures of the physical universe can be of only one form?

—Thomas

Dear Thomas,

It's a bold piece of metaphysics to claim that physical reality can be organized in just one way. Would naturalists be well advised to make such a claim? Let's look at a version of Naturalism that does so. We might call it *Single-Universe Naturalism*, because it says that physical reality can take only one form and that that form is life-supporting.

**Single-Universe Naturalism**: (1) There exists a self-organizing physical reality. (2) *The self-organization of physical reality can take only one form, and* (3) *that form is precisely the form we find in our universe.* (4) Some part of physical reality exists of logical necessity. (5) Leaving aside possible special cases (e.g., numbers), all entities are physical entities.

Of course the new clauses are clauses 2 and 3; the others are needed for reasons we've discussed previously.[10]

It seems to me that Single-Universe Naturalism is a deeply flawed hypothesis. First, consider the content of clause 3: "that form is precisely the form we find in our universe." What form is that? The form is summed up in the term *fine-tuned* or *life-supporting. In other words, Single-Universe Naturalism doesn't explain fine-tuning or the fact that our universe supports life, but rather simply presupposes these things.* Thus, Single-Universe Naturalism fails utterly as an explanatory hypothesis.

Second, Single-Universe Naturalism must be assigned a low prior probability, for several reasons.

   a. We must ask: "*Independent* of the fact that our universe is life-supporting (or fine-tuned), how likely is it that our universe could have only one form, *and that form one that supports life?*" As far as I can tell, apart from the fact that our universe actually does support life, we have no reason to suppose that physical reality would support life. So nothing in the background evidence lends plausibility to Single-Universe Naturalism. Note that we can't fix this problem by leaving clause 3 out. What is the likelihood of a life-supporting universe given that physical reality can take just one form? For all we know, *independent of the fact that our universe does support life,* if physical reality can take just one form, that form would *not* be one that supports life.

   b. Many physicists assume that physical reality could be structured in different ways. For example, this is assumed by those who advocate the Many-Universes Hypothesis. So the assumption that physical reality can have just one form is eminently questionable.

   c. Single-Universe Naturalism contains more theses than Necessity Naturalism. And the theses of Single-Universe Naturalism receive little or no support from one another. Thus, in terms of the fourth facet of simplicity, Single-Universe Naturalism is more complicated than Necessity Naturalism. Together with (a) and (b), this means that Single-Universe Naturalism must be assigned a significantly lower prior probability than Necessity Naturalism.

But we have already agreed that Theism and Necessity Naturalism have about the same prior probability. Hence, Single-Universe Naturalism has a significantly lower prior probability than Theism.

To sum up, Single-Universe Naturalism does not explain fine-tuning or our life-supporting universe, it merely presupposes these things. Moreover, it has a lower prior probability than Theism. Therefore, Theism does a better job of explaining our life-supporting universe than Single-Universe Naturalism does.

—Zach

Dear Zach,

After some reflection, I find myself substantially in agreement with your last letter. It does seem right to say that Single-Universe Naturalism presupposes (and so does not explain) the phenomenon of a fine-tuned (or life-supporting) universe. And it also seems right to say that Single-Universe Naturalism would have to be assigned a lower prior probability than Necessity Naturalism. So I must grant that Theism explains our life-supporting universe better than Single-Universe Naturalism does.

But I want to try to express something that's been bothering me: Scientists can tell us that if we start with the present basic physical parameters and change one, such as the force of gravity, the result would be a universe that won't support life. But what if we changed all or most of the parameters at once? In terms of the Creation Machine, instead of changing the setting of one dial, think in terms of changing the settings on all of the dials (there are over twenty dials, as I recall). When all the dials have been set a certain way, call that a *dial configuration*. Maybe there are lots of different dial configurations that would yield a universe that supports life—not necessarily life as we know it, but life of some sort. And if so, maybe the presence of a life-supporting universe isn't as amazing and improbable as it seems.[11]

What do you think?

—Thomas

Dear Thomas,

I think you are wondering about an approach I earlier referred to under the label "Percentage of Possible Universes." The basic idea is this, I take it: Some large percentage of the total number of *possible* physical universes is life-supporting (i.e., the basic structures in those possible universes would support life if the universes were actual). From this perspective, it seems that any actual universe would have a good chance of being life-supporting.

I like your idea of thinking in terms of dial configurations for the Creation Machine, one universe per configuration. These universes would presumably support different types of life (if any), including forms of life that would be quite different from any in our universe.

We can use these ideas to formulate another version of the Naturalistic hypothesis. For lack of a better name, I'll refer to this as *Per-*

*centage Naturalism*, since it affirms that some large percentage of possible universes would support life (if actual):

> **Percentage Naturalism**: (1) There is a self-organizing physical reality, (2) some part of physical reality exists of necessity, (3) the necessary part of physical reality generates additional parts of physical reality in a contingent manner (not of necessity), and (4) leaving aside possible special cases (e.g., sets or numbers), all entities are physical entities. (5) *A large percentage of possible physical universes are life-supporting* (i.e., *if* they were actual, these universes would support life).

The crucial clause is of course clause 5. The idea is this: *If* we assume that a large percentage of the possible universes is life-supporting, then it's not very surprising that our universe is life-supporting. Compare: If a large percentage of 50-year-old men are overweight, then it's not surprising if a particular 50-year-old man, Raymond Q. Bloggs, is overweight.[12]

But the prior probability of Percentage Naturalism is, I believe, low, for two reasons. First, we must ask this crucial question: "*Independent of the fact that our universe supports life*, how likely is it that a large percentage of possible universes are life-supporting?" In other words, if we didn't know that our universe supports life, would we have reason to expect a large percentage of the possible universes to be life-supporting? I think the answer is plainly "No, we wouldn't." As best as we can tell, many possible universes would contain only gases. And there is no reason to suppose that life of any sort can occur in an environment containing only hydrogen and/or helium. Many other possible universes would almost certainly be too hot or too cold to support life. Still others would not last long enough for life to develop; e.g., if the initial expansive force is too weak, a universe will quickly collapse back in on itself. And so on. But if, independent of the phenomenon (our life-supporting universe), we have no reason to suppose that a large percentage of possible universes are life-supporting, then the background evidence does not lend plausibility to Percentage Naturalism.

We can reinforce this first point by asking, "What percentage of possible universes is life-supporting?" Any number chosen would be completely arbitrary. There's no more reason to propose 75 percent than to propose, say, 0.0001 percent. There are simply no grounds for specifying any relevant percentage or even a range of percentages. Even a very vague specification such as "a large percentage" is completely ungrounded and arbitrary. Since any relevant specification of percentages is *wildly* speculative, the background evidence gives no probabilistic support to Percentage

Naturalism. (By contrast, Theism is not wildly speculative because, as we have seen, it is partly grounded in religious experience.)

Second, Percentage Naturalism contains more theses than Necessity Naturalism. And since the new thesis, clause 5, receives no support from the others, we must assign Percentage Naturalism a lower prior probability than Necessity Naturalism. Furthermore, Percentage Naturalism apparently presupposes a sixth thesis, along these lines:

(6) Each possible universe has an equal chance of becoming actual.

If a large percentage of possible universes are life-supporting but for some reason these universes are significantly less likely to become actual than non-life-supporting universes, then Percentage Naturalism has little explanatory power. But the assumption that all possible universes are equally likely to become actual is a nontrivial one and so should be built into the hypothesis, complicating it further. Thus, in terms of the fourth facet of simplicity (the number of theses having little or no support from the others), Percentage Naturalism (six theses) is substantially more complex than Necessity Naturalism (four theses).

For these reasons, Percentage Naturalism has a significantly lower prior probability than Necessity Naturalism. It follows that Percentage Naturalism has a significantly lower prior probability than Theism.

—Zach

Dear Zach,

But even if Percentage Naturalism has a low prior probability, it still might have a lot of explanatory power. Maybe its explanatory power can offset its low prior probability.

—Thomas

Dear Thomas,

I doubt it. Here are some things to consider. First, we know that the dial configuration for our universe is extremely sensitive. If we change just one basic parameter slightly (without changing the others), we get a configuration that won't support life. It would be entirely baseless to suppose that, if there are other dial configurations corresponding to life-supporting universes, those configurations are not similarly sensitive.

Second, as far as we know, there are a vast number of possible universes. Take just one basic physical parameter, say, the force of gravity: If we alter it by as little as one part in $10^{40}$ (and do not alter the others), we have a dial configuration (hence a possible universe) that would not support life. And as far as we know, we can specify a vast number of universes simply by changing the value of this one force. Think of all the settings there might be on that dial, for example, 1.1 part in $10^{40}$, 1.11 part in $10^{40}$, 1.111 part in $10^{40}$, and so on.

Third, given that life-supporting dial configurations are in general sensitive, it is not plausible to suppose that if we give the dials a spin, they are likely to come to rest on a life-supporting configuration. Here's an analogy to consider. Suppose we have a machine that throws darts at a painted number line, with the (horizontal) angle of launch being completely random. (See the following diagram.) How likely is it that the dart will hit 100, 200, 300, 400, and so on? Even though there are many such locations on the line, there's a lot of space between each of them, so isn't it likely that any given dart will strike *between* them? Clearly it is.

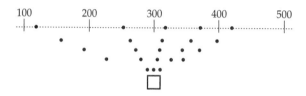

Thus, given that slight changes in the basic physical structures of a universe will remove its capacity to support life, one would naturally suppose that between any two life-supporting dial configurations (possible universes), there are *many* dial configurations that would not support life. If that's correct, clause 5 of Percentage Naturalism seems to be inaccurate—at odds with the phenomenon it's supposed to explain.

Where does this leave us? If Theism has a substantially higher prior probability than Percentage Naturalism, Theism has a marked initial advantage over Percentage Naturalism. But Theism also has considerable explanatory power—it provides good reason to expect a life-supporting universe—good enough, at least to make our life-supporting universe unsurprising. Furthermore, Theism, unlike Percentage Naturalism, is not at odds with the plausible claim that between any two life-supporting dial configurations there are many non-life-supporting ones. I conclude that Theism explains the presence of our life-supporting universe much better than Percentage Naturalism does.

—Zach

Zach,

I admit I don't see a good way to defend Percentage Naturalism. So let's move on. What do you take to be the Naturalists' best attempt to explain the fact that our universe is life-supporting?

—Thomas

Dear Thomas,

Well, the *Many-Universes Hypothesis* (MUH, for short) is getting a lot of attention these days. The basic idea of MUH is that there are lots of *actual* universes. And if there are lots of actual universes with their fundamental physical structures varying at random, it is not surprising that at least one universe is life-supporting. To illustrate the principle involved, if I throw a pair of dice thousands of times, it won't be surprising if I (at some point) have a run of doubles, e.g., roll doubles five times in a row. Similarly, if there are lots and lots of universes, it won't be surprising if at least one of them is life-supporting.

—Zach

Dear Zach,

How do advocates of MUH know there are lots of actual universes? Also, what makes one universe different from another?

—Thomas

Dear Thomas,

MUH is a hypothesis. No one has observed other universes. But remember that this doesn't rule MUH out. No one has directly observed quarks, but we believe they exist because they are postulated in our best physical theories. So the question is whether MUH explains the fact that *our universe is life-supporting* better than the alternative hypotheses do.

MUH may gain some currency because of the "famous and famously controversial, many-worlds interpretation of quantum mechanics—the idea that random quantum processes cause the universe to branch into multiple copies, one for each possible outcome."[13] While this interpretation of quantum physics is highly controversial, it is at least taken seriously by many physicists. I must add, however, that while this interpretation of quantum physics posits many universes, it does not (in standard versions) postulate universes that differ from ours so far as fundamental physics goes, i.e., laws of nature, constants, and initial conditions.[14]

What makes one universe different from another? The usual answer is: different physical constants, different laws of nature, and/or different initial conditions. For example, in describing the phenomenon of fine-tuning, I mentioned the force of gravity, the weak and strong nuclear forces, and the initial force of the Big Bang. We can describe other universes simply by specifying an increase or decrease in these forces. Go back to the Creation Machine. We have over twenty dials to play with, and each dial can be turned to a vast number of different settings. Set the dials anywhere you like; that specifies one universe. Then change one of the dials by one "click," and you have invented yet another universe. And so on. There would seem to be a vast number of possible universes, perhaps even infinitely many.

—Zach

Dear Zach,

If there are many universes, couldn't a Theist just say that they are all created by God?

—Thomas

Dear Thomas,

Yes. The idea of multiple universes is not contrary to Theism. An inventive and generous God might create more than one universe, for all we know. So MUH is not a *direct* threat to Theism.

But if there is a physical mechanism that generates multiple universes that vary in their fundamental physics, then we have an alternative to the design hypothesis (i.e., Theism). Such a mechanism could in principle explain the presence of our fine-tuned universe, in the way that the laws of probability explain that, if I role a die six times, I'll probably roll 2 at some point. So if there were good evidence to the effect that there is a physical mechanism that generates vast numbers of universes (differing in their fundamental physics), then fine-tuning design arguments would face a serious challenge.

Is there good evidence for multiple universes? John Polkinghorne, a physicist-turned-theologian, remarks:

> The many-universes account is sometimes presented as if it were purely scientific, but in fact a sufficient portfolio of different universes could only be generated by speculative processes that go well beyond what sober science can honestly endorse. An example of such a metascientific idea would be the hypothesis that the universe eternally oscillates, the big bang subsequent on each big crunch producing a world with totally different physical laws.[15]

Physicist Max Tegmark provides an alternative assessment. He states that the concept of a multiverse is grounded in well-tested theories such as relativity and quantum mechanics, and it fulfills both of the basic criteria of an empirical science: It makes predictions, and it can be falsified. Scientists have discussed as many as four distinct types of parallel universes. The key question is not whether the multiverse exists but rather how many levels it has.[16]

But Tegmark's claims are misleading at best. Just consider that his argument for other universes *that differ in their laws of nature* depends on the highly controversial metaphysical assumption that "all mathematical structures exist physically" (i.e., all mathematical truths have a physical realization).[17] Such an assumption is purely philosophical and highly speculative. (For example, if our universe conforms to Reimannian geometry, as Einstein taught, why suppose there is some other universe that conforms to an alternative geometry, such as Euclidean geometry?) Superstring theorist Brian Greene comments, "It will be extremely hard, if not impossible, for us ever to know if the multiverse picture is true."[18]

To sum up, relevant versions of MUH require a vast number of universes that differ with regard to their fundamental physics. And there is no compelling scientific evidence for the existence of a vast number of universes.

—Zach

Dear Zach,

But Naturalists are free to engage in metaphysical speculation, right? After all, Theism is not science but metaphysics.

—Thomas

Dear Thomas,

I fully agree. My point is just that both sides are offering metaphysics, not science. So let's look at a version of Naturalism that contains MUH:

**MUH Naturalism**: (1) There is a self-organizing physical reality, (2) some part of physical reality exists of necessity, (3) *the necessary part of physical reality randomly generates additional parts of physical reality that are distinct universes, and* (4) *the number of universes generated is vast—perhaps even infinite.* (5) Leaving aside possible special cases (e.g., sets or numbers), all entities are physical entities.

While backers of MUH typically suggest that some part of physical reality generates universes in a random fashion, they do not usually specify that the "universe generator" exists of necessity, but something along this line will be needed, as we've seen, if Naturalism is to rival Theism as an explanation of the presence of contingent beings.

Now, if we assume MUH Naturalism, are we led to expect a life-supporting universe? Advocates of MUH answer, "Yes, if you roll the dice enough times, you'll get some amazing series; similarly, if the universe generator produces lots of universes whose fundamental physics (laws, constants, initial conditions) varies at random, at least one of the universes will probably be life-supporting." Indeed, some advocates of MUH claim that a life-supporting universe is certain, on the assumption that MUH is true.

—Zach

Dear Zach,

At first, MUH seemed kind of far-fetched to me. But then I thought, "Is it really any more far-fetched than Theism?" Why *not* postulate many universes if doing so gives us a good explanation of the fact that our universe supports life?

—Thomas

Dear Thomas,

In evaluating a hypothesis, we always have to return to the two key issues of prior probability and explanatory power. Let me here make some observations about the prior probability of MUH Naturalism.

First, MUH Naturalism postulates a large number of entire universes that are not postulated by either Theism or the versions of Naturalism we've considered previously. Clearly, MUH Naturalism *completely* cancels Naturalism's initial advantage over Theism with respect to the first facet of simplicity (i.e., the number of things postulated).

Second, MUH Naturalism posits a necessarily existing entity that generates vast numbers of distinct universes in a random fashion—a universe generator. Like the contingent being generator of Necessity Naturalism, the universe generator is a *kind* of entity not postulated by Theism. (*Note*: Even if there were compelling empirical evidence for a universe generator, such evidence could not establish that the universe generator exists of logical or metaphysical necessity. There is no empirical test for logical or metaphysical necessity.)

Third, we can observe only one universe, but MUH Naturalism postulates *unobservable* universes. And unobservable universes are a *kind* of entity not postulated by the versions of Naturalism we've considered previously. (Think of a detective postulating that an unobservable burglar took the TV—not an *unobserved* burglar, but one that *cannot* be observed. Again, I've nothing against postulating unobservable entities, such as quarks, but it must be recognized that this adds to the complexity of a hypothesis.) Thus, from the standpoint of the second facet of simplicity (the number of *kinds* of things postulated), MUH Naturalism is more complex than the forms of Naturalism we've considered so far.[19]

Fourth, MUH Naturalism contains more theses than Necessity Naturalism. And the distinctive new theses, namely, 3 and 4, receive little or no support from other statements within MUH Naturalism. So, from the standpoint of the fourth facet of simplicity, we have yet another reason to view MUH Naturalism as more complex than Necessity Naturalism.

Now, we've already agreed that Necessity Naturalism has about the same prior probability as Theism. That was the upshot of our discussion of the Cosmological Argument. But MUH Naturalism has at least three additional layers of complexity beyond Necessity Naturalism: the number of entities postulated (many universes), an additional kind of entity (unobservable universes), and more theses (five rather than four). With this in mind, shouldn't we assign MUH Naturalism a significantly lower prior probability than Necessity Naturalism?

—Zach

Dear Zach,

I suppose so. But doesn't MUH Naturalism have more explanatory power than Theism? If there are infinitely many universes, at least one of them is *bound* to be fine-tuned. Theism cannot make so strong a claim. So, even if MUH Naturalism has a lower prior probability than Theism, its greater explanatory power may make it the better hypothesis, all things considered.

—Thomas

Dear Thomas,

Even if we suppose that there are infinitely many universes, we do not have a guarantee that at least one will support life. Consider this simple mathematical fact: There are infinitely many even numbers. So we can have an infinity of possibilities without covering every possibility—indeed, if we leave out all the odd numbers, we've omitted infinitely many possibilities.

Now, go back to our Creation Machine. If there are infinitely many universes, then there are infinitely many ways to set the dials (infinitely many dial configurations). However, we might have infinitely many universes but none of them life-supporting. To see this, consider an illustration. Suppose a life-supporting universe requires certain values ending in odd numbers, e.g., mass of the muon = 0.11 and mass of the up-quark = 0.0047; but we like the even numbers and always use them when we specify the settings. For this reason, *we don't know what to expect given only that there are trillions, or even infinitely many, universes.*

—Zach

Dear Zach,

Why not simply change clause 4 of MUH Naturalism to read as follows?

(4+) Every possible universe is generated.

With that revision, given MUH Naturalism, there is *bound* to be a life-supporting universe.

—Thomas

Dear Thomas,

Well, yes, if every possible universe is actual, then a life-supporting universe is actual. But we need to dig a little deeper here.

For one thing, the claim that *every possible universe is generated* strikes me as *ad hoc*. A mere infinity of possible universes doesn't do the trick, so let's be sure we cover all the bases! Honestly, does that strike you as a satisfying explanation? Unless you've got good reasons (other than the need to explain our life-supporting universe) to raise the number of universes generated, your revision of clause 4 appears both contrived and wildly speculative.[20] Here it is important to recall that Theism's prior probability is partly grounded in the experiences of the Theistic mystics.

More importantly, the Theistic hypothesis can be revised so that *it* guarantees a life-supporting universe:[21]

**Theism-Plus**: (1) There is exactly one entity that is (2) perfectly morally good and (3) almighty and who (4) exists of necessity and (5) has the purpose of creating a life-supporting universe.

Of course, adding this fifth clause would lower Theism's prior probability. But the prior probability of Theism-Plus remains higher than that of MUH Naturalism, for two reasons.

First, as we have already seen, clause 5 receives partial support from the other theses belonging to Theism-Plus. For, as we have seen, a perfectly good Deity would have good reason to bring life into existence, especially intelligent life. Hence, it isn't surprising that a perfectly good Deity would have the *purpose* of creating life. And we have seen that God would have reason to place intelligent life in a stable physical environment, governed by laws of nature, as a theater for action. Furthermore, a universe fine-tuned for life is a means to the end of bringing life into existence. Such a universe is not only an effective means to this end but an elegant system that contains much beauty. So, while the additional thesis number 5, undoubtedly gives Theism-Plus a somewhat lower prior probability than Theism, thesis 5 is not surprising given theses 1 through 4.

By contrast, consider the distinctive theses of MUH Naturalism: (3) *The necessary part of physical reality randomly generates additional parts of physical reality that are distinct universes, and (4+) every possible universe is generated.* As far as I can tell, these receive *no* support whatsoever from the other theses within the Naturalistic hypothesis. Moreover, as I've already indicated, clause 4+ seems to me very contrived, especially in comparison to Theism, which is motivated in part by the experience of the Theistic mystics.

Second, as we've already seen, MUH Naturalism has three levels of complexity beyond Theism. Theism-Plus only partly removes one of these levels. (It adds a thesis, but one that enjoys partial support from the others.) MUH Naturalism remains more complex, in two important ways: the number of entities postulated (a vast number of universes) and the number of *kinds* of entities postulated (*unobservable* universes in addition to a necessarily existing universe generator).

The upshot is this: MUH Naturalism has a lower prior probability than Theism-Plus, and MUH Naturalism does not have more explanatory power than Theism-Plus. So Theism-Plus is clearly the better hypothesis.

—Zach

Dear Zach,

So your whole argument rests on the prior probabilities? That's it?
—Thomas

Dear Thomas,

I could rest my case with the discussion of prior probabilities. Why shouldn't I? If two hypotheses are equal in explanatory power, the one with the higher prior probability is the better hypothesis.

But in fact I think there are problems with the alleged explanatory power of MUH Naturalism. Keep in mind that we are here regarding MUH as an explanation of the most fundamental laws, constants, and initial conditions science can (ever) discover. According to MUH, a universe generator produces many different universes, i.e., many physical systems differing in their fundamental physics. What is this process of universe generation like? Problems arise as we consider the details.

First, remember that the universe generator must produce every possible physical universe, and there may be infinitely many possible universes. How does the universe generator succeed in generating *every possible* universe? The story here might be *very* complex. And if no details are provided, we lack a satisfying explanation.

Second, in the current conjectures on offer, the universe generator does not produce all the universes at once. Rather the universes are produced sequentially—either singly or in clusters. But on this assumption, we have no way of knowing how many universes have actually been generated so far. Of course, the number of universes actually generated to date is not relevant if each "cycle" of the universe generator has an equal chance of producing a life-supporting universe. But if the process of universe generation is more like evolution, a process that builds gradually over time, then it's important to know what stage the process is in. For example, if the universe-generation process is evolutionary in nature but our life-supporting universe was the first universe to be generated, then our universe is a sheer fluke. So if the process of universe generation is analogous to evolution, an assumption about the stage the process was in when our universe was generated would need to be added to MUH. But given that there is no good reason (independent of the fact that our universe supports life) to make such an assumption, adding it to MUH would lower MUH's prior probability significantly.[22]

Third, given that universes are produced sequentially and that there are infinitely many possible universes, the universe generator must presumably function eternally, if it is to produce infinitely many universes. In that case, we have to assume that it is not subject to entropy, i.e., that it does not tend to "run down" over time (otherwise it would do so before producing infinitely many universes). But since the physical systems known to us are subject to entropy (the second law of thermodynamics), this assumption is implausible. The only alternative is the equally implausible assumption that infinitely many universes are generated at "one go." There is no known mechanism that could *at one "go"* generate infinitely many universes (much less every possible universe).

Fourth, to avoid the problems mentioned so far, MUH advocates might claim that the number of possible universes is finite or even relatively small. The problem here is that there is no good reason, independent of the fact that our universe supports life, for making such claims. Thus, adding such claims to MUH would lower its prior probability substantially.

To sum up, if we ask for details about how MUH Naturalism leads us to expect a life-supporting universe, problems arise. Sketchy versions of MUH are unsatisfying, but filling in the details involves adding questionable claims that would cause MUH's prior probability to plummet.

I must conclude that MUH Naturalism is inferior to Theism-Plus. Even if we grant—for the sake of the argument—that MUH Naturalism has as much explanatory power as Theism-Plus, Theism-Plus is superior because it is simpler and hence has a higher prior probability. But in fact, MUH Naturalism has less explanatory power than it is typically alleged to have. This leads to a dilemma: Either admit that Theism-Plus has more explanatory power than MUH Naturalism or elaborate MUH Naturalism (i.e., add theses), thus lowering its prior probability still further. All in all, I think the design argument is holding up well.

I've got to stop here and cook dinner. Our universe supports life, but one still has to eat!

—Zach

Dear Zach,

You've made some intriguing observations about the comparative strengths and weaknesses of Theism and MUH Naturalism—I'll give you that. But if a life-supporting universe cries out for an explanation, then so does a life-supporting God. (God must be at least as complicated as the universe.) So doesn't the design argument lead to an infinite regress of explanations? To illustrate: Who designed the universe? God. Who designed God? Super-God. Who designed super-God? Super-duper God. And so on.

—Thomas

Dear Thomas,

Ah, the "Who designed God?" objection! That objection would be fair if the design argument contained a premise along these lines: "Every complex event or entity has an explanation." But no such premise (or presupposition) is involved in the argument we've been considering.

Or again, the "Who designed God?" objection might have some force if Theism were proposed *for no other reason* than to explain the life-supporting universe. (We would at least need assurance that there was some explanatory advantage in postulating one complex entity to explain another complex entity. But keep in mind that scientists routinely hypothesize one complex entity to explain another; e.g., think of subatomic physics. So there's nothing wrong with doing this as long as there's a clear explanatory advantage to be gained.) But as we've seen, Theism is partly grounded in religious experience. It isn't just cooked up to explain our life-supporting universe. Theism also does a good job of explaining the presence of contingent beings. It purportedly explains additional phenomena as well—though we've not yet discussed these. To sum up, Theism gets some support from religious experience, and Theism is a metaphysical hypothesis that promises to explain a wide range of phenomena.

Finally, I thought we agreed long ago that no theory can explain everything. When theorizing, you have to start somewhere. There has to be an initial hypothesis, a claim that something or other has so-and-so features. And if this hypothesis is genuinely one's *initial* move in the "explanation game," then one will have no explanation for the state of affairs it postulates. And Theism is offered as an initial metaphysical hypothesis.

For all these reasons, the "Who designed God?" objection misses the mark, in my estimation.

—Zach

Dear Zach,

Your response to the "Who designed God?" objection is helpful. But now I'm having second thoughts about the explanatory power of Theism with regard to a life-supporting universe.

You've provided a solid list of reasons God would have to create a universe that supports life. But what do we really know about the mind of God? For all we know, God has better reasons to create something else we can't even imagine. So I fear that the design argument presupposes that we humans know more about what might motivate an all-knowing being than we do know (or could ever hope to know).

—Thomas

Dear Thomas,

I have to agree, of course, that an all-knowing God might well have reasons (for doing various things) that we could never guess. But I don't think this vitiates the Theistic explanation of our life-supporting universe, for two main reasons.

First, remember that we are talking about Theism as I've formulated it, not about someone's idea of a mysterious divine reality utterly beyond all human comprehension. The God of Theism is morally perfect, hence loving, generous, and wise. It is from these moral qualities, and especially from divine generosity, that we develop a list of reasons God would have for creating conscious, intelligent forms of life. It seems to me that the list of reasons I drew up previously makes a life-supporting universe *unsurprising*, on the assumption that Theism is true. "Unsurprising" is of course a long way from "certain" or "guaranteed," but it still indicates that Theism has genuine explanatory power.

Second, we regard similar explanations of human action enlightening. Suppose I am puzzled about why Bob said X. You provide a plausible reason why Bob said X. I nod and say, "Yes, that makes sense. That would explain it." Of course, you don't know all that's going on inside Bob—not by a long shot. It doesn't follow that your explanation is without explanatory power.

Of course, you might say that we know a lot more about possible human motivations than we do about possible divine motivations. No doubt that's true. But I do not think we are simply clued out about the nature of love and generosity. Creating humans in order to provide them with interesting activities, beauty, physical and mental pleasures, and satisfying personal relationships—that's something we might expect of a loving God. Of course such a God would have reasons to create other kinds of creatures (and God has done so, according to traditional Theism). Furthermore, God might well have reason to create other universes (or aspects of reality) separate from our universe. And, for all we know, God has done so. But none of this, it seems to me, removes the plausibility of the Theistic explanation of our life-supporting universe.

—Zach

Dear Zach,

What if an all-knowing God would have an excellent reason not to create humans? That could be so, for all we know. After all, we have made quite a mess of things.

—Thomas

Thomas,

I think our discussion is beginning to drift toward the problem of evil ("Why is there so much evil and suffering if God is both almighty and good?"). That's a topic we must discuss in the near future, but we need to set it aside for now. Suffering and evil belong to the list of phenomena that both Theism and Naturalism attempt to explain, and the problem of evil is a big issue that has to be treated in its own right. Our exploration of the problem of evil could conceivably lead us to conclude that God would have powerful reasons not to create conscious beings and place them in a setting such as we find ourselves in. But our question at the moment is simply whether God would have reason to create a universe that supports life—aside from (or independent of) these further facts about suffering and evil. And here it seems to me that, because we have some real grasp of the nature of love, we can see that God would indeed have very good reasons to create a universe that supports life, especially one that supports intelligent, conscious life. Thus, a life-supporting universe is not surprising, on the assumption that Theism is true.

—Zach

Dear Zach,

Fair enough. Let me try another line of questioning. Suppose—just for the sake of the argument—that Theism (or Theism-Plus) is a better explanation of our life-supporting universe than MUH Naturalism is. Still, we must keep in mind the Imperfect-Deity Hypothesis:

**Imperfect-Deity hypothesis**: (1) There is exactly one entity who is (2) morally imperfect and (3) almighty and who (4) exists of necessity.

And even if your design argument gives us a reason to accept Theism over the various forms of Naturalism, I cannot see that your argument gives any reason to accept Theism over the Imperfect-Deity hypothesis. A morally imperfect Deity might be pretty generous, even if not perfectly or always so; hence, such a Deity would have good reason to create intelligent conscious life.

Still doubting,
Thomas

Dear Thomas,

First, as always, my main concern is with Naturalism. If you are granting that there is a good design argument for the existence of an Imperfect Deity, you're granting that the design argument amounts to serious trouble for Naturalism. No Naturalist can accept the Imperfect-Deity hypothesis.

Second, I think you're overlooking something. As we've discussed previously, the deeper the moral flaws of the Imperfect Deity, the more apt this hypothesis is to undermine human knowing in general (in which case the hypothesis is self-defeating).[23] So the only relevant version of the Imperfect-Deity hypothesis is one in which the Deity is like a human being who is basically a good person but with some moral faults. However, there is no enduring tradition of religious experience indicative of a Deity of this type. In short, Theism receives support from Theistic mystical experience; the Imperfect-Deity hypothesis does not. For this reason, the Imperfect-Deity hypothesis has a lower prior probability than Theism.

I think the design argument for Theism holds up well under scrutiny.

—Zach

# CHAPTER 6

# An Argument from Free Will

Dear Thomas,

How are you? Are you ready for another argument? I'd like to try out an argument that depends crucially on some claims about free will.

Theists and Naturalists quite often disagree about the nature of free will and/or about whether humans have free will at all. The issues here are difficult and much fought over, but we should explore them, for at least three reasons. First, the free will issue forces both Theists and Naturalists to clarify certain aspects of their respective positions. Thus, by exploring this issue, we get a better understanding of both Theism and Naturalism. Second, while the free will issue is not an easy one to sort out, as we work through the issues, I believe that an interesting argument for Theism will emerge. Third, Theists generally make crucial assumptions about free will in responding to the problem of evil ("Why is there so much evil and suffering in the world, given that God is almighty and good?"). And since the problem of evil is generally considered the most important objection to Theism, we need to discuss it eventually. So, even if we disagree about the value of my "argument from free will" for Theism, our discussion will facilitate an exploration of the problem of evil.

Because the free will issue is complex, we'll need to work through a series of preliminary issues before my "argument from free will" can usefully be set forth. And here as elsewhere it will be helpful to bear in mind Marilyn Adams' observation that the "defense of any well-formulated philosophical position will eventually involve premises which are fundamentally controversial and so unable to command the assent of all reasonable persons."[1]

—Zach

Dear Zach,

Sounds like you plan to climb one of the higher peaks in the philosophy mountain range. Well, I've got my hiking boots on, so let's hit the trail. What is free will?

—Thomas

Dear Thomas,

*Free will* is traditionally characterized as the power to do otherwise than one in fact does. Let's say you recently voted in a meeting by raising your right arm. If you performed this action freely, then you had the power to do otherwise, to refrain from raising your right arm. If you have free will, then when you face a decision between incompatible courses of action (such as speaking and refraining from speaking), although you cannot take more than one of them, *each* of them is within your power. Another way to put it: If you have free will, then when you are confronted with mutually exclusive courses of action, which one you take is genuinely up to you.[2]

There are two main philosophical views of the nature of free will. **Incompatibilism** is the view that free will is incompatible with (i.e., logically inconsistent with) determinism. By **determinism** I mean the view that "the past determines a unique future."[3] The state the world is in today—right down to the minute details, including all human thoughts and actions—results from (and is fully guaranteed by) the state the world was in yesterday and also by the state the world was in a year ago or a million years ago. Nowadays determinists typically regard physical reality as governed entirely by laws of nature, especially the laws of physics, chemistry, and/or biology.[4]

If determinism is true, then given the state of the world at any moment, there is exactly one physically possible future. As I write I am sitting down. It's 9:08 A.M. Given the state of the world yesterday and the laws of nature, my current posture is guaranteed. Given the past and the laws of nature, standing or lying down are not possible for me at 9:08 A.M. today—if determinism is true. Incompatibilists claim that if determinism is true, then we do not have free will; and if we have free will, then determinism is false.

Long ago, I described three kinds of explanations: scientific, personal, and conceptual. Roughly speaking, whereas scientific explanations are given in terms of laws of nature (and initial conditions), personal explanations are given in terms of the beliefs, desires, reasons, and choices of persons. Incompatibilists place a special emphasis on personal explanations. From the incompatibilist point of view, personal explanations cannot be replaced with scientific ones, for there is no way to translate talk about laws of nature into talk about free choices. The clearest forms of incompatibilism, in my view, ascribe to persons a fundamental power or ability to originate their own purposes or goals, to form their own intentions—that is, to make choices. A fundamental power is not a combination of other powers, and what it produces (in this case, a choice or intention) cannot be fully accounted for via other causal factors. Thus, free will is not a combination of other powers, as my power to walk is a combination of my power to move my legs, keep my balance, swing my arms, etc. And when an agent exercises free will, her choices cannot be fully accounted for by anything other than herself. She simply forms an intention, usually or at least often after considering various alternatives. From this perspective, just as physical particles, such as electrons, have fundamental causal powers of a mechanistic sort (e.g., electrical charge), free agents have a fundamental power of a nonmechanistic sort. (Recall that a mechanistic power is one that operates without purpose or choice, such as the force of gravity.)

I should add that incompatibilists do not deny that many things influence our choices, e.g., desires, beliefs, biology, and environment. Just as a president or prime minister may be influenced by advisors while still making his or her own final decisions, so a free agent may be influenced by various factors while making a real decision between alternative courses of action.

Many philosophers reject incompatibilism. They follow Hobbes, Hume, and Mill in asserting that free will is compatible with (logically consistent with) determinism. This view of freedom is called **compatibilism**. Compatibilists offer various analyses of freedom, but you can get the basic idea of compatibilism by considering the following version: One's act is free if (and only if) one performs the act because one wants to (all things considered). Here a free act is contrasted with one that is coerced or impeded—as when a stronger person overpowers me and forces me to do something I do not want to do. The "all things considered" clause is needed because we often want more than one thing at a given time and it is often impossible to satisfy all of our wants or desires. For example, I may want to finish reading a novel tonight but also to watch a movie; however, the evening is short, so I cannot do both. Assuming I'm not coerced, hypnotized, drugged, or anything of that sort, I will presumably do what I most want to do, and that is what I want, *all* *things considered.* As long as I do what I want to do, all things considered, I act freely.

Some compatibilists emphasize that one's acts are not free unless one's deliberations are responsive to reasons.[5] These compatibilists stress that making a decision is not a matter of being overcome by a strong desire. For example, suppose you are contemplating a contribution to a charitable organization because you think the organization is really helping people. But suppose that, prior to making a donation, you find out that the organization is fraudulent—the contributions mostly wind up in the pockets of the organization's leaders. With this information in hand, you probably won't make a contribution. So, when I speak of what a person wants, "all things considered," I'll assume that among the things considered will be relevant *reasons* for acting.

Note that, given the compatibilist definition of *free act*, your desires and thoughts can be caused by factors over which you have no control. For instance, your wanting to do X (all things considered) might be the consequence of the operation of laws of nature, and you have no control over which laws of nature hold. Suppose Sue steals a candy bar on Tuesday at 11:27 A.M. because she wants to, all things considered. Could she have done otherwise? Compatibilists typically answer along these lines: "Yes, she could have done otherwise in this sense: She would have done otherwise *if* she had wanted to do otherwise." (This type of analysis of "could have done otherwise" is called a *conditional analysis*.) But could she have wanted to do otherwise on Tuesday at 11:27 A.M.? Not if determinism is true. Even so, Sue's act is free, according to compatibilists.

—Zach

Dear Zach,

The conditional analysis puzzles me. Let's assume that given the state the world was in on Monday *and* the laws of nature, the only possible future included (a) Sue wanting (all things considered) to steal the candy bar on Tuesday at 11:27 A.M. and (b) Sue taking the candy bar from the store at that time without permission. Obviously, Sue would not have stolen the candy bar if she had wanted to do something else, but her wanting to steal was determined (we're to assume). *Whatever it was* that Sue wanted (and did) at 11:27 A.M. on Tuesday, it was physically necessary, given the past. Alternative "wantings and doings" were not physically possible for Sue, given the past. This being so, Sue was not free, it seems to me. So the conditional analysis seems to me inadequate. It doesn't capture the sense of "could have done otherwise" needed for genuinely free action.

—Thomas

Dear Thomas,

You've very nicely expressed the incompatibilist's misgivings about the conditional analysis of "could have done otherwise." Such analyses seem inadequate to me also. And as far as I know, the only argument in support of such analyses is along these lines: "Given that we are both free and determined, the only sense in which we 'could have done otherwise' in any particular case is the sense captured by a conditional analysis." Obviously, this argument can have no appeal to the incompatibilist, who denies that we can be both free and determined. In short, the argument begs the question.

Your comments also suggest a very important problem for compatibilism. If determinism holds true, then human acts result from laws of nature operating on past states of the physical world. But we humans do not control which laws of nature hold. Nor do we control the past states of the world. Therefore, given determinism, it seems that our actions are not "up to us," not within our control. If we do not control today's weather because it results from the operation of laws of nature on past states of the physical world, it seems we do not control our present actions if they result from those same factors.[6]

—Zach

Dear Zach,

That looks like an interesting problem for anyone who wishes to claim that humans are both free and determined. But why exactly are we talking about determinism? According to contemporary physics, past states of the world do not determine a unique future. Quantum physics leaves us with more than one possible future.

—Thomas

Dear Thomas,

The compatibilist/incompatibilist distinction was originally drawn up when laws of nature were regarded as deterministic. **Deterministic laws** are of the form "Given $p$, $q$," where $p$ is a proposition summarizing the initial conditions and $q$ describes the result. Example: "Given that the water is heated to 212° Fahrenheit at sea level, it will boil." Given the initial conditions, only one result can occur if a deterministic law applies in a closed system. A system is **closed** if no energy is introduced from outside it.

Contemporary physicists view laws of nature as statistical rather than deterministic. For present purposes, we can regard **statistical laws** as having roughly this form: "If $p$, then $q$ is very probable but $r$ could also result—though it is much less probable." Thus, statistical laws allow for more than one possible result, given the initial conditions. For example, take a quantity of radium 226 over a period of 3,240 years; each atom of the radium has a .75 probability of decaying and a .25 probability of not decaying (within that period of time).

So you're right: Contemporary science does not support determinism. Hence, scientifically informed Naturalists will presumably not be determinists. However, Naturalists are often *mechanists*. Let me explain what I mean by this technical term. First, let's say that a causal factor is *mechanistic* if it does not involve purpose, choice, volition, or the like. For example, the negative charge of an electron is a mechanistic factor. Laws of nature may be viewed as descriptions of how physical entities behave when only mechanistic factors are at work. So the factors involved in a scientific explanation (as I've characterized it) are mechanistic. Now, **mechanism** is a view about the causal history of events in general, including those events we call "human acts." Mechanists claim that the causal history of any event can be traced back ultimately to purely mechanistic factors. In particular, each part of the causal history of any human act can be traced back to purely mechanistic factors. For example, suppose Frank raises his right arm because he desires to vote and believes that raising his arm is the way to do that. According to mechanists, each part of this act has a causal history that can be traced back to entirely mechanistic factors. Frank's desire to vote has such a causal history; perhaps it can be traced back to neural activity in his brain. (Of course, the neural activity can in turn be traced back to prior mechanistic factors within Frank's body and outside it.) Frank's belief ("Raising my arm is the way to vote") also has such a causal history, as does the upward movement of his right arm. Note that, even if we count mental states such as desires, beliefs, and choices as causes, each such mental state will in turn have a causal history that terminates ultimately in purely mechanistic factors.[7]

The compatibilist's view of free will is consistent with mechanism, just as it is consistent with determinism. For the sake of illustration, suppose you are currently in brain state B1. And there's a law of nature to this effect: Given B1, brain state B2 has a probability of .90 while brain state B3 has a probability of .10. Further, suppose that anyone in brain state B2 wants a chocolate chip cookie (all things considered), while anyone in brain state B3 wants vanilla ice cream (all things considered). Given this scenario, you'll probably wind up wanting the cookie (all things considered), but you might wind up wanting the ice cream (all things considered). In any case, even if your "wantings" are fully governed by the laws of nature, you still act freely, says the compatibilist, as long as you do what you most want to do.

Notice that the problem I described earlier still seems to apply. True, given that the laws of nature are statistical, the universe is an indeterministic system and the past does not determine a unique future. But this does not guarantee human freedom. If each part of my act (beliefs, desires, bodily movements) has a causal history that traces back to purely mechanistic factors, then it seems I'm not in control of my act. After all, I do not control the laws of nature—whether they are deterministic or statistical. Nor do I control the past events that form the causal chains leading to the various aspects of my act.

—Zach

Dear Zach,

But some of the events leading up to my actions of today may be acts I performed in the past. Won't the compatibilist say that I was in control of those?

—Thomas

Dear Thomas,

Yes, but of course saying it doesn't make it so. And compatibilists will agree that each part of any act has a causal history that traces back to mechanistic factors, such as the movement of atoms. Moreover, eventually that causal history traces back to times prior to your birth. And clearly, we humans do not control the remote past. But present events have causal histories that are linked to the remote past. If what I call my desires, beliefs, choices, etc., each result ultimately from entirely mechanistic factors linked to the remote past, then, again, it appears that my acts are not really under my control. This is so, in brief, because I control neither the laws of nature nor the past.

—Zach

Dear Zach,

All right. If compatibilists say that free will is compatible with determinism, they will certainly say that free will is compatible with mechanism. Since incompatibilists claim that free will is incompatible with determinism, will they claim that free will is incompatible with mechanism?

—Thomas

Dear Thomas,

Some incompatibilists have suggested that free will is compatible with mechanism, assuming that the laws of nature are statistical. But this seems to me a mistake. If the laws of nature are statistical, the universe is an indeterministic system: There is more than one physically possible future. Thus, indeterminism opens up the possibility that I, on a given occasion, might perform *either* act A *or* some alternative act, B. *But the crucial question is whether I control which of the acts occurs.* Suppose I perform act B simply because of the operation of certain statistical laws of nature. Then I fail to see how I can be credited with controlling which act I perform. Notice that indeterminism by itself doesn't give me a new kind of control over my acts; it simply replaces deterministic laws of nature with statistical ones.

So I think incompatibilists *should* claim that free will is incompatible with mechanism. When a free act occurs, its causal history cannot be traced back to mechanistic factors *alone*. But how could this be? Well, I think we know something about this through introspection. Suppose I have a reason to perform act A ("It's right") but also a reason to perform act B ("It's fun"). I have the power to consider these reasons and to form an intention to act on one of them. If I act freely in the incompatibilist sense, the causal history of my act will trace back, in part, to my exercise of this power. Suppose I form the intention to perform act A because it's right. I simply form that intention. It does not "come over me." It is not fully caused by the operation of laws of nature. As we trace back the causal history of the act, part of that history ends simply with my exercise of the power to form an intention to act.[8]

—Zach

Dear Zach,

But won't compatibilists (and others) say that your formation of an intention is ultimately due to the operation of laws of nature? The situation seems to be this. From your perspective, incompatibilism is false if mechanism is true. But I would guess that many scientists or science-minded thinkers believe that mechanism true. Is there any sort of positive case for incompatibilism?

—Thomas

Dear Thomas,

Yes. The main argument for incompatibilism depends on the link between free will and moral responsibility. People are not morally responsible unless they act freely. For example, Dave stole a car yesterday. If we hold him morally responsible, don't we assume the following?

a. Dave chose to steal the car—he formed an intention to do that, and he might well have formed some other intention incompatible with stealing the car; the intention Dave formed was up to him, within his control.
b. Dave could have done something other than steal the car.

If these assumptions do not hold in Dave's case, most people, I think, would say that Dave was not responsible for stealing the car.

Could Dave have done something other than steal the car, if Dave's act was determined? It seems not. All his bodily states at the time of the theft—including even his brain states—were fully guaranteed by the past and the laws of nature. Given the past and the laws of nature, *only one future is physically possible*, assuming determinism is true.

The situation is a bit more complicated if we assume that mechanism is true and that the laws of nature are statistical. These assumptions allow for more than one physically possible future. But as we've seen, indeterminism does not guarantee freedom. Given mechanism, Dave's bodily states, including his brain states, result from the past plus the operation of laws of nature. Dave doesn't control the past and Dave does not control the laws of nature, *whether they are deterministic or statistical*. It seems, then, that Dave's act is not under his control, assuming that mechanism holds.

So if people are morally responsible, it appears that they have free will, in the incompatibilist sense. And while people may disagree quite a bit about just what our moral responsibilities are, hardly anyone denies that we humans are sometimes morally responsible. Here then, we have a positive argument for the proposition that humans have free will, in the incompatibilist sense.

Perhaps I should add that, if humans are never morally responsible, many ordinary moral beliefs appear to be false. For example, if I regard myself as guilty for some action, then I regard myself as morally responsible, as blameworthy, for performing it. And if you forgive me for some wrongdoing, you are assuming that I am morally responsible for it, that I deserve blame. Similarly, if you are indignant over some injustice, then you are assuming that the person who committed the injustice is morally responsible for it, is to blame for it.[9]

To sum up: People are at least sometimes morally responsible. To deny this is to deny many widely held beliefs about morality. But people are morally responsible only if they are free. And it appears that the relevant sort of freedom here is incompatibilist freedom.

—Zach

Dear Zach,

You've outlined a prima facie case in favor of the incompatibilist view. But a prima facie case is by definition incomplete. You've got to deal with the inevitable objections or evidence to the contrary. Some people deny free will altogether. And others accept the compatibilist view. Furthermore, the incompatibilist view of free will seems a little mysterious to me. So you've still got plenty of work to do.

Let's take a closer look at compatibilism. I've been doing a little reading on my own, and the compatibilist view has more to recommend it than you let on. Consider this: In rendering a verdict, a jury doesn't need to know whether determinism or mechanism is true. Juries need only know the types of things compatibilists emphasize. Did the defendant perform the act because he wanted to? Was he coerced by others? Or hypnotized? Was he able to reason or was he mentally impaired? In short, the compatibilist view seems quite adequate for practical purposes. And free will in the incompatibilist sense hardly seems necessary for moral responsibility if the compatibilist view is adequate for practical purposes.

—Thomas


Dear Thomas,

You've nicely summarized a standard argument for compatibilism, but I think the argument is open to several objections.[10] First, although it's true that courts don't try to settle the issue of determinism, I suspect that most people (including most judges and jurors) assume that human actions are not usually determined. They also assume, I think, that people have a power to form intentions and that a person's intentions do not result entirely from factors beyond her control, such as the operation of laws of nature (whether deterministic or statistical). Such assumptions may not be held consciously, but they can be brought to light under questioning. They are background assumptions—not ordinarily made explicit.

Second, when judges and jurors do become convinced that a defendant's behavior was caused by factors beyond his control, this is apt to affect their assessment of the case. A defense of insanity should succeed if the jury concludes that, because of a mental disease or defect, the defendant was "not sufficiently able to control his [or her] conduct so as to be held accountable for it."[11] And remember that, according to the compatibilist, a person's all-things-considered wants can be *fully* caused by factors beyond his or her control, such as the past and the laws of nature.

Third, suppose you are indignant about something; e.g., someone trips you on the bus. But later you find out that the person's behavior was due to factors beyond her control, such as a nervous disorder. You will realize that being indignant is no longer an appropriate response. And if each person's thinking and behavior is entirely governed by laws of nature operating on past conditions, isn't each human act due to factors beyond the agent's control? So it seems to me.

—Zach

Dear Zach,

Let me try a different tack. Let's suppose you are playing chess with a computer—one of the sophisticated types programmed for "self-improvement." We assume of course that the inner workings of the computer are entirely mechanistic. After all, humans designed, built, and programmed it. However, if you are playing chess with such a computer, you may not always be able, in practice, to regard its workings as mechanistic. That is, the details of its operations are so complex that you could never anticipate its next move in mechanistic terms (the terms in which the program is written). Instead, you will need to think of the computer as a player intent on winning the game. For instance, you are apt to find yourself thinking along the following lines: "If I move my pawn here, the computer will move its bishop over there to put my king in check."[12]

Such examples suggest to me that our concept of free will arises out of (or is reducible to) complexity. Once the behavior of a physical system becomes sufficiently complex or complex in a certain way, we say it is "free." From this perspective, free will does seem to be compatible with mechanism. And if *free will* is really just a form of complexity within systems, we'll never know otherwise. Moreover, as far as I can see, it won't make any difference. We can go on using the term *free will* or *choice* just as we always have.

—Thomas

Dear Thomas,

Consider an example of Peter van Inwagen's.[13] Suppose Martians implant a tiny brain monitor into every human being at birth. The brain monitor is undetectable to us, given the current state of our science, and it is programmed to take control of human decision-making processes. Whenever a person has to make a choice, the brain monitor causes that person to choose in accordance with its program. (Each program is conditional in nature, to cover all the kinds of situations humans must face, e.g., "If attacked by a human, run if the attacker is larger; otherwise counterattack.") But we humans never feel interfered with because the monitor causes us to form beliefs and desires that naturally lead to the choices it causes us to make.

Now, by hypothesis, if the Martians have implanted such brain monitors in us, we would not know this. We would go on applying the words *free act* to various behaviors—but we would be mistaken in doing so. That seems clear to me, even though human behavior and human thought processes would remain very complex. Therefore, it seems to me that you are wrong in supposing that complexity equals freedom and wrong in supposing that it makes no difference if freedom is merely complexity. If we are like humans under the control of Martian computers, we lack freedom and our situation is pathetic.

—Zach

Dear Zach,

The Martian-brain-monitor example is interesting and helpful. I concede that free will can't rightly be equated with internal complexity.

But I want to go back to your main argument for incompatibilism. You claimed that one is morally responsible only if *one can do otherwise than one in fact does*. Consider, however, the example of a person who is locked in a room but does not know she is locked in. She considers leaving the room in order to help a friend who is in need but decides not to. Isn't she responsible for staying in the room? She seems both free and responsible, even though (unknown to her) *she could not leave the room*.[14] What do you make of that?

—Thomas

Dear Thomas,

Although the woman may not be able to leave the room, she is certainly capable of doing something other than just sit there. For example, she can form the intention to leave the room. And she can try to leave the room.

I think that moral responsibility depends fundamentally on the intentions we form. Suppose Boggs fully intends to shoot Smyth, when doing so would be morally wrong. Boggs aims and pulls the trigger, but by chance the gun fails to fire. Clearly, in such a case, Boggs is morally blameworthy. He has done something wrong, even though his intention was not ultimately fulfilled (due to the malfunctioning gun). Similarly, in the case of the woman locked in a room, to describe the woman's actions we can't simply focus on the fact that she remains in the room—we have to consider her intentions.

Your case actually backs up an important point favorable to incompatibilism. The woman needs to get out of the room in order to help a friend. Suppose she tries her best to escape but cannot. Would we blame her for not helping her friend under these circumstances? Of course not. We could reasonably blame her if she didn't even try to get out of the room, but we cannot blame her for remaining in the room if leaving is not within her power.

By the way, philosopher Harry Frankfurt called attention to special cases in which the agent seems morally responsible but could not "do otherwise." These types of cases—now commonly referred to as *Frankfurt cases*—have been intensely scrutinized by philosophers in recent years. I'll send you some readings on this.[15]

—Zach


Dear Zach,

Thanks for sending the material about Frankfurt cases. I found one of Pereboom's examples particularly intriguing.[16] Let me paraphrase it: Deb is considering whether to cheat on her taxes. She can do so simply by checking a box on her tax form. And let us assume that Deb knows she can cheat without being caught. So the only reason she has not to cheat is a moral reason, namely, that cheating is wrong. Furthermore, assume that Deb's psychology is such that she won't choose not to cheat unless she considers this moral reason very carefully so that it becomes vivid to her. (Deb won't be motivated by the mere fleeting thought that cheating is wrong.) Indeed, let us suppose that even if Deb considers this moral reason carefully, she may still decide to check the box and thus to cheat on her taxes. To sum up, Deb will cheat for sure if she does not consider the moral reason carefully, but she may cheat even if she does consider the moral reason carefully.

Now, a mad scientist has implanted a device in Deb's brain. The device tracks Deb's deliberations, and it indicates if she considers the moral reason carefully. Not only does the device track Deb's deliberations, but if Deb considers the moral reason carefully, the device is activated: It takes control of Deb's brain and makes her check the box (i.e., cheat on her taxes). Thus, the device is set up to ensure that Deb cheats on her taxes.

However, as a matter of fact, when Deb sits down to fill out her tax form, she never considers the moral reason ("Cheating is wrong") carefully—it remains only a fleeting thought. Much more vivid to Deb is the thought that she can keep a lot of money by cheating on her taxes. So she checks the box and the device is never activated. Does Deb act freely? Yes. Is she morally responsible for cheating? Yes. But can she do otherwise? No, she cannot. The device is set up so that she cannot choose not to cheat. If she so much as considers the moral reason carefully, the device is activated and it makes her cheat.

What do you think of this "mad scientist" case? Does it show that one can be morally responsible for an action even though one cannot do otherwise? And if so, doesn't this undermine your main argument for free will in the incompatibilist sense?

—Thomas

Dear Thomas,

The mad scientist case is very interesting. Here are a few observations.

First, in my opinion, Frankfurt cases tend to be tricky and confusing. I would caution against placing too much weight on them. Nevertheless, I am inclined to agree that Deb would be free and responsible as long as the device is not activated.

Second, the mad scientist case is not, strictly speaking, a case in which the agent "cannot do otherwise." Deb can do something besides cheat by considering the moral reason carefully. True, Deb cannot choose *not* to cheat, because the device will be activated before such a choice can occur. But she can at least consider the moral reason carefully, and in that case her freedom will be taken away when the device is activated. Then she's merely a tool in the mad scientist's hands and hence is not responsible for cheating. Indeed, I would say that checking the box doesn't count as cheating if the device is activated.

Third, if we accept the givens of the case, *refraining from cheating* is a three-step process that involves (1) considering the moral reason carefully, (2) forming the intention not to cheat, and (3) acting on that intention. Therefore, *part* of the action of choosing not to cheat is within Deb's power—specifically, the first step is within her power. And since Deb does not take that first step, we rightly judge her responsible for cheating. After all, she does not know she cannot perform steps 2 and 3.

In conclusion, your example is interesting and fun to consider, but I don't think it refutes the principle that one is morally responsible only if one can do otherwise.

—Zach

Dear Zach,

You've admitted that Deb is responsible for cheating even though she cannot choose not to cheat, cannot form the intention not to cheat, and cannot intentionally refrain from cheating. True, Deb can consider the moral reason carefully. But having considered it carefully, she might still cheat. And merely considering a moral reason (even doing so carefully) does not rid one of blame, does it?

—Thomas

Dear Thomas,

Interesting point. Normally, the power to "do otherwise" than X is taken to include the power to form an intention not to do X and to intentionally refrain from X. The mad scientist case suggests that these powers can be absent while the agent remains free and responsible. But I think we need to dig a little deeper.

Let's begin by considering an analogy. Suppose Kim drinks a bottle of whiskey and goes for a drive. Being drunk, Kim is unable to get his foot on the brake in time, and so he hits another car. We of course hold Kim responsible, even though he can rightly claim that he was unable to operate the brake in time. Why do we hold him responsible? Because of his earlier choices to drink the whiskey and to drive while intoxicated. We assume that he could have refrained from drinking and/or from driving while intoxicated. In other words, he is responsible for being in a state in which he cannot operate the brake properly. He is in that state by his own free choice.

Now go back to the mad scientist case. Deb does not give careful consideration to the principle that cheating on her taxes is morally wrong. We have to ask why she is so little concerned with moral reasons. How did she get into a state in which she can cheat so casually? Your case doesn't fill us in on Deb's history, but we need to know something of her history to determine if she is really responsible. Perhaps she has cheated a lot in the past and no longer gives serious consideration to the principle that cheating is wrong. Cheating has become a habit. If so, Deb is responsible for the immoral state she's in. Like Kim, she's responsible for her actions because she's responsible for the morally deplorable state she's gotten herself into. Previous choices have resulted in that state. Earlier in Deb's life there were presumably cases in which she could have formed the intention not to cheat and, indeed, cases in which she could have intentionally refrained from cheating. If not—if Deb is abnormal in some way; e.g., if she's a mentally impaired person who has never been able to appreciate moral reasons, then I would not consider her morally responsible for cheating.[17]

I don't think the mad scientist case destroys the link between moral responsibility and being able to do otherwise, but perhaps it calls for a more subtle account of that linkage. Typically, agents do have the power to do otherwise, and this power results in part from the power to originate purposes or intentions. A bank robber forms the intention to rob a particular bank. He might have entertained the possibility of robbing the bank but, after thinking matters over, have formed the intention to refrain. And in a typical case, he could have intentionally refrained from robbing the bank. In exceptional cases, such as the mad scientist case, the power to form an alternative intention may be absent (along with the power to intentionally refrain from the relevant act). *But in such cases, if we judge that the agent is free and responsible, we presuppose earlier (relevant) situations in which the agent "could have done otherwise"—at least in the sense that the agent could have formed alternative intentions.* Or so it seems to me.

In my opinion, then, the Frankfurt cases don't undermine the link between moral responsibility and being able to do otherwise. They merely require a more subtle understanding of that linkage. And therefore, the Frankfurt cases do not undermine the main argument for incompatibilism.

—Zach

Dear Zach,

Your response to the mad scientist case is plausible, though I'll need some time to think it over. But now I want to turn to some empirical issues.

I assume that the human brain is a physical organ. And so, like any physical object, it is composed of atoms. But atoms are governed by the laws of physics. So the brain is governed by the laws of physics, right? Therefore, the brain is a mechanistic system.

I further assume that the mental state I'm in at any particular moment (e.g., my current thought that I'd like a coffee) is correlated with some specific brain process (e.g., a series of neuron firings). The mental state cannot occur unless the correlated brain process occurs.

It follows, doesn't it, that our mental states are "on a tether." They are tied to brain processes that are in turn tied to laws of physics. At the micro level, your brain is just an arrangement of atoms. The laws of physics dictate the state your brain will be in tomorrow. So the state of your brain at any time results from past states of the world (including past states of your brain) plus the laws of physics.

I don't see any room for free will in this picture.

—Thomas

Dear Thomas,

Many people have thought that such empirical considerations undermine the case for incompatibilism. But for several reasons, I don't agree.

First, the brain is a very complex organ and there is much that we do not know about its operations. So we have a right to be skeptical about sweeping claims regarding the detailed operations of the brain.

Second, in one very important respect a brain is like no other type of physical object. Specifically, a brain—a human brain, anyway—is clearly linked to mental states, such as desires, beliefs, emotions, pains, and pleasures. Moreover, it is extremely plausible to suppose that mental states are causes. For example, pain can cause a person to cry out. Beliefs and desires can lead a person to act. Therefore, a human brain, unlike other physical objects, is intimately linked to mental causes. For this reason, we cannot simply assume that the brain operates as other physical objects do. It is manifestly a special case.

Third, the brain may well be a chaotic system.[18] In a chaotic system, minute changes in one part of the system can cause massive differences in the entire system. The weather is an example of a chaotic system. The proverbial butterfly flaps its wings and a tropical storm ensues. Chaotic systems are unpredictable even when they are deterministic. But physical systems are at bottom indeterministic, according to physicists. Now, normally, quantum-level (subatomic) indeterminacies are thought to cancel one another out at the macro level. But a chaotic system that amplifies nondetermined events would be unpredictable in a special sense. It would be unpredictable, not only because we cannot get enough information about the initial conditions of the system, but because the initial conditions actually allow for multiple outcomes, i.e., because more than one result is physically possible.

Why is this relevant? If the brain is a chaotic system that amplifies nondetermined events, free will might be operative without producing any violation of laws of nature. Here is a simple analogy. Let's suppose that, at the micro level of the brain, there is a state S1. A law of nature tells us that given brain state S1, brain state S2 has a probability of 90% while brain state S3 has a probability of 10%. (We can go on to imagine that S2 corresponds with telling a lie while S3 corresponds with refraining from the lie.) This means that, in the long run, in 90% of the cases, S1 will result in S2 (and the person will lie). Now imagine that we can press a button to put a person's brain into state S1. We try this ten times. In how many cases will S1 yield S2? You might be tempted to answer, "Nine." But that answer is not necessarily correct. In our experiment, S2 might result only eight times or even fewer, for the law tells us the frequencies in the long run; it does not guarantee what will happen in the relatively short run. So if a nonmechanistic cause were to affect outcomes of this sort, laws of nature would not *necessarily* be violated.

Some argue, however, that it is implausible to hold what might be called the *coincidence thesis*, namely, that free will operates in such a way as to coincide with probabilities laid down by physics. Pereboom compares the coincidence thesis to Kant's implausible claim that the choices of noumenal selves just happen to coincide perfectly with determined events in the phenomenal realm.[19] Pereboom has a point: If free will is a causal factor in addition to mechanistic causal factors, it would be rather surprising if free will (in the long run) *never* produced effects that diverge in some way from the effects of mechanistic causal factors. And he rightly observes that it "is far from acceptable in physics or neurophysiology to count such a belief [i.e., a belief in moral responsibility and free will] as evidence for a hypothesis in these sciences."[20] However, I think it is well to keep the following three points in mind.

First, it is true that we don't expect a physics textbook to contain arguments along these lines, "Since we are morally responsible and free, electrons must behave in such-and-such ways." We don't expect physicists, in their role as physicists, to employ premises regarding the moral life. But when we are doing philosophy, we can't confine ourselves to the evidence physicists, qua physicists, employ. We have to take into account the full range of evidence, including evidence from the moral life.

Second, given the very great plausibility of the case for moral responsibility and free will, we ought to be extremely reluctant to give up these beliefs. We ought to demand very strong—I would say overwhelming—contrary evidence before doing so.

Third, the evidence for fundamental physical theories "is gathered by analyzing relatively simple, decomposed physical systems." And if "some scientists say that they believe these results to hold quite generally, regardless of the macro-level complexity in which a microphysical system is embedded, . . . they are merely expressing their faith in reductionist metaphysics."[21] Simply put, we can't rightly assume that minute physical particles embedded in the brain behave precisely as they would in every other context.

To sum up, we don't know enough about the workings of the brain to conclude that those workings rule out free will. The currently available facts about the operation of the brain do not overturn the main argument for free will in the incompatibilist sense.

—Zach

Dear Zach,

I'm mulling over your reflections on the empirical issues. I do admit that there is much we don't know about how the brain works. So, given our present state of knowledge, I suppose it *would* be hasty to conclude that scientific findings rule out free will. But I still have questions about the incompatibilist view. It's not that I'm thrilled with compatibilism—in fact, I'm not. But I am somewhat puzzled by incompatibilism. Here are my questions.

A. If incompatibilism is true, then there can be no fully scientific account of human action. Right?
B. In fact, if incompatibilism is true, then human acts must be totally unpredictable. But we can often accurately predict what humans will do. For example, I predict that at 5:00 P.M. today, nearly all of my fellow workers will leave work and go home. And I'm willing to bet on that!
C. If we have free will in the incompatibilist sense, an agent's choice just appears on the scene. It has no antecedents. Right? So it's just a random occurrence.

All in all, free will *in the incompatibilist sense* seems rather mysterious to me.

—Thomas

Dear Thomas,

Let me take up your questions in order.

A. "If incompatibilism is true, then there can be no fully scientific account of human action." Well, *free* action (in the incompatibilist sense) cannot be accounted for in purely mechanistic terms. Free will is a nonmechanistic power. So if science deals only with mechanistic powers (or causes), then there can be no complete scientific account of free action. That said, there's still a lot of room for science to explore the various factors involved in human motivation. Incompatibilists don't deny that many causal factors influence our choices. Furthermore, it may be that a great many human actions are not free. For instance, perhaps we are often on "automatic pilot" in the course of a day—not really making choices at all. One can be an incompatibilist and yet hold that many human actions are not free.

B. "If incompatibilism is true, then human acts must be totally unpredictable." I disagree. Even if humans are free in the incompatibilist sense, there can be useful generalizations about human behavior. We often know what people will probably do, because we know a good bit about their desires, beliefs, and purposes. For example, you know your fellow workers will probably go home at 5:00 P.M. because you know that they strongly desire to go home and (usually) are not faced with a more attractive (or pressing) alternative. Anyone can make such predictions, including the incompatibilist. Of course, human behavior is much harder to predict in certain types of cases, e.g., when the agent has two or more conflicting desires of approximately equal strength, or when a desire is in conflict with the (perceived) demands of prudence or morality.

C. "If we have free will in the incompatibilist sense, an agent's choice just appears on the scene. It has no antecedents. So it's just a random occurrence." The conclusion does not follow. A choice is not a random occurrence. To be sure, a free act might appear to be random to an outside observer, but what results by choice is plainly not a random occurrence. Right now, you can choose to think about philosophy or instead to think about, say, football. If you choose to go on thinking about philosophy, that's not a random occurrence, is it? Come on, Thomas, you've got the inside scoop on making choices—you've been doing that all your life!

—Zach

Dear Zach,

We understand the causal interactions between physical objects pretty well. Billiard ball X strikes billiard ball Y, and Y rolls away at a predictable speed in a predictable direction. But how are we to understand the causal interaction between an agent (a decision maker) and its brain? How do we get from "I choose the object on the left" to some particular brain state?

—Thomas

Dear Thomas,

First, in anybody's view, there is ultimately a mystery about causation. Consider the causal interaction of two billiard balls, X and Y. You say, "The movement of X *causes* the movement of Y." Someone else responds, "I see that their movements are correlated, but I see no *necessary connection* between these events. X moves toward Y, we hear a loud 'clack,' and Y moves away at a certain speed in a certain direction. But as far as I can see, Y might just as well have exploded or have vanished. The behavior of the billiard balls is a mystery." Hume of course said just this sort of thing about causation.

A scientific law (in effect) gives a description of how a thing behaves. But why does the object behave that way and not some other way? At the fundamental level we can say nothing more than, "We've observed this many times, and that's just how the thing behaves." There is a mystery about causation, but that is certainly not a good reason to deny its presence.

Second, there is a further mystery about mental causation in general. How does the feeling of intense pain—that familiar, unpleasant sensation—cause my mouth to emit a noise, a scream? It's no good talking about neural events. How does that felt experience of pain bring about any neural process at all? No one knows. But the felt experience of pain—the mental state—surely does cause events in the brain (as well as in other parts of the body).

So there is a mystery about causation in general, but that's not a good reason to deny that causation occurs. And there's a special mystery about mental causes in particular, but that's not a good reason to deny their presence. It appears that the concept of causation is ultimately one we cannot analyze—we must simply grasp it as a primitive. And causal connections cannot be arrived at *a priori*; we know about them by observation. But, then, don't we observe things occurring via free will, via our power to form intentions? I admit I don't know how forming an intention or making choices brings about a process or event in the brain. But apparently it somehow does. The fact that there is mystery here is not a good reason to deny the presence of free will, right?

—Zach

Dear Zach,

You've given me a lot to think about. I don't pretend to have it all sorted out. But this morning I had the following thought: "I firmly believe that people are sometimes morally responsible. But that belief seems to presuppose free will *in the incompatibilist sense*. And although there is much I don't pretend to understand about free will, I do believe that I have it and that other people do too. I very much doubt that I could give that belief up."

Well, that's just a statement of "where I'm at," so to speak. I'm sure I will go on having questions about free will, all the while believing I and others have it. And given my belief in free will (in the incompatibilist sense), I would be very interested in the argument you promised long ago—an argument for God's existence based on free will. How does the argument go?

—Thomas

Dear Thomas,

I think many people, Theists and non-Theists alike, are in your shoes. They find free will puzzling in various ways, but they nevertheless find themselves believing that we humans have it. And under questioning it becomes clear that by *free will* they mean free will in the incompatibilist sense. (Indeed, I'm struck by the fact that, when I discuss free will in my classes, students quite often express the opinion that compatibilist freedom "isn't really freedom at all.")

So, in spite of the questions we may have about free will, an argument from free will for God's existence can hope to appeal to a wide audience. How might such an argument proceed? Let me provide a rough outline here. I'm sure you'll have some questions, and we can take it from there.

My argument from free will is an argument-to-the-best-explanation. Thanks to our detailed discussion of free will, we can summarize the phenomenon succinctly:

*Phenomenon*: Humans have free will (in the incompatibilist sense). And humans do at least occasionally exercise this power—they sometimes act freely.

Now we need to compare Theism, as an explanation of this phenomenon, with a competitive form of Naturalism. Given our discussion of the design argument, I suggest that MUH Naturalism is as strong a version of Naturalism as any we've considered:

> **MUH Naturalism**: (1) There is a self-organizing physical reality, (2) some part of physical reality exists of necessity, (3) the necessary part of physical reality randomly generates additional parts of physical reality that are distinct universes, and (4) the number of universes generated is vast—perhaps even infinite. (5) Leaving aside possible special cases (e.g., sets or numbers), all entities are physical entities.

If you judge that, based on our discussion of the design argument, some other form of Naturalism (such as Single-Universe Naturalism) is better than MUH Naturalism, that's not a problem. With fairly minor changes, the argument will be the same.

> **Premise 1**. Theism has a significantly higher prior probability than MUH Naturalism.

I won't rehearse the arguments for this in great detail, since doing so would be repetitious. But there are two main points to keep in mind. First, recall that, in our discussion of the Cosmological Argument, we agreed there is no good reason to assign Theism a lower prior probability than Necessity Naturalism (provided we take Theistic mystical experience into account).[22] But MUH Naturalism is much more complicated than Necessity Naturalism. It postulates many more entities (namely, lots of universes), it postulates more kinds of entities (*unobservable* universes in addition to a "universe generator"), and it contains more theses. So, given the complexity of MUH Naturalism, we must assign it a lower prior probability than Theism:

> **Theism**: (1) There is exactly one entity that is (2) perfectly morally good and (3) almighty and that (4) exists of necessity.

But a second reason also comes into play. In our discussion of the design argument, I argued that Theism has more explanatory power with regard to our life-supporting universe than MUH Naturalism does. For example, the Many-Universes Hypothesis doesn't do a good job of explaining the presence of a life-supporting universe unless every possible universe is postulated. (As far as we know, there might be infinitely many universes that are not life-supporting.) But it's not plausible to suppose that every possible universe is generated "at one go" (no known mechanism could produce such a result); and if the universes are generated sequentially, the "universe generator" must presumably operate *forever* to produce every possible universe; however, it is implausible to suppose that any physical system operates forever since the physical systems of our acquaintance tend to run down over time. *In short, with the evidence of design included in our background evidence (for present purposes), the prior probability of Theism gets a boost.* (One of the main advantages of a cumulative case approach is that the gains achieved through one argument provide a basis for assigning more favorable prior probabilities for the next argument.)

**Premise 2.** Theism does a better job of leading us to expect the presence of free will (in the incompatibilist sense) than MUH Naturalism does.

There is, as far as I can see, nothing in MUH Naturalism to lead us to expect the presence of free agents. The many universes of MUH Naturalism are entire physical systems, distinct from one another because of differences in their basic physical laws, physical constants, or initial conditions. Events in these physical systems are presumed to be either governed by laws of nature (operating on past conditions) or else random (uncaused). But as we've seen, humans control neither the laws of nature nor the past. And humans don't control random (uncaused) events either, for if humans controlled these events, they would not *be* random. Accordingly, there's nothing indicative of free will (in the incompatibilist sense) in the MUH Naturalist's scheme. There's nothing in MUH Naturalism to lead us to expect free agents.

An analogy might be useful here. From the standpoint of MUH Naturalism, events in general—including those events we call *human actions*—may be viewed in the way most of us view the weather. We assume that the state of the weather yesterday, together with the laws of nature, accounts for today's weather. But of course back of yesterday's weather was the weather of the day before yesterday and of the day before that, etc., going all the way back to days belonging to the remote past, prior to the existence of any human beings.

By contrast, the presence of free agents is not surprising, on the assumption that Theism is true. A morally perfect Deity would have good reason to give persons the opportunity to live significant lives. And, other things being equal, a life involving important choices is more significant than a life involving no choices. So God would have reason to give us the power to make important choices, such as the choice to help or harm ourselves and others. For this reason, a morally perfect Deity would have reason to give persons responsibility for themselves and others—prudential and moral responsibility. Furthermore, while an almighty God could create conscious robots and program them to behave in accord with the divine will, a loving God would have reason to create beings capable of a free response to divine love, for surely a free response to God's love is much more significant than a programmed response. A programmed or "robotic" devotion to the Deity would seem to pale in significance as compared to a freely chosen devotion.

Conclusion: Theism explains the presence of human free will better than MUH Naturalism does; hence, the phenomenon of free will provides evidence in favor of Theism over MUH Naturalism.

—Zach

Dear Zach,

It's an interesting argument. I grant your first premise, that Theism has a higher prior probability than MUH Naturalism. But I do have some questions about your second premise.

You assume something like this: "If all events are either random or the result of laws of nature operating on past conditions, and if humans don't control what's random, don't control the laws of nature, and don't control the past, then humans don't control their own actions." But let's take this down to specifics. Suppose I walk into a store to buy a candy bar. I think it over and decide to buy the candy bar. I certainly seem to be in control of my action. And MUH Naturalists aren't denying that such events occur, right?

—Thomas

Dear Thomas,

Of course not. But MUH Naturalism posits only mechanistic causal factors, such as the laws of nature. The only sort of control this would give you is the sort compatibilism gives you. You buy the candy bar because you want to (all things considered). But could you have wanted to do otherwise? Only in the sense that, because physical laws are indeterministic, there may be some probability that you would not have wanted the candy bar (all things considered). But whatever you wind up wanting (all things considered), it will be due to the operation of the laws of nature (or perhaps to chance), not to your nonmechanistic power to originate choices. So MUH Naturalism does not lead us to expect acts that are free in the incompatibilist sense.

—Zach

Dear Zach,

But why stick with MUH Naturalism? Why not formulate a version of Naturalism that postulates free will in the incompatibilist sense?

—Thomas

Dear Thomas,

We could do that, but there would be a price to be paid. Here's a version of Naturalism that posits free will (note clause 6).

> **MUH-Naturalism-Plus-Free-Will**: (1) There is a self-organizing physical reality, (2) some part of physical reality exists of necessity, (3) the necessary part of physical reality randomly generates additional parts of physical reality that are distinct universes, and (4) the number of universes generated is vast—perhaps even infinite. (5) Leaving aside possible special cases (e.g., sets or numbers), all entities are physical entities. (6) *Organisms with highly complex brains, such as humans, have free will in the incompatibilist sense.*

Let me make a few comments about this version of Naturalism. First of all, I do not think that most Naturalists want to postulate free will in the incompatibilist sense. Many Naturalists deny free will altogether, precisely because they see it as incompatible with a world governed by natural law. Many other Naturalists endorse freedom in the compatibilist sense while denying freedom in the incompatibilist sense.

Second, because of clause 6, MUH-Naturalism-Plus-Free-Will has a *much* lower prior probability than Theism. As we have already seen, MUH Naturalism has a significantly lower prior probability than Theism. But MUH Naturalism-Plus-Free-Will contains an additional thesis that receives no support from the other theses belonging to that hypothesis. And, as we saw in our discussion of the fourth facet of simplicity, adding a thesis to a hypothesis will lower its prior probability, except in very special cases not relevant here.[23]

Third, MUH-Naturalism-Plus-Free-Will does a poor job of explaining the presence of free will. It asserts that free will is present and suggests that free will somehow results from the complexity of the human brain. But the mere fact of brain complexity does not lead us to expect free will in the incompatibilist sense. In fact, van Inwagen's Martian case shows that creatures as complex as human beings might very well lack free will. Furthermore, no knowledge of brain structure or brain processes will lead us to expect free will. There is simply no information we could have about neurons, synapses, electrochemical laws, etc., that would justify us in saying, "Oh, now that I know *that*, I can see that this organism has free will." (If we know that humans have free will, it is not because of what we know about human brains.) In short, Naturalism is in principle incapable of explaining free will.[24]

By contrast, Theism isn't limited to explaining the presence of free will *by appeal to mechanistic factors*. Instead, Theism provides reasons for expecting there to be creatures with free will *by appeal to the reasons a good God would have for bringing such creatures into existence.* So it seems to me that Theism explains the presence of free will better than Naturalism does.

—Zach

Dear Zach,

This may surprise you, but I think you're right about Naturalism's inability to explain free will. But I feel you've been rather easy on Theism. After all, historically speaking, many Theists have denied free will in the incompatibilist sense. Calvinists, for instance, are compatibilists, because they claim that human actions are determined by God *and yet free.* Furthermore, there are well-known arguments showing that God's knowledge of the future rules out human freedom. So I'm not so sure that Theism explains free will. Maybe Theism implicitly denies that humans have free will.

—Thomas

Dear Thomas,

Fair enough. I have been skirting the problem of theological determinism. We must take it up. I'm all the more willing to do so because this issue has a definite bearing on the problem of evil—which we really must discuss sometime soon.

The most impressive argument for theological determinism may be briefly summarized as follows.[25]

> God is omniscient, so God knows the future and has always known it (in detail). Now, consider a specific future time, say, next Friday at 1:31 P.M. My friend Al will either tell a lie at that time or not. Let's just suppose, for the sake of the argument, that *Al will tell a lie next Friday at 1:31 P.M.* Then God knows this and always has known it. Moreover, if God knows this, it is true and God believes it. Indeed, God believed it long ago—hundreds, thousands, even millions of years ago. Now consider the following key premise:
>
> **Key Premise**: If God believed long ago that Al will tell a lie next Friday, and if it is in Al's power to refrain from lying next Friday, then next Friday it will be in Al's power to bring about one of the following: (a) that God held a false belief long ago or (b) that God did not believe long ago that Al will lie next Friday.
>
> Since God is infallible, Al will not have the power (next Friday) to bring about (a). And since humans cannot change the past, Al will not have the power (next Friday) to bring about

(b). So it seems that Theists must draw the conclusion that, next Friday, Al will not have the power to refrain from lying. And we can of course generalize this conclusion to all human acts. Hence, if God is omniscient, we can *never* "do otherwise" and so we lack free will.

Let's call this *the foreknowledge argument* for short. It's a formidable argument! And if it works, my "argument from free will" for Theism is a total flop, of course.

—Zach

Dear Zach,

You call it the foreknowledge argument, but you state the key premise in terms of what God *believes*. Why?

—Thomas

Dear Thomas,

Most philosophers accept the following partial analysis of knowledge: "If one **knows** that $X$ (where $X$ is any proposition), then one believes that $X$, $X$ is true, and $X$ is justified or warranted in believing that $X$." Knowledge is success in the cognitive realm, which is why one cannot know a falsehood. (You can *think* you know something that turns out to be false, but you don't really know it.) And to know something you must believe it—a true proposition that never enters your mind is not something you know, nor do you know a proposition simply because you've entertained it. Finally, knowledge is not just a lucky guess—it's more than an opinion that turns out to be true. To count as knowledge, a belief must be grounded, justified, or warranted. (Of course, there is plenty of room for disagreement about the conditions under which a belief is grounded, justified, or warranted.)

The foreknowledge argument makes reference to God's beliefs because it seems especially clear that we cannot change past *beliefs*. For example, when I was four, I believed that Santa exists. I gave that belief up later on (you'll be glad to know!), but nothing can now change the fact that I once held it. Similarly, according to the foreknowledge argument, whatever God believed long ago is not within our control. We can't change history.

—Zach

Dear Zach,

Maybe I'm missing something, but isn't there an easy answer to the foreknowledge argument? To know something is not to cause it. For example, suppose I observe someone rob a bank. I know he's robbing the bank, but I'm not *causing* him to rob the bank. Similarly, why can't God know what Al will do next Friday without causing Al to do it?

—Thomas

Dear Thomas,

You make a good point: One can know that something is true without causing it to be true. Unfortunately, this point is not relevant to the foreknowledge argument. The argument does not say that God causes Al to lie. Roughly speaking, the problem results from these claims: God held a certain belief long ago, Al cannot alter the fact that God held that belief (because Al can't change the past), and Al cannot render the belief false (because God is infallible). *To sum up, the problem isn't that God causes Al to lie; the problem is that Al can't cause God to believe falsehoods and Al can't cause the past to change.*

—Zach

Dear Zach,

All right. My "easy answer" doesn't work. Do you have a better one?

—Thomas

Dear Thomas,

Let me summarize a possible response and get your reaction. Recall our original discussion of the Theistic hypothesis. I argued that a maximally powerful being would be very knowledgeable, because knowledge is a form of power. In fact, I argued that a maximally powerful being would know all propositions *that can be known*. So let's say that an **omniscient** being is one who knows all propositions that can be known.

Now, the foreknowledge argument says that God cannot infallibly foreknow what Al will do *freely*. If God infallibly foreknows that Al will lie, then Al will not lie freely, given the assumptions of the foreknowledge argument. So propositions of the form "Al will do $X$ freely" (where $X$ is any action) *cannot* be infallibly foreknown. Such foreknowledge is logically or metaphysically impossible. But God remains omniscient, given the foregoing definition, as long as God knows all the truths that *can* be known.

From this perspective, the error in the foreknowledge argument occurs right at the outset, in the move from "God is omniscient" to "God knows the future (in detail)."[26] An infallible God does not hold beliefs about the future *free* acts of creatures, because infallible beliefs about future *free* acts are logically (or metaphysically) impossible. Just as God cannot create a colorless green frog, God cannot infallibly foreknow the future free acts of creatures.

Employing a customary term, I'll refer to this proposal as the *Open Theism* solution, since in this view God does not hold beliefs about all details of the future. The future is open, in the sense that it is not foreknown in all details.

—Zach

Dear Zach,

You can't be serious! Your "solution" is totally unacceptable from the standpoint of traditional Theism. And for good reason: A God who does not know the future in complete detail is a God who is not in control of the world. Furthermore, such a God cannot reveal the future to prophets, as God has often done, according to traditional Theists.

—Thomas

Dear Thomas,

I think the proposed solution is more defensible than you suggest. But let me start by saying that my main purpose here is to construct an argument for Theism. And the Open Theism solution is extremely useful from that standpoint. It is fully consistent with Theism (as I've formulated it). In fact, we don't have to add any theses to Theism to take this option, we merely need to apply the original definition of maximal power to the givens of the foreknowledge argument. Moreover, the Open Theism solution is simple and clear. *In effect, I'm saying that my free will argument for Theism works as long as we don't insist on a God who infallibly foreknows the future acts of free creatures. And if that result is correct, it's dramatic, philosophically speaking.*

But I also think Open Theism is nearer to *traditional* Theism than you suggest. First of all, God does not need knowledge of the future in order to be in control of the world. God's *power* ensures that God is in control. For example, suppose a dictator is about to press a button that will launch nuclear missiles and destroy the world. God does not need foreknowledge to prevent this from happening—assuming God wants to prevent it. God knows what the dictator is currently thinking and God can interfere at any point: God can break the wiring in the missile launcher, cause the dictator to lose consciousness, disable the missile in midflight, and so on.

Second, foreknowledge is not a form of control. If God really knows that X will happen, then of course X will happen. Foreknowledge is not merely knowledge of *possibilities* such as: (a) Al might freely lie at 1:31 P.M. this Friday, (b) Al might freely choose not to lie at that time, and (c) Al might drink poison and collapse at that time. If God knows something will happen—really knows it—then (so to speak) it's too late for God to prevent it. To put this point negatively, if God does prevent X, then God obviously did not *know* that X was going to happen. (One can know only truths.)

Third, prophecy is still possible, given Open Theism. Divine prophecies are often statements about God's plans or intentions; for example, a prophecy to the effect that God will judge the world may be taken as a statement of God's intention to judge the world. And God's knowledge of his own intentions is fully consistent with Open Theism. To cite a Biblical example: At God's command, the prophet Jonah cries, "Yet forty days, and Nineveh shall be overthrown" (Jonah 3:4). But Nineveh does not get overthrown, because the Ninevites repent. Such prophecies appear to be conditional in nature: They require only that God knows what God intends to do if free creatures do (or do not do) something within a specified period of time.

Finally, given Open Theism, God can infallibly predict what any creature will do if God decides to interfere with the creature's freedom. God cannot infallibly predict that Al will tell a lie *freely* next Friday, but God can infallibly predict that Al will tell a lie next Friday if God is prepared to cause Al to tell a lie *should Al decide freely not to do so*. Of course, if God interferes and causes Al to tell the lie, then Al would not be morally responsible for telling it. But God can remove free will temporarily if it suits God's purposes.[27]

To sum up, Open Theism provides a solution to the foreknowledge problem. And it does so in a way that supports the argument from free will for Theism. Of course, Open Theism denies something traditional Theists affirm, namely, that God has infallible knowledge of every true proposition about the future. But Open Theism can satisfy the most important theological concerns of the traditional Theist.[28]

—Zach

Dear Zach,

OK. Open Theism has more going for it than I initially thought, but I'm sure many traditional Theists won't accept it. Why not adopt a solution that fully supports traditional Theism?

—Thomas

Dear Thomas,

Solutions that fully support traditional Theism seem to me much more problematic than Open Theism. As you noted previously, one traditional solution is Calvinism, which employs a compatibilist view of human freedom. This approach inherits all the philosophical difficulties of compatibilism. It also creates special difficulties with regard to the problem of evil. For if we combine Theism and determinism, then human acts, including the most evil ones, are determined (directly or indirectly) by God. Thus, God is the author of evil.

Two other attempted solutions loom large in the tradition: the divine timelessness solution and the middle knowledge solution. But they are both highly problematic, in my opinion.

—Zach

Dear Zach,

I assume the divine timelessness solution involves the idea that God is outside of time. I've always found that idea rather attractive, myself.

—Thomas

Dear Thomas,

I'm open to the idea that God is timeless, but I don't think it provides a good answer to the foreknowledge problem, for two main reasons.

Let me first clarify the concept of timelessness a bit. If God is **timeless**, then there is no sequence, no "before and after," in the divine life. God's life does not come in temporal phases. God has no past, present, or future; God's life somehow transcends all that. God does not perform different acts at different times or think different thoughts at different times. God doesn't first create, then later reveal things to prophets, yet later work miracles, and so forth. God does not will one thing now and another thing later. Whatever God wills, God wills "all at once" in a timeless "moment" or eternal "now."

Some traditional Theists hold that God is timeless, but others hold that God is everlasting. God is **everlasting** if God existed at each past moment, exists now, and will exist at each future moment. If God is everlasting, then there is sequence, "before and after," in the divine life; God can will one thing now and another later on, etc.

How is the thesis of divine timelessness supposed to solve the foreknowledge problem? Well, from this perspective, we cannot literally speak of what God believed "long ago," for (taken literally) that way of speaking implies that God is in time. (The very term "divine *fore*knowledge" is a misnomer.) Thus, the foreknowledge argument contains a false presupposition; accordingly, the argument never gets off the ground. Furthermore, since God is outside of time, God can be directly aware of all times "at once." God is like a person in a tall tower, looking down at the road below. Just as the person in the tower can see at a glance what is happening all along the road below, so God can "see" past, present, and future "at a glance."

Here's one problem with the timelessness solution. Even if God is not in time, the proposition "God timelessly knows that Al tells a lie on May 14, 2097" was true *long ago* if it is true at all. And so, if the past can't be changed, the problem has not been solved. (Some philosophers deny that propositions can be true *at a time*; then the problem can be restated along these lines: Many years ago the English *sentence*, "God timelessly knows that Al tells a lie on May 14, 2097," expressed a truth; and this fact about the past cannot now be changed.)[29] In this connection, also consider the possibility that God reveals the future to a prophet. Then a timeless God's beliefs are in the mind of a prophet, who is in time, and the problem persists. The prophet's beliefs can be in the past even if God's own mental states cannot be.

A second problem is that the timelessness solution apparently involves a blatantly false presupposition about time. Supposedly, God doesn't (strictly speaking) have *fore*knowledge, because all times are present to God, and thus God can be directly aware of the past, the present, and the future. The problem here is that one cannot be directly aware of something that does not exist. (I am directly aware of the tree outside my window, but I couldn't be directly aware of it if it weren't there.) And the future does not exist. The future, by definition, hasn't happened yet. To put this point vividly, if God knows my future sins by direct awareness of them, I've somehow already committed them—but of course I haven't.

In conclusion, while God may be timeless, the idea of divine timelessness is of no help whatsoever in solving the foreknowledge problem.

—Zach

Dear Zach,

Your first criticism of the divine timelessness solution is well taken. But concerning the second, couldn't advocates of the view claim that the future exists for God but not for us?

—Thomas

Dear Thomas,

I can make no sense of that claim. My future acts have to be *my* acts. If those acts exist "for God," then it seems to me that I must somehow have already performed them, but that can't be—by definition, the future hasn't happened yet.

—Zach

Dear Zach,

I see what you mean. The idea that the future is somehow present to God is pretty hard to swallow.

You mentioned a "middle knowledge" solution. How does that work?

—Thomas

Dear Thomas,

The middle knowledge solution was developed by Luis de Molina, a Spanish Jesuit (1535–1600). Through "middle knowledge God knows what every possible person would do freely (in the incompatibilist sense) in every possible situation."[30] For example, if God has middle knowledge, God knows the following propositions if they are true (and if they are false God knows they are false):

1. If you were to become fabulously wealthy, you would freely give large sums to charitable organizations.

2. If Tom Cruise were to insult Jackie Chan, Jackie would freely give Tom a karate chop.

Notice that these conditionals (if-then statements), if true, do not *by themselves* tell us what the future holds.[31] Since you aren't fabulously wealthy, Thomas, we cannot apply proposition 1 to predict your future actions. And, as far as I know, Tom Cruise has not insulted Jackie Chan, so I can't use proposition 2 to predict that Jackie will actually give Tom a karate chop.

Middle knowledge also concerns merely possible (nonactual) persons, persons God might have created but did not. Let Betty be such a merely possible person (who has never existed and never will exist). According to the doctrine of middle knowledge, God knows (infallibly) whether the following conditional is true:

3. If God were to create Betty, place her on Earth, and command her not to eat any apples, Betty would freely obey God's command.

Now, for the sake of the argument, let's suppose God has middle knowledge, and revisit the Key Premise of the foreknowledge argument:

If God believed long ago that Al will tell a lie next Friday, and if it is in Al's power to refrain from lying next Friday, then next Friday it will be in Al's power to bring about one of the following: (a) that God held a false belief long ago or (b) that God did not believe long ago that Al will lie next Friday.

If God has middle knowledge, God knows all the circumstances under which Al would tell a lie and all the circumstances under which

Al would not tell a lie. But if Al is free and has the power to refrain from lying, then Al has the power to do something (namely, refrain from lying) such that, if Al were to do it, God would not (long ago) have held the belief that Al will lie next Friday. In fact, Al won't refrain from lying—he has the power to but he won't, and God knows this because God has middle knowledge. In short, *it will be in Al's power next Friday to perform an act that is such that if he were to perform it, then God would never have believed that Al would lie next Friday.* This possibility is not acknowledged in the foreknowledge argument, but it should be, for middle knowledge secures it.

—Zach

Dear Zach,

I have two questions and a comment. My questions are: Where does the name *middle knowledge* come from? And how does God come by this amazing form of knowledge?

My comment is simply that I don't see how the alleged solution works. Suppose that on Thursday God believes that *Al will lie on Friday.* I can see that the *truth* of God's belief depends on what Al chooses on Friday, but I cannot see how the mere fact of God's holding that belief (on Thursday) could depend on anything that happens on Friday. (Just as you can't now change the fact that you once believed there's a Santa.)

—Thomas

Dear Thomas,

*Re your first question:* Middle knowledge "lies between" natural knowledge and free knowledge. Natural knowledge is God's knowledge of necessary truths, which are beyond God's control, such as "No circles are squares." Free knowledge is God's knowledge of contingent truths that are within God's control, such as "I exist." Middle knowledge is God's knowledge of contingent truths that are *beyond* God's control. God doesn't control the truth of conditionals such as "If I were offered a bribe, I would freely accept it" because the conditional describes what I would *freely* do.[32]

*Re your comment on the middle knowledge solution:* You're in good company! For the very reasons you give, Richard Swinburne, a leading philosopher of religion, also doubts that middle knowledge reveals a problem in the foreknowledge argument.[33]

*Re your second question* ("How does God come by middle knowledge?"): This question is a very important one. But those who offer the middle knowledge solution do not take on the burden of answering it. In general, they would say, "We humans can't know how God knows what he knows. We should not expect to."[34] I think, however, that your question spells big trouble for the middle knowledge view. To see this we need to do a little epistemology—a little thinking about ways of knowing.

We can know necessary truths in two ways. When they are relatively simple, we can know them simply by grasping the concepts involved, e.g., "All wives are married." More complex necessary truths, such as theorems of mathematics, can be known by deriving them logically from simpler ones. Since we humans have some knowledge of necessary truths, there's no particular problem in claiming that God has this type of knowledge. Similarly, it doesn't seem hard to accept that God knows things under his direct control. For example, if God creates something and sustains its existence, then surely God knows that it exists.

But the conditionals God knows via middle knowledge are beyond God's control, since they concern the free choices of persons. Of course it is up to God whether a given person exists or not. But if a person performs an act freely, God cannot fully cause the action to occur. The agent has to make a contribution of his or her own, i.e., originate an intention. Otherwise the act is not free.

The conditionals God knows through his middle knowledge cannot be known in the way necessary truths are known, just by grasping the concepts involved (or by logical derivation). Take a conditional such as:

4. If Judy thinks she can cheat on her taxes without getting caught, she will freely cheat on her taxes.

If Judy has free will in the incompatibilist sense, there is no necessary connection between the if-clause and the then-clause of this conditional. You can *fully* grasp all the concepts involved and still not know whether the statement is true or false. And you cannot, by using logic, derive the then-clause from the if-clause.

Conditionals such as statement 4 cannot be known certainly or infallibly by induction, either. When we know a person well, we can often make good guesses about how they will behave under various circumstances. We are reasoning from past behavior to future behavior. But if the behavior is free (in the incompatibilist sense), this type of reasoning can never yield certainty. There's always a chance the agent will act out of character, in which case our prediction will be mistaken. Now, in the case of God, who is presumably a superlative judge of character, the predictions might be very reliable, *but they could not be certain or infallible, by the nature of the case*. To say that such inductions (based on a sample of past behavior) *cannot be mistaken* is to deny that the acts are truly free.

If God knows statement 4, there must be some causal relationship between God's belief and Judy's choice. It can't be that God (or God's belief) causes Judy's choice, because then her act would not be free. But remember, Judy may not have been created yet. Indeed, she may be a merely possible person who never gets created—God has middle knowledge of every possible person *before God creates any persons* (and even if God never creates anyone or anything). Think about that! It is implausible to suggest that nonexistent agents can somehow cause God to believe something. And to me it is extremely implausible to suggest that merely possible agents, who will never exist, can cause God to believe something. How can merely possible persons exercise control over what God believed billions of years ago or prior to creation? As Swinburne remarks, "What does not happen can cause nothing."[35] In short, middle knowledge presupposes a form of causation that is metaphysically impossible.

So I think the middle knowledge "solution" fails. And we have already seen that the timelessness "solution" fails. Fortunately, the Open Theism solution has much to recommend it. Even those who dislike it for theological reasons can agree that it plays a useful role in our discussion: In the absence of a plausible reply, the foreknowledge argument undermines the argument from free will for Theism, but the Open Theism solution provides a philosophically elegant and plausible reply. And so the argument from free will for Theism is successful, though it may not deliver everything the traditional Theist wants. And our exploration of free will, though long and involved, does in the end give us some reason to accept Theism over Naturalism.

—Zach

Dear Zach,

I have less confidence in your free will argument for Theism than you do, mostly because I feel the issues are so complex. So I want to review our correspondence again soon and do some additional reading on my own. That said, I will admit that your argument has *some* value. Although the issues are complex, at the end of the day I do believe that humans have free will—and I mean free will in the incompatibilist sense. (At this point, I'm not much attracted to compatibilism.) And while I can't consider your argument a "slam dunk" by any means, it does seem that Theism does a better job of explaining the presence of free will than Naturalism does. In short, I'm not fully convinced by the argument, but I do feel it has *some* force.

—Thomas

# CHAPTER 7

# Theism and Evil

Dear Zach,

I know it has been a long time since I wrote. I've been traveling a lot—all work related, unfortunately. But now I'm eager to continue our discussion. Where are we?

—Thomas

Dear Thomas,

Long ago we began by comparing Theism and Basic Naturalism. We saw that Basic Naturalism, due to its relative simplicity, has a higher prior probability than Theism. But Basic Naturalism also has a very limited degree of explanatory power. To explain the presence of contingent beings, Naturalists must adopt Necessity Naturalism (or something similar). But Necessity Naturalism is almost as complicated as Theism. And hence, if we grant that Theistic mystical experience provides even a very modest amount of support for Theism, then Theism and Necessity Naturalism seem about equally justified.

We then considered how well Theism and Naturalism explain the phenomenon of our life-supporting universe. Again, we saw that relatively streamlined forms of Naturalism have limited explanatory power. Something like MUH Naturalism is needed if Naturalism is to compete with Theism. But MUH Naturalism is much more complex than Necessity Naturalism, so MUH Naturalism has a lower prior probability than Theism. (In drawing this conclusion, I'm taking for granted the upshot of my Cosmological Argument: Necessity Naturalism and Theism are "tied.") Furthermore, I argued, MUH

Naturalism has less explanatory power regarding our life-supporting universe than does Theism. So a "design" argument gives some positive support to Theism.

Next, we discussed the free will issue. This issue is very complex, but we wound up agreeing—I think—that humans have free will, in the incompatibilist sense. I argued that MUH Naturalism has no explanatory power with regard to free will. Once again, Naturalists can move to a more complex version of their hypothesis; they can add a thesis regarding free will, but that thesis will lower the prior probability of Naturalism, and it also has little explanatory power. Theism, on the other hand, leads us to expect the presence of free will *unless* the foreknowledge argument succeeds. The foreknowledge argument does not succeed if an omniscient being is one who knows all that *can* be known (and future free acts cannot be infallibly foreknown).

To sum up, the Cosmological Argument, together with Theistic mystical experience, puts Theism on a par with Naturalism. The design argument provides a significant, positive reason to accept Theism over Naturalism. And the argument from free will adds yet another positive reason to accept Theism over Naturalism. Therefore, the evidence we've considered so far favors Theism, on balance.

—Zach

Dear Zach,

But we've been arguing on territory that's often thought to be favorable to Theism, right? Maybe it's time we got onto territory more favorable to Naturalism. Indeed, I think it's high time we talked about the problem of evil.

As I see it, the presence of evil creates two related problems for Theism. First, evil counts as direct evidence against Theism. Given all the evil in the world, Theism seems very unlikely. If God is all-powerful, then God can eliminate all the evil in the world. And if God is perfectly good, then God wants to eliminate all the evil, right? *A good God is opposed to evil.* But if God wants to eliminate something and God can do so, then surely it is eliminated. Therefore, on the assumption that Theism is true, it seems there would be no evil or, at any rate, nowhere near the amount actually present.

Second, even if my first point is somehow mistaken, I don't see how you can reason from (1) a world containing massive amounts of wickedness and suffering to (2) the existence of a *perfectly good* God. In other words, the presence of evil would seem to throw a wrench in any attempt to develop a positive case for Theism, with its claim that God is both all-powerful *and* perfectly good.

Let me know what you think.

—Thomas

Dear Thomas,

Yes, it's time we discussed the problem of evil. I'd like to begin by offering some clarifications about the meaning of *evil*.

In this context, **evil** refers to badness in general, including such items as moral wrongdoing, suffering, loss, and being under systematic illusion about important matters. **Moral evil** is the wrongdoing for which humans are responsible *and* the suffering (and loss) that results from it. For example, lying, stealing, and murder count as moral evil, and so does any suffering or loss that results from such acts. **Natural evil** is the suffering (and loss) due to nonhuman causes, such as earthquakes and tornados. I realize that in ordinary English we don't use the word *evil* in reference to suffering caused by natural factors, but the term has long been used this way in philosophical circles. (We do commonly speak of "bad things" happening to people, and *evil* means "bad" in this context.)

It may be useful to make three observations at this point. First, note that natural evil occurs only when suffering (and/or loss) occurs. The suffering (and/or loss) may result from earthquakes, tidal waves, hurricanes, tornados, extremes of temperature, drought, mudslides, avalanches, forest fires, volcanic eruptions, viruses, and so on. But it is important to note that, by our definition, *these causes are not themselves evils*; the instances of suffering and loss they bring about are the evils (i.e., bad things). So earthquakes, tornados, floods, etc., are not themselves natural evils; and whenever such natural events occur without causing any suffering or loss, no natural evil occurs.

Second, the distinction between moral and natural evil is not very sharp. To illustrate, the suffering due to disease is often regarded as a natural evil. But if a person gets an infectious disease, she may by *wrongful choice or culpable negligence* pass that disease along to others. Those infected via wrongful choice or culpable negligence are, at least in part, victims of moral evil. Also, people often take foolish chances with respect to nature, e.g., hiking high in the mountains despite authoritative warnings about adverse weather conditions. Foolishness being a moral vice, any suffering or loss that results in such cases is at least in part a moral evil. When natural and moral evils are (as it were) intertwined, it may be difficult or even impossible to specify the extent to which the suffering in question is properly assigned to human causes or to "natural" causes.

Third, some of the suffering of nonhuman animals counts as moral evil and some counts as natural evil. When humans inflict suffering on nonhuman animals without a morally sufficient reason for doing so (e.g., abandoning a pet dog or cat), the suffering counts as moral evil. On the other hand, when a nonhuman animal suffers as a result of disease, accident, or attack by another animal, the suffering counts as natural evil.

I've got to break off here and catch a bus. Hope everything is going well.

—Zach

Dear Zach,

The concept of suffering seems rather vague and subjective. I have a feeling this may hinder an attempt at rational discussion.

—Thomas

Dear Thomas,

It needn't—as long as we can agree on some rather homespun observations about suffering. Here's a short list.

- Suffering is a very unpleasant conscious state.
- Suffering comes in both mental and physical forms. For example, intense anxiety is a form of mental suffering; and the long-lasting pain common in diseases such as cancer is a form of physical suffering.
- Because suffering is a conscious state, many types of entities cannot suffer. For example, I assume that rocks and plants cannot suffer because they lack the sort of conscious awareness suffering involves.[1]
- Suffering comes in degrees. For example, suffering can be trying, intense, unbearable, etc.

Opinions may differ, of course, about whether a given type of suffering is, say, very trying or intense, but I don't think we need to worry too much about such disagreements. Virtually everyone agrees that there is a great deal of suffering in the world, some of it truly horrifying: the carnage of modern warfare, torture, rape, child abuse, diseases that wipe out entire populations, tsunamis that devastate entire regions, and so on.

Let me add a comment about loss. A *loss* occurs when a person is deprived of something of value, such as her life or sanity. Such deprivation commonly causes suffering, but it need not. And in any case, loss can be a bad thing in addition to any suffering it causes. For example, the early death of a person is normally a loss to that person and to others. And such a loss is a bad thing even if no suffering is involved, as can happen in the case of certain kinds of natural catastrophes; e.g., an isolated village is suddenly and completely wiped out by a tornado.

—Zach

Dear Zach,

That gives me a better idea of what is meant by *suffering* and *loss*. But people disagree quite a bit about what counts as moral evil. Will this disagreement hamper our discussion?

—Thomas

Dear Thomas,

First, in evaluating Theism, we can employ the Theist's own conception of moral evil. This won't stack the cards in favor of Theism, because the traditional Theist regards the world as full of moral evil. And the list of moral evils is largely the same among the major Theistic religions: murder, stealing, injustice, cruelty, adultery, dishonesty, and so on. In short, Theists readily agree that there is a great deal of moral evil in the world—otherwise known as *sin*.

Second, I don't think we need to concern ourselves with matters of controversy *within* traditional approaches to morality, i.e., the kinds of issues that appear in anthologies on "contemporary moral issues," such as abortion, euthanasia, affirmative action, and the death penalty. We don't need to worry about such controversial issues because, regardless of how these issues are settled (if at all), there are *vast amounts* of moral evil in the world—speaking from the standpoint of any traditional moral code.

—Zach

Dear Zach,

It seems to me that there is an argument from evil that favors Naturalism over Theism. It's a best-explanation type of argument—your favorite! The phenomenon would be *all the moral and natural evil in the world*, including the most horrible things, such as genocide, torture, child abuse, starvation, and epidemics. Theism leads us to expect little or no evil, for reasons I've already mentioned: A perfectly good God would be opposed to evil and would want to eliminate it. And an almighty God would be able to eliminate every instance of evil.

Naturalism, on the other hand, doesn't need to reconcile suffering and evil with the presence of a perfectly good Power. From the Naturalist's perspective, we humans evolved from simpler forms of life and we are involved in the struggle for survival. As we struggle to live and flourish in a situation involving scarce resources (land, food, water, etc.), it's not surprising that we harm one another. That explains moral evil, in a nutshell. As for natural evil, we have plainly evolved in an environment that is in many ways hostile to us. So natural evil is just what we should expect if Naturalism is true.

Strikes me as a very plausible argument.

—Thomas

Dear Thomas,

Many philosophers have found your argument quite impressive. In fact, you have stated the most important argument against Theism. That said, I do not think the argument holds up well under scrutiny.

The problem of evil is complex, and I think we need to focus on the major parts of your argument in turn: (1) the Theistic explanation of evil and (2) the Naturalistic explanation of evil. Furthermore, at some point we'll need to discuss something you didn't mention: (3) the prior probabilities of Theism and Naturalism. After all, even if Naturalism does a better job of leading us to expect evil than Theism does (a point I wish to dispute), this advantage of Naturalism might be offset by a lower prior probability.[2]

I don't have time for a long letter today but I want to make one observation. We cannot simply assume that if God is almighty and perfectly morally good, then there is no evil. What we can assume, I believe, is that if God is almighty and perfectly morally good, then there is no evil *unless there is a reason that would justify God in allowing it.*[3] The qualification is crucial. Much of the traditional discussion of the problem of evil concerns the alleged reasons—possible or actual—that would justify God in allowing evil.

—Zach

Dear Zach,

I'd love to see your Theistic explanation of the presence of evil and suffering.

—Thomas

Dear Thomas,

Let's start with moral evil.[4] Suppose a loving God creates intelligent finite beings. Such creatures could be "puppets" responding to God's love and goodness in a predetermined fashion. Or they could be allowed to respond to God's love and goodness freely. Now, a freely chosen, affirmative response to God's love and goodness is surely a higher good than a programmed or robotic response. It seems absurd to suggest that God would place much value on a puppetlike devotion to God that is *fully caused by God*. So a perfectly morally good Deity would have good reason to create beings possessing a capacity to choose between devotion to God and some alternative(s).[5]

Now, for all practical purposes, there is no choice between two alternatives if the agent desires to take one (and/or has significant reasons to take it) but the agent has no desire to take the other alternative (and no reason to take it). Perhaps in theory I have the choice, when I leave my office today, of (a) using the door or (b) trying to exit through the wall. But (b) is so unattractive to me, and so silly, there's really no choice here worthy of the name. Thus, one must have a significant reason or desire to take a course of action if it is to count as a genuine alternative. It follows that we can freely choose to devote ourselves to God only if we have a significant reason and/or desire to adopt a different way of life. Therefore, if God has reason to allow us to choose whether we will devote ourselves to God, then God also has reason to provide us with reasons and/or desires to take some alternate path through life.

No one will deny that, as a matter of empirical fact, human individuals are deeply self-interested, so much so, in fact, that they are tempted to devote themselves to their own pleasures, purposes, and interests. They are often tempted to act in self-serving ways. I submit that this is not surprising if a perfectly good God exists. Rather, it is the sort of thing we should expect. There is at least one attractive alternative to devotion to a perfectly good God, namely, devotion to one's self.

I am *not* suggesting that one must be either devoted to God or selfish. I am merely pointing out that if we are to *choose* to devote ourselves to God, there must be an attractive alternative and that such an alternative is in fact available: Devotion to self surely seems attractive to all of us. And this is the sort of thing we ought to expect if a perfectly good God exists.

—Zach

Dear Zach,

Are you saying that God created us with desires to do evil? If so, isn't God to blame for the whole moral mess we find ourselves in?

—Thomas

Dear Thomas,

Again, I don't see how we can have a significant choice to devote ourselves to a good God if there is nothing attractive about turning away from God. So if one has a significant, free choice to be devoted to God, then one's motivational structure must include desires (and/or reasons) for some alternative form of life. If the alternative form of life is unattractive in every way, I fail to see that we have any real choice.

I am not suggesting that God must create us with desires to do terrible things, e.g., innate desires to maim, torture, and kill. But we do seem to be born with strong, innate desires to serve our own interests—such desires are manifest very early in life. (You can visit any local preschool if you want to test this claim empirically!) I would not say that a strong desire to serve one's own interests is evil, but I would say that such a desire clearly provides temptations to do wrong. And it is predictable that wrong actions will occur given the familiar human motivational structure: Sensible parents don't have children on the assumption that their children will never do anything morally wrong.

—Zach

Dear Zach,

So God created us knowing full well that we would fall into sin? In your view, then, isn't God like a parent who places her young children in a room full of candy and then complains when they eat the candy?

—Thomas

Dear Thomas,

I think your analogy is flawed. It fails to recognize the unique position God is in as creator. We simply have to face up to this point: *God cannot give us a genuine choice to devote ourselves to God unless there's an alternative we find attractive.* And there can be no attractive alternative unless we have a desire or reason to opt for it. Thus, a genuine choice to devote ourselves to God requires an attractive path away from God.

Parents are procreators, not creators, and there's a big difference. A Creator must determine the basic structure of the created realm, including the fundamental sorts of options to make available to free creatures. No one else is in a position to do that. Human parents lack the requisite power and knowledge. The God-parent analogy is useful, but it is misused if it is taken to mean that God has precisely the same responsibilities a human parent has.

—Zach

Dear Zach,

Isn't it the traditional view that humans "fell" from a state of perfection? That is, God gave the first humans a morally pristine motivational structure, but they blew it by rebelling against God. And as a result (or punishment), they and their descendants were saddled with wrong desires and made subject to harmful forces in nature.

—Thomas


Dear Thomas,

Well, that version of the fall has been commonly held by Christians. It can be traced back to St. Augustine (354–430). But Augustine's version of the fall is not official doctrine and not the only version of the fall within the Christian tradition. Prior to Augustine, Irenaeus (c. 130–202) offered a view of the fall that, in my opinion, makes better sense. Irenaeus regarded the first humans as immature creatures endowed with a great capacity for moral and spiritual development. He saw them as having been created with desires that could lead them into temptation.[6]

I think a view along the lines Irenaeus suggested is preferable, for at least two reasons. First, as I have been pointing out, we don't have any real choice to devote ourselves to God unless we have desires (and/or reasons) for taking some other path in life. And in Irenaeus' view, God created humans with the kind of strong self-interest that can tempt them to be devoted to themselves rather than to God. In Augustine's view, by contrast, the fall is utterly mysterious. If the earliest humans had no desires that could lead them into temptation (and no reason to do wrong), what explains their lapse into sin? There seems to be no way they could have been tempted to do wrong, given Augustine's account of their motivational structure.

Second, Irenaeus' view fits much better (than Augustine's) with the modern scientific picture of the human past. According to modern biology, humans evolved from simpler forms of life. Our ancestry can be traced back to apelike creatures and from there to yet simpler forms of life. From this perspective, humans are animals (which is of course compatible with our having special capacities other animals lack). And all animals are caught up in the struggle for survival. Thus, the earliest humans would have found themselves in a situation in which temptations were bound to arise. For example, shortages of food and water predictably tempt self-interested humans to be selfish.[7]

—Zach


Dear Zach,

Let's back up. I think I missed something. I didn't see any moral standards in your formulation of Theism. How can there be moral evil without moral standards?

—Thomas

Dear Thomas,

Moral standards are implicit in the claim that God is perfectly morally good. God is not perfectly morally good unless God has such virtues as love, justice, and wisdom. Thus, implicit in Theism is the claim that love, justice, and wisdom are morally good.

I don't think you're asking me to work out a detailed scheme of ethics, but let me just note some connections between the claim that love, justice, and wisdom are virtues and some traditional claims about right and wrong.

- *Love* involves a concern for the long-term best interests of others. Plainly, many of the acts traditionally regarded as morally wrong tend to be contrary to the long-term best interests of others, e.g., murder, stealing, and bearing false witness.

- *Justice* involves giving each individual his or her due. There can be much discussion about what individuals are due, but moral agents are *at least* due a profound respect. That respect is typically denied when people are beaten, ridiculed, lied to, cheated, or treated as mere sex objects.

- *Wisdom* involves the knowledge of what's worth achieving and how to achieve it. Wisdom excludes patterns of behavior that hinder worthwhile achievement, such as being frivolous or lazy.

Again, these examples are merely illustrative. The main point is that Theism, in its claim that God is perfectly morally good, implicitly contains far-reaching moral standards.

There is a long-standing problem in ethical theory regarding reliable standards for actions in particular situations. For example, lying seems to be wrong in most cases but not all, and is there any reliable way to discern the exceptional cases? Attempts to derive answers logically from abstract moral principles seem to falter. Some philosophers have suggested that the moral thinking of virtuous persons is a reliable process for assessing what is right and wrong in particular situations. Of course, virtuous humans are not infallible, but their ways of thinking about concrete cases might generally yield moral truth.[8] The moral assessments of a perfectly virtuous, omniscient God would of course be an even more reliable standard of right and wrong action.

—Zach

Dear Zach,

Very well. If God is perfectly morally good, then the Theistic hypothesis implicitly contains moral standards by which human action may be evaluated. And if God is perfectly morally good, God has reason to provide us with a fundamental choice between (1) a life devoted to a perfectly good God and (2) a life devoted to something else (such as ourselves). But we can have such a choice only if we have desires (and/or reasons) to pursue a way of life distinct from that of devotion to a perfectly good God. In short, God has reason to provide us with a motivational structure that allows us to be tempted to turn away from God and God's goodness. This much, I can buy.

But logically speaking, we can have wrong acts without any resulting suffering, can't we? If I take a swing at you, God can create the illusion that I harmed you while preventing any actual harm; nevertheless my intent would be wrong or evil.

—Thomas

Dear Thomas,

If we believe we can harm others but in fact we cannot, then we are systematically deceived about something extremely important to our lives, and such massive deception would itself be a bad thing, i.e., an evil. So a perfectly good God surely would not set up a world involving such deception.[9]

—Zach

Dear Zach,

But couldn't an almighty God simply prevent harm from occurring? For example, suppose I'm in a situation in which food is scarce and I selfishly hoard the small amount of food available. God can simply create more food. Or suppose I steal someone's purse. Well, God can provide a new purse, with the same contents.

—Thomas

Dear Thomas,

I think there are problems with such inconsequential wrongdoing. First, it's far from clear that there would be anything wrong with the acts in question if God could be counted on to intervene in the way you describe. The very significance of the acts has been removed.

Second, a loving God would have good reason to place persons in a situation in which they can achieve lives that are rich in meaning and significance. And, other things being equal, a life that involves significant choices is more significant than one that does not. Furthermore, the significance of a choice is linked to its consequences or expected consequences.

If God creates free agents, God can confine them to trivial choices or entrust them with highly significant choices. I submit that a God of love would do the latter. If God creates free agents, then, we ought to expect a situation in which the free agents are entrusted with highly significant choices. And that is the situation we find ourselves in.

Third, if God gives us a choice about whether we devote ourselves to God and to God's goodness, how wide a range of alternatives will God grant? Our motivational structure might allow only for the alternative of a life of trivial pleasures, for example. Or it might allow for progressively unloving choices—for example, indulging one's self-interest at others' expense might tend to make one more self-interested and so more easily tempted to disregard the welfare of others. I suggest that God would have multiple reasons to give creaturely freedom a relatively wide scope.

1. Love consists partly in a profound respect for persons. One way to show respect for persons is to entrust them with great, and even dangerous, powers. As a simple illustration, think of the first time your parents entrusted you with driving the family car on your own and of how you valued that trust.

2. The deepest kinds of loving relationships involve mutual vulnerability. But how can almighty God be vulnerable? There's not much that free creatures can do to harm almighty God directly, but we could harm God indirectly, if we could harm those God loves, just as we can harm parents by harming their children. Thus, a loving and almighty God would have reason to give free agents the latitude to mistreat one another.[10]

3. As mentioned earlier, the significance of our choices is linked to their consequences or expected consequences. I think this linkage is in part metaphysical: Our choices simply wouldn't *be* significant if they didn't (at least often) have significant consequences. But the linkage is also epistemological: We *understand* the seriousness of our choices by seeing their consequences. The wrongness of a wrong choice is often revealed through its consequences.[11] But couldn't God just hardwire us so that we have an innate, accurate, firmly entrenched set of moral convictions? Yes, but here again respect enters the picture. In our actual circumstances, we are given the freedom and responsibility to "figure out" many things for ourselves, including many aspects of the moral life. By contrast, the more God hardwires beliefs into us, the more we are simply required to believe.

I've used the word *significance* often in this letter. Let me emphasize that, in speaking of significance, I am not speaking merely of *feelings* of significance. I take it that genuine significance can be achieved in meeting certain kinds of challenges well, in overcoming certain sorts of obstacles, and in performing certain types of actions. Robert Nozick invented the idea of an *experience machine* that can give us feelings and experiences of any sort, including feelings of significance. We can opt to "plug into" the experience machine and "experience" whatever sort of life we wish, e.g., the life of a rock star, a famous athlete, etc., even though all the while we are really just sitting there, hooked up by wires to the machine. Clearly, a life spent sitting in an experience machine has little or no significance compared to a life involving actions with consequences in the real world.[12]

—Zach

Dear Zach,

But so many specific cases of wrongdoing seem completely un-necessary for any conceivable divine purpose! Just to cite one exam-ple: Yesterday I read in the newspaper about a teenager who was killed in a "drive-by" shooting. Am I supposed to believe that this murder is logically necessary for some greater good?

—Thomas

Dear Thomas,

I do not think it wise to assume that each wicked act is allowed as a means to some greater good. Instances of wickedness are better re-garded as "collateral effects" of divine creative activity rather than necessary means to divine ends. If God gives us significant choices (in part) by giving us important moral choices, some wrong acts are an unsurprising result. But there is no reason to suppose either that God wants any specific wrong act to occur or that God plans for some greater good to arise from each wrong act. At any rate, I see no reason to make such assumptions. Wrong acts, taken collectively, are simply *the unsurprising result* of creating agents with very significant moral choices; and wrong acts, taken individually, need not be the necessary means to any greater good.

—Zach

Dear Zach,

Let me try again. First, I agree that there is something good about our having free will, significant choices, and moral responsibility. And if we are given moral responsibility, we must be able to do at least some wrong acts. I'm willing to go that far. But second, I don't think you've shown that Theism can explain the extremes of wickedness—genocide, torture, child abuse, rape, and so on. Obviously, we can have significant choices without being able to inflict such horrible suffering on others.

—Thomas

Dear Thomas,

Do the divine purposes require genocide and other extremely wicked acts? Here are some points to consider.

First, as we've seen, the meaning or significance of human life is in large measure a function of the significance of the choices humans make. And moral choices are especially significant ones. This being so, if a loving God exists, it does not seem surprising to me that God would place us in a situation in which there are many opportunities to make important moral choices. But the significance of the choices is in large measure a function of the benefit or harm the acts are apt to bring about (or prevent). Therefore, if a loving God exists, we ought to expect there to be opportunities to make choices between good acts that will provide great benefits (or prevent great harms) and evil acts that will inflict great harms (or prevent great benefits). So if a loving God exists, it is not surprising that we have opportunities to freely perform very wicked acts.

We've noted two additional reasons why a perfectly good God would grant us the power to help and to harm. (1) Granting us such power shows respect for us as free agents; it confers a kind of honor on us. And (2) by granting such power to us, an almighty God can make possible a certain type of relationship between God and free creatures—the very deep sort of loving relationship that involves mutual vulnerability, for God is harmed when creatures God loves are harmed.

Second, the suggestion that we could have *as much* meaning or significance in our lives *as we actually do* without certain types of wickedness, such as genocide, is problematic. If there were no genocide, no doubt we would be discussing some other example of wickedness, such as murder or rape. And if murder and rape were beyond human capability, I suspect we would be discussing still other forms of wickedness. Some humans would probably be satisfied with a situation in which the consequences of our acts would be trivial; but such a world would pale in significance to the world we find ourselves in—a world full of drama, in which acts have enormous significance—significance that is partly a function of their consequences.

A world with less significance has its attractions, because such a world contains fewer risks. But I believe it remains unsurprising that we find ourselves in a situation in which acts have enormous significance—assuming that God exists. Such a world has many risks, but it is also replete with meaning. What we do—and do not do—really counts for something. When we wish for this or that type of wicked act to be removed from the human repertoire, it seems to me that we are wishing for a world in which human action has less significance than it does in the world we have got.[13]

I think it comes down to this. We can see that a good God would have multiple good reasons for permitting us to make choices that can have harmful effects on other creatures. However, we find the degree of vulnerability that is actually present among humans quite scary. We may feel that a loving God wouldn't let free creatures "go that far." But just how much power should God give us? How is that line to be drawn? Are we in a good position to draw it? And do keep in mind that death sets a limit on the harm we can inflict on one another.

—Zach

Dear Zach,

Well, if we're not in a good position to specify the amount of harm a loving God would allow us to inflict, doesn't that mean your Theistic explanation falters with respect to extremely harmful wicked acts?

—Thomas

Dear Thomas,

Perhaps so. But it seems to me that the argument that a loving God clearly would not allow, say, genocide, falters also. In any case, my strategy is not to argue that Theism explains *all* evils well. *My goal is to show that Theism explains evil at least as well as Naturalism does.*

—Zach

Dear Zach,

I want to press a slightly different issue. Let's suppose God does grant us the power to inflict great harm. We have to ask whether a God of love can rest content with the destructive results of wickedness. Suppose an innocent child's life is ended by violence or a victim of torture goes permanently insane. Can a God of love simply regard such wickedness as the price of significance—end of story? "Well, if you want omelets, you've got to break eggs?" That doesn't sound like love to me. We are talking about lives utterly destroyed by wickedness. And this sort of thing is a daily or even hourly occurrence.

—Thomas

Dear Thomas,

You're right: Love will not accept tragedies and horrors as final if there is any alternative. What matters is not only the "big picture" but each individual person. Marilyn Adams has suggested that a good God would be "good to each created person, by insuring each a life that is a great good to him/her on the whole."[14] (I would only qualify this by replacing *insuring* with *offering*, since I want to leave open the possibility that persons may freely reject the life God offers.) Adams also notes that God cannot make up for great suffering in an individual's life simply by adding pleasant experiences to it. The significance of intense suffering must be transformed by the role it plays in one's life as a whole, as an ugly splotch of color in an impressionist painting may add to the beauty of the whole painting.

—Zach

Dear Zach,

I agree with Adams, but her standards make Theism appear hopeless to me. So many young lives have been cut short in human history! And so many others effectively destroyed by severe injuries that leave the victim permanently and tragically disabled!

—Thomas

Dear Thomas,

Let me make a suggestion and get your response. I assume that an almighty being is able to raise creatures from the dead; thus, life after death is possible, from the standpoint of Theism.[15] Indeed, life after death is probable, from the standpoint of Theism, at least in part because divine love will not give wickedness the last word. A loving God seeks the fulfillment of his creatures. And from the standpoint of Theism, the only thing that can prevent the fulfillment of an individual creature *in the long run*, I take it, is the individual's free rejection of divine love.

I'm suggesting (in effect) that we add a thesis to the Theistic hypothesis:

**Afterlife Theism**: (1) There is exactly one entity that is (2) perfectly morally good and (3) almighty and that (4) exists of necessity. (5) *If there is an almighty and perfectly good entity who has purposes for its creatures and the creatures die before those purposes are fulfilled, then the purposes will be fulfilled (insofar as possible) after the death of the creatures.*

Clause 5 provides an assurance that those whose lives are wrecked by wickedness in this earthly life will have opportunities to reclaim the fulfillment denied them. Beyond this, clause 5 provides for the possibility that God may have some purposes for *each person* that are not (or cannot) be fulfilled prior to death, in which case all persons would have a life after death.[16]

Note that clause 5 is a conditional (if-then) statement; hence its truth does not depend on the existence of God. A non-Theist can accept this if-then statement as true, because it is merely hypothetical in nature. It doesn't say that an almighty and perfectly good being exists, it just says that *if* such a being exists, then certain consequences hold.

Indeed, because clause 5 is a conditional statement, I think we should grant that it is highly probable. A perfectly good being will have good purposes for its creatures, and it will not lose interest in those good purposes. So, unless one denies that an almighty being can raise creatures from the dead, one ought to assign clause 5 a very high probability. Now, generally speaking, when we add statements to a hypothesis, we lower its prior probability. But one exception is when the statement to be added has a probability of 1. I suggest that clause 5 has a probability close to 1. For this reason, it can be added to Theism at little cost to Theism's prior probability.[17] It will be important to keep this in mind.

—Zach

Dear Zach,

I'm not sure that Afterlife Theism meets Adams' high standards. In effect, you're saying that God can neglect the free creatures during their earthly lives as long as God is "nice" to them later on. God is like a workaholic husband who neglects his wife for years but thinks he can "make up for it" by being attentive in his retirement years. As Adams says, God can't make up for an individual's horrible suffering simply by adding good experiences, activities, etc., after death.

—Thomas

Dear Thomas,

I thought your main point was something like this: "Many wicked acts destroy lives—either by ending them prematurely or by decreasing their quality dramatically. And even if the significance of our actions is in part due to the fact that they can have serious consequences (harmful as well as helpful), a God of love cannot ignore the life-destroying toll that wickedness takes." And I agree. But it seems to me that clause 5 goes a long way toward addressing this concern.

It's not that God is indifferent to suffering and loss. It's not that God is neglectful, like the workaholic husband in your example. Rather, God seeks to provide us with the opportunity to live lives of great significance, and so God endows us with moral responsibility. But if we are to have highly significant moral choices, we must be able to harm others as well as to help them. Obviously, wrong acts often have dire consequences. A God of love will allow many such consequences to occur, because they are indeed the price of great significance, but such a God will not abandon those whose earthly lives are destroyed or marred by evil. As a loving being, God seeks the (long-term) best interests of free creatures. And since the life-destroying effects of wickedness are so often allowed to stand in this earthly life, a loving God will ameliorate things (insofar as possible) in a life after death.

I said *ameliorate* things, make them better—not just tack on some pleasant experiences. For example, suppose that early in life Lisa was a victim of assault—she received a severe brain injury that left her with a very low IQ. After death, her intelligence might be fully restored or even enhanced, and she might be allowed to use it in some important, fulfilling way. Or suppose Ben was placed in a concentration camp during the war. The horrifying experiences left him permanently weak, frightened, and deeply depressed. After death, his health is restored and enhanced, he is vigorous and given challenging and useful tasks to perform. Successful completion of the tasks leads to confidence and joy.

Obviously, I'm speculating wildly about the details. These are just illustrations.

—Zach


Dear Zach,

I'll admit that, if God exists, there is likely an afterlife. And in that case we have to take into account a much longer view of things than we ordinarily do. Most importantly, given Afterlife Theism, tragedies and horrors don't have the terrible *finality* they would otherwise have. I'll go that far. But I wonder if you haven't created a new problem for Theism. There's no free choice in heaven, right? No possibility of doing wrong. But then, by your logic, isn't life in heaven pretty insignificant?

—Thomas


Dear Thomas,

I don't think that follows, for at least four reasons. First, heaven should be viewed as the resolution of a larger story. So the significance of one's life in heaven is, in part, a function of the significance that is grounded in the choices of this earthly life.

Second, some of the significance of one's life in heaven could be grounded in choices between good things (experiences, activities, relationships), where each choice is morally permissible. I have not denied that choices between good things can be significant.

Third, I've not claimed that significance is merely a function of choices. For example, significance is partly achieved by having interesting experiences, fulfilling relationships, and worthwhile activities.

Finally, I am not sure it is quite right to say that there will be no opportunities for wrongdoing in heaven. Those in heaven may look back on their earthly lives, rather in the way that most of us can look back on some earlier stage of our earthly life, and see that we were engaged in a pattern of foolish or wrong actions. We could in principle return to that foolish or wrong behavior, but we've "learned our lesson." We could turn back, but we won't.

—Zach

Dear Zach,

I still think your Theistic explanations come up short as regards the extremes of wickedness. And a worse problem looms. I don't see how Theism can explain any natural evil at all. Remember, the factors that cause natural evil are in God's hands—if there is a God. By your own admission, Theists claim that the laws of nature are present because God sets them in place (presumably by endowing physical entities with certain mechanistic powers, to borrow your lingo).

So let's say a tornado wipes out a village. That sort of thing happens only because God created and sustains the physical universe, which is governed by laws of nature. The same goes for those dreadful hot viruses: They operate in accord with laws of nature, held in place by God. And why is nature "red in tooth and claw"? Why must some animals live by killing and eating others? Theists must answer, "Because God set it up that way."

Yes, I know some Theists will say, "No, God didn't set it up that way. Natural evil is one of the results of the fall." But this is bogus for a couple reasons. First, there is no *logical* connection between "Adam sins" and, say, "Tornadoes hit towns" or "Hot viruses kill children" or "Wolves eat rabbits." So if there is a connection, it has to be one God set up. I see no way out of that. Second, according to the theory of evolution, animals (including both carnivores and herbivores) existed millions of years before humans arrived on the scene. These animals undoubtedly suffered from disease, accident, and attack from other animals. Thus, natural evil predated the so-called "fall."

When it comes to natural evil, Theism can't compete with Naturalism.

—Thomas

Dear Thomas,

In my opinion, quite a bit of natural evil is unsurprising, on the assumption that Theism is true. But I certainly do not think this is obvious.

Let's take it from the top. First, if God exists, God has strong reasons to create both nonhuman animals and human beings. In general, if God exists, God has reason to create good things, that is, things that *merit* such responses as wonder, admiration, and delight. And physical or biological life is a good thing in this sense. Plants, animals, and humans are all things that *merit* such responses as wonder and delight—and in fact living things commonly do elicit these responses. As we have already seen, God would have especially strong reasons to create relatively intelligent forms of biological life, such as human beings, for they are capable of experiences, activities, and relationships of enormous worth and significance. And a generous God would therefore have strong reason to bring such creatures into existence so that they might enjoy these goods, these blessings.

Second, nothing counts as physical unless it is governed by laws of nature. So it is logically impossible for there to be physical life unless it is governed by laws of nature. Moreover, not just any set of natural laws will support life. As we have already seen, physical or biological life cannot occur unless the universe is "fine-tuned." In fact, universes without natural laws and physical constants very, very similar to those in our universe are universes that probably will not support forms of life similar to those known to us, and perhaps they will support no life of any sort. Furthermore, natural evils are a function of the operation of natural laws (or of the mechanistic powers that ground those laws). So, as best we can tell, in any universe containing forms of life similar to those known to us, many natural evils are bound to occur in the absence of supernatural intervention (i.e., miracles) on a massive scale. And we have no reason to suppose that there are natural laws that (a) differ from those in our universe and (b) support intelligent life *while involving less natural evil than occurs in the actual universe.*

At this point, the key question is this: "Why wouldn't an almighty, perfectly good God intervene *miraculously* to prevent the natural evils?" Of course, according to traditional Theists, God sometimes does intervene. But since natural evils occur quite often, it is apparent that God often does not intervene. Why not?

My answer, in a nutshell, is that there is a link between natural evil and the moral life, and more generally, a link between natural evil and certain types of significance. Insofar as God has reason to provide us with the opportunity to achieve certain types of significance, including the significance of moral responsibility, God has reason to allow natural evils.[18]

As a first step, let's think a bit about moral responsibility in the form in which it actually exists. The moral life is played out within society and between societies. Why do we band together into societies? We need each other. For what? We each need a few people as companions, but why band together in large groups? Directly or indirectly, it seems to me, the answer involves natural evil. In large measure, societies can be regarded as organizations formed to cope with challenges from the natural environment. If we are to eat well, the natural environment must be cultivated. For protection from the elements, we must build shelter and make clothing. To stay healthy, we need medical assistance. To avoid discomfort, we need technology (at least in simple forms). To avoid boredom, we need entertainment. To flourish in the natural environment, we need research and education. To make the most of diverse talents and abilities, we need a division of labor that includes many different types of work. We can achieve all of these things better if large numbers of us cooperate. So we form into societies.

Of course we also band together in large groups to protect ourselves from other large groups of people. And the threat of war is a moral evil. But what are the underlying reasons for war? Often wars are fought to obtain better natural resources—land, water, lumber, minerals, oil, and so on. That is to say, wars are often fought because of the scarcity of natural resources. Sometimes wars are fought to enslave others. But why enslave them? So the conquerors can have a more comfortable life. But what makes their lives uncomfortable? Natural evils. Sometimes wars are fought out of hatred. But typically, behind the hatred, there is injustice—scarce goods were unfairly distributed. And scarcity is ultimately due to the fact that most of the things we want "don't grow on trees"; i.e., given the natural environment, it is hard for us to obtain all the things we want.

Again, the moral life, as we know it, is lived out within societies and between societies. But our need for societies is largely based on the presence of natural evils, and the size and organization of societies, as we know them, are largely determined by pressures from the natural environment. I submit that, if the natural evils were removed, societies, and hence the moral life, would be so dramatically altered as to be scarcely recognizable to us.

We've agreed that a loving God would have good reason to provide us with lives of great significance. And we've agreed that a loving God would therefore have good reason to endow us with moral responsibility. But, as I hope this letter makes clear, the moral life, as we know it, depends on natural evils.

—Zach

Dear Zach,

Yes, the moral life, as we know it, depends on natural evils. But surely an almighty God can provide a moral life that is independent of natural evils?

—Thomas

Dear Thomas,

That's a good question. But before attempting an answer, I'd like to reflect a bit further on the link between significance (in forms familiar to us) and natural evil.

First, consider how much important human thinking, decision-making, experience, and action occurs within the process of preparing for work (i.e., education), finding work, and working for a living. And many jobs exist because of the threat of natural evil. For example, without food, clothing, shelter, and medical assistance, we cannot live for long or flourish, given the natural environment. But a great many forms of employment exist to meet these needs, some directly (e.g., farming, carpentry, plumbing, nursing) and others indirectly (e.g., shipping, trucking, teaching, research).

Second, forms of work that may not seem to be connected with the natural environment generally do depend on it indirectly. For example, humans need entertainment because they find boredom unpleasant. But people can easily become bored even when they have plenty of food, adequate shelter and clothing, and good medical assistance. In short, boredom is often a natural evil or else indirectly produced by natural evils, as when one is bored by dull work needed to earn money so one can pay for food, shelter, and clothing.

Third, one reason we work, and work very hard, is simply that we must in order to have food, shelter, clothing, medical assistance, and so on. There are other reasons to work, of course. Some people enjoy their work (though many do not). Others want to work because they value being of use to others. But if we did not need to work for food, shelter, etc., I think it is plausible to suppose that many would not work at all, or they would work very little. Many people would in all probability spend their lives in relatively trivial pursuits.

Fourth, work and the preparation for work (that is, education) shape most human lives profoundly, so the meaning and significance of the lives of most humans is intimately bound up with their work. We find significance by being of use to others, and many of our most important decisions are connected with work.[19]

So far I have emphasized the connection between significance, work, and natural evil. I am not suggesting that our lives would be insignificant without natural evil. But I am pointing out that we humans often find great significance in the work we do, and the work we do is usually linked to some natural evil, so the work would not be needed if the natural evil (or threat thereof) were absent. And I suggest that the kind of significance humans achieve in their working lives is a very good thing. A mode of existence in which this type of significance is available *at some stage* seems to me a very good thing, even if it does depend on natural evils. If that's correct, then a good God would have reason to provide us with the opportunity to achieve such significance.

—Zach

Dear Zach,

All right, there is a *de facto* connection between certain types of significance and natural evil. But my question stands: "Isn't there some other way for an almighty being to provide us with significant lives?" Moreover, I hope you're not suggesting that you've explained why God would cause a hurricane to destroy an entire city or bring about a tsunami that kills thousands upon thousands of people.

—Thomas

Dear Thomas,

You recently remarked, "I don't see how Theism can explain any natural evil at all." I'm trying to explain why I think God would place us in an environment that contains at least some natural evils.

I presume that God could make creatures whose lives consist simply in pleasant experiences and activities. If this is what we expect a good God to bring about, we are bound to be puzzled by moral and natural evil. I have been suggesting that lives of great significance result from meeting challenges and having great responsibilities. I find it implausible to suppose that equally significant lives can be achieved without similar challenges and responsibilities. Challenges similar to those provided by the natural environment could in principle be provided by free agents, such as angels, I suppose, but those challenges would raise more or less the same questions, as far as I can see.

We find ourselves in a situation in which it is possible to have lives of great significance. This great significance is partly a function of meeting the challenges of the natural environment and of meeting our moral responsibilities (which in large measure are what they are because of the threat of natural evil). My claim is that a perfectly good God would have good reason to provide us with the opportunity to achieve lives of great significance. And such an opportunity is in fact present.

—Zach

Dear Zach,

I admit that the moral life, *as we know it*, depends on natural evil. But even if there were no natural evil, we could still insult one another. We could still lie to each other. We could still break promises. Rivals in love could still hate each other, even to the point of committing murder. We could clearly have a significant sort of moral life without natural evil.

Furthermore, we certainly do not need the extremes of natural evil (tsunamis, tornados, hot viruses) in order to have significant lives.

—Thomas

Dear Thomas,

While we may be able to imagine scattered elements of a truncated or fragmented moral life independent of societies of the sort we are familiar with, I doubt we have any sort of clear grasp of alternative types of moral life. And I'm sure we have no clear grasp of the degree of significance such alternatives would offer. So it's far from clear to me that a perfectly good God would provide us with some alternative sort of moral existence.

Some Theists have suggested that extreme natural evils make us deeply aware of the fragility of our lives and of the shallowness of seeking a purely materialistic happiness. Thus, natural disasters prod us to seek deeper values and to think seriously about our lives, about death (including the possibility of an early death), and about our place in the world (including the possibility of there being a God or gods). Now, it does seem to me that natural disasters have this effect. But we must ask such questions as "Is there no better way for an almighty God to stimulate us to think seriously about our lives? And in any case, do we really need so many disasters (and so many different kinds of disasters) for this purpose?" Not easy questions to answer.

Some Theists suggest that natural disasters are punishment for sin. I'm not thrilled with this idea. The suffering that results from natural disasters falls on babies, innocent children, the mentally impaired, and nonhuman animals—as well as on ordinary human adults, the "just and the unjust" alike. Thus, natural disasters strike me as too indiscriminate in their effects to count as plausible instances of divine punishment.[20]

Some Theists will point out that natural disasters often bring out the best in people. A kind of noble compassion and self-sacrifice arises in response to the tremendous suffering and loss. Of course, such disasters also bring out the worst in people—when the police are otherwise occupied, moral chaos surfaces with shocking speed.

God might have placed us in a hedonistic paradise. No natural evils. Everything we want at our fingertips. No effort needed. Assuming a good God exists, I don't find it at all surprising that we are not in a hedonistic paradise, but rather in circumstances that challenge us, involve moral responsibility, and call for us to develop moral virtue. We understandably dislike it when those challenges become extreme, frightening, and deadly. But a Creator who creates free agents must set the bounds of their existence, decide what their environment will be like, determine the kinds of challenges they will face. Are we in a good position to see clearly that this or that sort of challenge (or degree of hardship) is too much? I don't think so.

—Zach

Dear Zach,

*If we are not in a good position to see just what challenges a good God would give us, then the Theistic explanation of natural disasters falters. We can't be sure what a good God would cause or allow.*

Moreover, there's another gap in your discussion of natural evil. What you've said so far applies only to natural evil that befalls humans. What about all the suffering of nonhuman animals? Why would a *loving* God create animals that can live only by killing and eating other animals? Why would God let animals die in a forest fire?

—Thomas

Dear Thomas,

Again, let me emphasize that my goal is not to show that Theism explains all evils well. I'm trying to show that Theism can explain more evil than is often supposed and, ultimately, that Theism explains the presence of evil at least as well as Naturalism does.

Your questions about the suffering of animals are tough ones. Let me start with some preliminary observations.

It is widely agreed that many kinds of animals are wonderful life forms. Most of us feel the world would be impoverished without them. From this standpoint, it is surely not surprising that God would create ducks, deer, beaver, and buffalo. Wolves, lions, wolverines, sharks, and grizzly bears are wonderful too, but when it comes to predators, our feelings are mixed. Yes, they are wonderful in a sense, but aren't they also dreadful inflictors of pain and death? Thus, the phenomenon of predation can seem surprising, from the standpoint of Theism. How could a loving God set up a system that runs on massive amounts of pain and killing?

First, let me acknowledge that many people, Theists and non-Theists alike, do not see predation as a phenomenon crying out for explanation. Indeed, many people do not fault themselves for eating meat even though they know (a) that they can readily attain a balanced diet without it and (b) that eating meat involves death and suffering for animals. Since such people are predators by choice, it would seem hypocritical for them to regard predation as evidence of divine callousness. *Nevertheless, in my opinion, the suffering of animals is a matter of great seriousness. Perfect love is not indifferent to any form of suffering.*

Second, it is not very plausible to suppose that an animal ought to live forever if at all. Thus, it is not clear that the death of an animal is something God ought necessarily to prevent. But isn't death itself a bad thing? If it is, it is a bad thing easily outweighed by good things in many cases; e.g., plants are killed when eaten, and *that* is not a problem for Theism. God isn't required to set up a natural order free of the death of plants. Similarly, I suggest, the death of many animals, such as bacteria, insects, and crustaceans, is plausibly justified simply on the grounds that it serves to keep more complex life forms (e.g., birds and mammals) well nourished. More generally, as far as I can see, God is under no obligation to provide a death-free environment for animals. *The serious problem with respect to animals is not death but the suffering that can occur among the more complex forms.*

Third, Theists should not be expected to account for what amount to mere *speculations or guesses* about the intensity and extent of animal suffering. And we humans ought to admit there is much we do not know about animal suffering. The next two observations indicate, in an admittedly imprecise and partial way, what I do (and do not) regard as mere speculation about animal suffering.

Fourth, while there is little doubt that very complex animals, such as birds and mammals, can suffer, there is good reason to doubt that relatively simple forms of animals, such as insects and mollusks, can suffer. Consider the following.

- Damage to body parts does not necessarily cause pain even in humans. And a nervous response, such as withdrawal from a stimulus that causes damage, is not by itself good evidence that pain or suffering has occurred. Even in humans an automatic nervous response can occur in the absence of pain.

- Generally speaking, the more limited the behavioral repertoire of the animal, the less reason there is to suppose it has conscious mental states. On this ground there is much less reason to suppose that a jellyfish is conscious than to suppose that, say, a dog is.

- The differences in the central nervous systems of animals must also be taken into account. For example, a nervous system composed of ganglia linked by nerve fibers (as in a worm) is vastly different from a nervous system involving a spinal column and a large brain 40 percent of which (by weight) is composed of a highly developed cerebral cortex.

- As we have already seen, suffering is an unpleasant *conscious* state. Only animals capable of conscious *awareness* can suffer. But it is far from obvious that simpler types of animals are capable of such awareness.

- Suffering requires memory and anticipation. A sharp but momentary pain is not a case of suffering. To be capable of suffering, an animal must be able to remember pain and to anticipate that it will continue.

To sum up, while we can confidently claim that highly complex animals (such as birds and mammals) suffer, there is good reason to doubt that animals below the evolutionary level of fish possess centers of consciousness of the sort required to suffer.[21]

Fifth, it may be easy to overestimate the amount of suffering involved in predation. We can take one clue here from studies of shark attacks on humans. For example:

> Shark attacks do not have to be violent encounters to seriously wound the victims. Slicing of flesh by shark teeth can be as gentle and painless as that by a surgeon's scalpel. About one-fourth of the victims experienced little or no turmoil, and many didn't even realize that anything of significance had happened to them.[22]

And again:

> [Ten-year-old Steven Samples, attacked by a shark near Palm Beach, Florida] said later that he knew from the first that he was being attacked by a shark, at one time feeling a "crunching" sensation in his back and buttocks as he was pulled underwater. He felt no severe pain—"it hurt, but not enough to make me cry."[23]

The point of course is that what one might assume to be quite painful may not be very painful or even painful at all. In this connection, consider the following remarks of the noted ethologist, Jane Goodall, who can scarcely be accused of a lack of sympathy for animals:

> That was the first hyena hunt that Hugo and I watched and we were horrified to see, for ourselves, how they ate their prey alive. Since that night we have seen the same gory drama enacted time and time again, for Cape hunting dogs, commonly known as wild dogs, and jackals also kill by the method of rapid disembowelment. We still hate to watch it and yet, though it seems longer at the time, *the victim is usually dead within a couple minutes and undoubtedly in such a severe state of shock that it cannot feel much pain.*[24]

My point here is not to deny that predation sometimes involves suffering, but I do wish to cast doubt on the notion that predators typically inflict much pain on their prey. For all we know, in the overwhelming majority of cases, the victim rapidly goes into severe shock and as a result feels little or no pain. Indeed, death due to predation may involve less suffering than death due to disease or old age. But again, the key point is that Theists should not be expected to account for the amount of animal suffering merely *guessed* to be present in the world.

This letter is on the way to becoming a book! I've got to stop for now.

—Zach

Dear Zach,

I don't disagree with anything you said in your last letter, but I can't see that you've explained *any* animal suffering at all.

—Thomas

Dear Thomas,

You're right. I didn't explain any animal suffering in my last letter. I was just trying to lay some groundwork. Now on to the explanations.

The drama of animal life is closely connected with the dangers animals face, including predation, accidents, shortages of food and water, and natural catastrophes. And although I do not think animals are capable of moral action, they are capable of significant action, and it seems to me that their lives are worth living in part because of the significance attained through such actions. We feel— rightly so, in my judgment—that caging a wild animal is wrong in the absence of a strong justification. It is wrong at least in part because it deprives the animal of the opportunity to take a significant part in the drama of nature. But the drama of nature involves hardships and dangers. So it seems to me that the significance of the lives of sentient animals is bound up with hardship and danger. If we insist on a safe and comfortable life for animals, we seem to be opting for a value system that weights safety too strongly relative to other values, such as significance.[25]

I should also note that clause 5 of Afterlife Theism seems to apply to animals as well as humans: "If there is an almighty and perfectly good entity who has purposes for its creatures and the creatures die before those purposes are fulfilled, then the purposes will be fulfilled (insofar as possible) after the death of the creatures." Now, earlier I made the point that if God creates a nonhuman animal, God is not duty bound to keep it in existence forever. Nevertheless, clause 5 indicates that if God has purposes for a nonhuman animal that are unfulfilled at the time of its death, God will fulfill those purposes (insofar as possible) in a life after its death. For example, to the extent that animal suffering and death are *rightly* viewed as tragic or lamentable, a perfectly good God would presumably have the purpose of ameliorating the situation. And in many cases such amelioration could presumably be provided only in a life after death (e.g., if tragic death is the problem). Humans disagree strongly about the extent to which animal suffering and death are tragic or lamentable, but clause 5 provides a strong reason to suppose that, to the extent such events are genuinely tragic or lamentable, matters will be set right, even if that involves a life after death for some (or all) nonhuman animals.

—Zach

Dear Zach,

Doggie heaven? Seriously?

—Thomas

Dear Thomas,

How can we rule out that possibility, if we accept clause 5 of Afterlife Theism? Everything depends on God's purposes for animals. Perhaps in the case of most or all animals, God's purposes are fulfilled by the time the animal dies. (I'm personally confident that this is so in the case of mosquitoes and gnats! And, for the record, I strongly oppose any afterlife for these critters.) But if God's purposes are not fulfilled prior to death, clause 5 supports some sort of life after death. By the way, the idea of an afterlife for animals has received careful and sympathetic treatment by some very well-known religious thinkers, such as John Wesley.[26]

I know my explanations of animal suffering do not cover all the ground. Suppose an animal is injured in a forest fire or a landslide and that it dies slowly and in pain. Why doesn't God either heal the animal or euthanize it? I don't know.

—Zach

Dear Zach,

There's good news and bad news. The good news is: You've convinced me that Theism can explain quite a bit more evil than I thought it could. The bad news is: Your attempts to explain evil from a Theistic perspective falter at several points, e.g., extremes of moral and natural evil, and certain types of animal suffering. I wonder if alternate forms of Theism might do a better job of explaining evil. What about the idea of a God who is limited in power? Or indifferent to human suffering?

—Thomas

Dear Thomas,

If we postulate a God who is too weak to eliminate moral and natural evil, we postulate a God who is too weak to create and sustain the universe. If God can't stop the Mafia or halt a tornado, God surely cannot bring the entire universe into existence.[27]

We've seen the problems with postulating an evil God. If an evil God controls the processes that form our cognitive faculties, we have reason to doubt their reliability.[28] The same goes for an indifferent Deity. A being who is indifferent to human suffering can hardly be assumed sufficiently concerned with us to guarantee that we have reliable cognitive faculties. So these forms of theism are self-defeating from an epistemological point of view. To hold these views is to hold beliefs that call all of our beliefs into question.

How about the idea of a God who is morally so-so, not perfectly good but more good than bad? Such a God might care about us only up to a point or only care about us intermittently. Such a God *could* eliminate extremes of moral and natural evil but simply does not care enough about us to do so.

**Imperfect-Deity hypothesis**: (1) There is exactly one entity who is (2) morally so-so (more good than bad), and (3) almighty and who (4) exists of necessity.

It seems to me that this version of Theism has several problems. First, the idea, I take it, is that if God were perfectly good, God would eliminate most evil or at least the extremes of moral and natural evil. And since God obviously doesn't do this, we need to think in terms of a God who is less than perfectly good. But how plausible is this picture? The Imperfect Deity behaves like a weak-willed human, who knows what is right but often fails to do it. But since the Deity is almighty, that's mysterious. An almighty being presumably doesn't get worn out, scared, confused, distracted, or overcome by desire. So why does the Deity so often fail to meet his moral responsibilities? I see no answer to that question. The element of mystery in this hypothesis lowers its prior probability.

Second, focus for a moment on very wicked acts and natural disasters. These things happen constantly, so if the Deity is almighty and sees that they ought to be eliminated, he is constantly "falling down on the job," morally speaking. The Deity knows he ought to eliminate great suffering but just can't be bothered to do that. And since the Deity is almighty, it's not as if he gets tired or has too much to do or anything like that—he just doesn't care very much. To me, an almighty being who thinks he ought to eliminate extreme suffering but *on a daily or even hourly basis* fails to do so is morally deplorable. He has a bad character—he's not decent or so-so.

Third, with the previous point in mind, the Imperfect-Deity hypothesis is arguably self-defeating. If the Deity cares so little about us as to abandon us hourly to intense suffering *when the Deity knows it ought to help us,* why should we suppose that this Deity would bother to ensure that we have reliable cognitive faculties? I don't see a convincing answer to that question.

Fourth, unlike Theism, the Imperfect-Deity hypothesis does not enjoy support from a tradition of Theistic mystical experience. For this reason also, the Imperfect-Deity hypothesis has a lower prior probability than Theism.

Here is an additional observation that, I believe, underscores the first three points. Moral theorists generally agree that the strongest reasons favor moral action. For example, suppose I'm late to work and have no good excuse but that a plausible lie occurs to me. In such a situation, I may have reason to lie—perhaps I know that my lie will placate my boss. But of course I also have a moral reason not to lie, "Lying is wrong." And assuming lying *is* wrong in this type of case, moral theorists would generally agree that, although I have a reason to lie, I have a *stronger or overriding* reason not to lie. In general, *if one is morally required to do X, then one has overriding reason to do X.* Therefore, the Imperfect Deity chooses to act on weaker, inferior reasons whenever it fails to be morally perfect. That's irrational. This underscores the element of mystery in the hypothesis and also casts doubt on the trustworthiness of the Imperfect Deity.

—Zach

Dear Zach,

OK. The Imperfect-Deity hypothesis is encumbered with problems. So I guess we're back to Theism vs. Naturalism. But you've
admitted that Theism does not explain all evils well. In my opinion,
that means there's a big question mark over Theism.

I know you think that Naturalism also has difficulty in explaining
the presence of evil. But *why* do you think that?

—Thomas

# CHAPTER 8

# Naturalism and Evil

Dear Thomas,

So far we've considered the problem of evil just as a problem for Theism. In this respect, our discussion has been typical. Anthologies in the philosophy of religion commonly treat the problem of evil simply as a problem for Theism, the main question being "Are Theistic replies adequate?" One seldom sees arguments to the effect that non-Theistic views have difficulty accounting for evil. Moreover, Naturalists commonly regard the problem of evil as a special problem for Theism and not as a problem for Naturalism at all. I think this is a mistake.

In my opinion, Naturalists face a dilemma. The streamlined forms of Naturalism do not explain any evil at all. But as Naturalists add theses to increase the explanatory power of their view, it becomes increasingly complicated. The complications lower the prior probability of Naturalism dramatically. In the end, I claim, we've no good reason to regard the Naturalistic explanation of evil as superior to the Theistic explanation. The upshot is this: The problem of evil does not give us a reason to accept Naturalism over Theism.[1]

—Zach

Dear Zach,

Why should Naturalism have any difficulty at all in explaining the presence of *natural* evil?

—Thomas

Dear Thomas,

Let's start with Basic Naturalism:

> **Basic Naturalism**: (1) There is a self-organizing physical reality (i.e., there is a physical reality whose nature is not imposed by a god or by any other force or agent), (2) physical reality exists either necessarily, eternally, or by chance, and (3) leaving aside possible special cases (e.g., sets or numbers), all entities are physical entities.

Recall that hurricanes, viruses, earthquakes, etc., do not count as natural evils; it's the suffering (and loss) these natural events bring about for sentient beings that counts as natural evil. But does Basic Naturalism lead us to expect the presence of sentient beings? No. As we saw in our discussion of the Cosmological Argument, Basic Naturalism does not even lead us to expect the presence of contingent beings, let alone a life-supporting universe and conscious living things. And if Basic Naturalism does not lead us to expect conscious living things, then it does not lead us to expect any suffering (or loss) at all. Hence, Basic Naturalism does not lead us to expect any natural evil.

—Zach

Dear Zach,

Well, of course, Basic Naturalism is too streamlined to explain much. We've long since agreed on that. I think MUH Naturalism is the best of the various Naturalistic hypotheses we've considered, so let's focus on it:

> **MUH Naturalism**: (1) There is a self-organizing physical reality, (2) some part of physical reality exists of necessity, (3) the necessary part of physical reality randomly generates additional parts of physical reality that are distinct universes, and (4) the number of universes generated is vast—perhaps even infinite. (5) Leaving aside possible special cases (e.g., sets or numbers), all entities are physical entities.

MUH Naturalism was developed to explain our life-supporting universe. And at this point we surely ought to be working with a form of Naturalism that can explain the presence of living things. Given that MUH Naturalism explains the presence of life, it surely leads us to expect the suffering of living things.

—Thomas

Dear Thomas,

The upshot of our discussion of the design argument was that Theism provides a better explanation of our life-supporting universe than MUH Naturalism does.[2] And this is for two reasons. First, MUH Naturalism has a lower prior probability than Theism because it's more complex. For example, it postulates more entities (many universes) and more kinds of entities (*unobserved* universes and a necessarily existing universe generator).

Second, and more important for present purposes, MUH Naturalism does not do a good job of leading us to expect a life-supporting universe. Suppose we assume that the universe generator somehow generates infinitely many universes. Does that lead us to expect a life-supporting universe? No, because, as far as we know, there may be infinitely many non-life-supporting universes. (Just for the sake of illustration, if we could number all of the universes, we might find that all of the even-numbered ones are non-lifesupporting and that perhaps all but a few of the odd-numbered ones are also non-life-supporting.)

So, apparently, we must stipulate that the universe generator produces every possible universe. Of course, that's a staggering suggestion. There seem to be infinitely many possible universes. How does the universe generator succeed in producing each and every one of them? "It just does" is not a satisfactory answer. The usual suggestion is that the universe generator produces universes randomly—singly or in groups. But this means that the process of universe generation must go on forever if it is to produce every possible universe. From this perspective, MUH Naturalists must postulate a physical system or process that does not run down over time, for a system that does run down over time obviously won't function forever. The problem of course is that all physical systems of our acquaintance do run down over time; i.e., they are subject to entropy.

The only alternative seems to be the even more implausible suggestion that the universe generator produce every possible universe at once—whoosh! No one has any idea how a physical system could produce every possible universe at once.

Now, MUH Naturalism does seem to be the best of the Naturalistic hypotheses for explaining the presence of fine-tuning. But the proposed explanation is highly problematic. It is far from clear that MUH Naturalism leads us to expect a life supporting universe. And clearly, if MUH Naturalism falters in explaining the presence of our life-supporting universe, then it falters in explaining the presence of life, and hence it falters in explaining the presence of suffering.

There are some further problems with the Naturalistic explanation of natural evil, but I've got to close for now.

—Zach

Dear Zach,

You haven't shown that life is impossible, given Naturalism. What prevents the Naturalist from claiming that life is just a "lucky accident"? After all, in anybody's view, improbable things happen every day.

Also, what "further problems" do you have in mind?

—Thomas

Dear Thomas,

Improbable things do happen, of course. But if, for a given hypothesis, life is a "lucky accident" (hence, improbable), then on that hypothesis, life is surprising. In other words, that hypothesis has very little explanatory power with regard to the phenomenon of life. And if Naturalism has very little explanatory power with regard to life, it has very little explanatory power with regard to the presence of suffering in the world.

Moreover, even if Naturalism can explain fine-tuning, there are at least two additional questions that arise about the Naturalistic explanation of natural evil. Let me briefly outline one of them in this letter.

MUH Naturalism's "universe generator" produces physical systems that differ in terms of their physical constants, laws of nature, and/or initial conditions. And a "universe fine-tuned for life" is a physical system capable of producing the chemicals necessary for life as we know it, such as hydrogen, oxygen, carbon, and nitrogen. Put simply, *if* MUH Naturalism works as a hypothesis, it explains the presence of the chemicals necessary for life, but it does not explain how lifeless chemicals developed into living things. This issue, the origin of life (or *abiogenesis*), remains a matter of scientific speculation.

In Darwin's day, scientists imagined that the simplest forms of life were very simple indeed, mere homogeneous globules. But as it turns out, the cell, which is the basic unit of life, is quite complex. Each cell has many parts: Amino acids must be put together in just the right, lengthy sequences to form protein molecules; and a living cell contains perhaps 200 protein molecules functioning together in accordance with a set of instructions, which are stored in genes, the latter being composed of DNA. Even the simplest (i.e., prokaryotic) cells, such as bacteria, have a number of structural elements, including the cell membrane, the cell wall, the nucleoid region (containing DNA), ribosomes (which synthesize proteins), and cytoplasm. Many prokaryotic cells also have a flagellum (a sort of propeller used for locomotion).[3]

Scientists have offered a number of hypotheses meant to explain how lifeless chemicals were transformed into living cells: the idea that some inherent attraction would cause amino acids to line up in sequences necessary for life; the idea that life arose via the intense conditions surrounding hydrothermal vents on the ocean floor; the idea that the first organisms consisted of RNA (which is simpler than DNA); the idea that life fell to Earth aboard meteorites; and so on. But these hypotheses remain speculative or incomplete (or both).[4]

Attempts to generate life in laboratory conditions thought to simulate conditions on Earth 3.5 billion years ago have not yet succeeded. Stanley Miller's famous experiment showed that amino acids could be generated under conditions (temperature, atmosphere, etc.) thought to be similar to those on Earth about 3.5 billion years ago. But Miller's assumptions about the Earth's atmosphere are now in doubt. And more importantly, amino acids are not living things. Indeed, as I've just indicated, in the simplest known forms of life, many proteins have to function together as a unit, and each protein is composed of a very complex sequence of amino acids.[5]

I'm not suggesting that living things *can't* arise by natural causes from nonliving matter. But we are asking how well MUH Naturalism accounts for the presence of living things. And Naturalists can only speculate about how lifeless chemicals developed into living cells. And, again, if Naturalism falters in explaining the presence of life, it falters in explaining the presence of suffering.

—Zach

Dear Zach,

But Theists cannot explain how life arose from mere chemicals either, right?

—Thomas

Dear Thomas,

Right. But unlike Naturalists, Theists don't assume that life arose by natural causes *independent of divine design or guidance*. The Theistic explanation of the presence of life appeals fundamentally to divine purposes. It doesn't depend on the success of scientific hypotheses about life's origin. Let me hasten to add that if life did arise from natural causes, there is no reason for Theists to deny this. According to Theists, God brings about many things indirectly through "secondary" (i.e., previously created) causes. (One's parents are a good example of a secondary cause.)

Let me mention another complication in the Naturalists' attempt to explain the presence of suffering (and, hence, natural evil). Note that Naturalism must explain not only the presence of life, but the presence of *conscious* life, for suffering is a conscious mental state. And we must bear in mind that many living things lack consciousness—surely this is true of all plants, and presumably it is also true for the simpler forms of animal life.[6]

I assume Naturalists will grant that there can be no conscious mental states apart from complex nervous systems.[7] So it is not enough for Naturalists to explain the presence of very simple forms of life. We must ask whether Naturalism leads us to expect forms of life having complex nervous systems of the sort that are correlated with consciousness or sentience. In essence, this means we must ask how likely complex life forms (e.g., mammals) are, on the assumption that they evolved through entirely natural causes (apart from any divine design or guidance). And the answer is a matter of debate, even among experts in evolutionary biology. Some argue that animals with complex brains, such as those found in humans and other mammals, are inevitable (or at least, likely), while others regard the evolution of such animals as a fluke.[8]

The idea that life has an inherent tendency to progress to more complex forms belongs to a Lamarckian conception of evolution, which is not endorsed by contemporary biology. According to Darwin, variations occur at random; e.g., in a litter of pups, there will be differences in color, size, strength, etc. If a variation confers an advantage for survival (and reproduction), then that variation will tend to be preserved (i.e., passed along to the next generation). As a matter of fact, life has evolved from very simple forms, such as bacteria, to very complex forms, such as mammals. But to what extent is the path of evolution inevitable or at least likely, and to what extent is it a fluke—a lucky accident? As Harvard paleontologist Stephen J. Gould once remarked, "Wind back the tape of life to the early days of the Burgess Shale; let it play again from an identical starting point, and the chance becomes vanishingly small that anything like human intelligence would grace the replay."[9] And if we wind the tape of life back to the Precambrian era and let it play again, conscious life would probably not have evolved, according to Gould.[10] If he is right, then the appearance of intelligent, conscious life is surprising from the perspective of Naturalism.

According to Gould, evolution might never have reached the stage of multicellular animals. For the first *2.4 billion* years of the history of life, all organisms were of the simplest single-celled (prokaryotic) type. (Eukaryotic cells, which compose multicellular organisms, did not appear during this time.) But the entire history of life is about 3.5 billion years. With these facts in mind, it is at least natural to doubt that complex forms of life were inevitable or even very probable from the beginning. Furthermore, Gould also notes that the course of evolution seems to depend on unpredictable extinctions. For example, the dinosaurs apparently became extinct because a large asteroid struck the Earth about 65 million years ago, sending up an enormous cloud of dust that blocked the sun (thus lowering temperatures and suppressing photosynthesis). Large mammals would probably never have evolved if the dinosaurs had not died off.[11]

My point here is simply this. Naturalism leads us to expect complex life forms only on the following assumption: "Given simple life forms, very complex forms (with brains as complex as those found in mammals) are fairly likely to appear eventually due to entirely natural causes (apart from any special divine activity)." But this assumption is a matter of debate among those with the relevant scientific expertise. Therefore, *even if* Naturalists can explain the presence of fine-tuning and *even if* they can explain the origin of life, it is not clear that Naturalism leads us to expect the presence of living things complex enough to suffer.

Let me sum up the situation. To explain natural evil, MUH Naturalists must explain the presence of sentient life. But the explanation falters at three levels. First, and most important, MUH Naturalism's explanation of fine-tuning is highly problematic. MUH Naturalism doesn't really lead us to expect a fine-tuned universe. Second, MUH Naturalists must assume, on the basis of little evidence, that lifeless chemicals developed into living cells apart from any divine design or guidance. Third, MUH naturalists must make the controversial assumption that, given unicellular life, life forms with complex nervous systems are at least fairly likely to evolve in the long run (apart from divine design or guidance). In short, the Naturalistic explanation of natural evil falters at the outset (in its attempt to explain fine-tuning) and is also laden with speculative or controversial assumptions.

If my arguments so far are on the right track, I fail to see that Naturalism gives us a better explanation of natural evil than Theism does.

—Zach

P.S. Perhaps I should mention that a tiny minority of Naturalists deny that there are sentient beings in the world. The so-called *eliminative materialists* deny that humans (or any other animals) have conscious mental states.[12] Rather than trying to explain the presence of suffering, these Naturalists in effect explain it away. Of course most philosophers, including most philosophers sympathetic to Naturalism, find eliminative materialism implausible in the extreme.

Dear Zach,

Haven't the natural sciences established that conscious living things were caused to exist by entirely natural factors? Wouldn't most scientists answer that question in the affirmative?

—Thomas

Dear Thomas,

The natural sciences operate under the assumption of **methodological naturalism**, i.e., that only *natural* factors should be considered in scientific explanations. Put simply, most scientists think you are doing theology and not science if your hypothesis involves divine activity. Therefore, the statement "Conscious living things were caused to exist by entirely natural factors" is not established by science; rather, it is *presupposed* by scientists who attempt to explain the origin of consciousness. I do not object to methodological naturalism as a restriction on science. But you can't count a methodological *assumption* as a result of science.

And remember, even if we grant that conscious living things were in fact caused to exist by purely natural factors, it does not follow that this event was likely or probable or at all to be expected. Indeed, it might have been a fluke of nature—something highly unlikely and quite surprising.

You might reply that Theists are also apt to have difficulty providing an adequate explanation of the presence of consciousness. But unlike Naturalists, Theists don't have to explain the presence of consciousness through purely natural causes. From the standpoint of Theism, the presence of conscious creatures is ultimately explained in terms of the reasons God would have for creating conscious life. And we have already seen that, if God exists, God would have good reasons to create conscious life, especially very intelligent conscious life.

—Zach

Dear Zach,

Some of the questions you've raised about the Naturalistic explanation of life may be answered by science in the near future. For example, if life is generated (under the relevant conditions) in a laboratory, that would settle the origin-of-life issue.

—Thomas

Dear Thomas,

Yes, I agree, some of the questions I've raised may be answered by scientists in the near future. But what are we to do in the absence of solid scientific answers? Pretend that they already exist? It seems to me that our assessment of Naturalism must take into account points at which it involves ungrounded or weakly grounded assumptions.

Anyway, my primary claim is that Naturalism falters right at the outset in explaining fine-tuning—which means it also falters in explaining whatever depends on fine-tuning—namely, life, complex life, and conscious life. I've drawn attention to the further assumptions Naturalists must make only as a supplement to this primary claim.

—Zach

Dear Zach,

I admit that the Naturalistic explanation of natural evil is more open to question than I had supposed. Do you see further problems for Naturalism in explaining the presence of moral evil?

—Thomas

Dear Thomas,

Recall that moral evil is the wrongdoing for which humans are responsible and the suffering (and loss) that results from it. If, as I have just argued, Naturalism falters in explaining the presence of beings who can suffer, then of course it falters in explaining moral evil in general. We must have conscious beings if we are to have moral agents. And we must have conscious beings if we are to have any suffering in the world at all.

Furthermore, in order for there to be any moral evil in the world, there must be a moral standard, that is, a standard of good and evil and of right and wrong actions. Also, there must be free agents. For, as we saw in our discussion of free will, agents are morally responsible only if they are free.[13]

Now, we have already discussed the issue of free will at length. I think you agree that agents are morally responsible only if they are free, *in the incompatibilist sense*. And there is nothing in MUH Naturalism to lead us to expect that agents are free in this sense. Free will, I have argued, involves a nonmechanistic power to form intentions.

And as we have seen, no amount of information about physical systems, brain processes, electrochemical laws, and so on leads us to expect the presence of free will. If we know that humans have free will, we know it by introspection or by reflection on the nature of moral responsibility, not by studying the human brain (or any other physical system). In short, MUH Naturalism does not lead us to expect free agents.

Naturalists can take various points of view with regard to free will. As you know, some Naturalists simply deny that humans are free, and hence, by implication, they deny that humans are morally responsible for anything. This is clearly a very problematic position and not one that many people will accept.

Other Naturalists claim that humans are free only in the compatibilist sense. But I've argued that the compatibilist view of freedom does not underwrite moral responsibility, for, in that view, I'm free as long as I do what I most want to do (all things considered); but my all-things-considered wants may be caused entirely by factors beyond my control, such as the laws of nature and the past.[14]

Perhaps the best move for Naturalists is simply to affirm the presence of free agency in the world, based on reflection on moral responsibility (and/or based on introspection). The naturalistic metaphysic does not lead us to expect free agency, but free agency does seem to be present. And Naturalists can accept its presence as a brute fact. Of course, in my view, this will involve admitting that Theism explains a key aspect of moral evil (namely, free will) better than Naturalism does. (As we've seen, from the Theistic standpoint, God would have good reason to create free agents.)

—Zach

Dear Zach,

I've just time for a short note. First, many Naturalists don't buy your line regarding free will. So they certainly won't feel that your last letter creates any serious trouble for their view. Second, what are the Naturalist's options with regard to a moral standard?

—Thomas

Dear Thomas,

The issue is not "Can we convince Naturalists?" Rather, the point to keep in mind is that the Naturalists' proposed explanations of evil are at least as controversial or problematic as the Theists'.

Now, regarding moral standards, Naturalists can take a variety of positions. Perhaps it's helpful to look at this from the standpoint of the metaphysics of morality. (I should note that these positions may also be taken by non-Naturalists.) **Moral antirealists** deny that there are any moral facts, i.e., objective truths about right and wrong, good and evil, etc. (By an "objective" moral truth, I mean one that holds whether we humans believe it or not.) For example, you might think that *Slavery is wrong* or *Booth murdered (unjustifiably killed) Lincoln* are moral facts, but not so, according to moral antirealists— there are no objective moral truths. The so-called **Ethical Naturalists** claim that moral facts are a species of natural fact; thus, moral properties (such as goodness or wrongness) are properties whose existence can be confirmed by the natural and/or social sciences. As a simple illustration, one might hold that wrongness is the property of *being disapproved of by society*. (Scientific opinion polls could tell us what actions are disapproved of by the members of a given society.) The so-called **Ethical Non-Naturalists** deny that moral properties are identical with any natural properties; rather, moral properties are unique, evaluative properties. Evaluative properties explicitly or implicitly involve rightness, wrongness, goodness, badness, "oughtness," and so on.[15]

Plainly, Naturalists can adopt a variety of positions regarding the presence and nature of moral standards. But if Naturalism makes no claims about the presence and/or nature of moral standards, then Naturalism explains no moral evil at all. I think that's obvious, so I won't dwell on it. But I also think that some positions regarding moral standards, such as moral antirealism, are very problematic.

—Zach

Dear Zach,

I've heard of moral antirealism, but I'm curious as to why some philosophers take that position. Are there any good arguments for it?

—Thomas

Dear Thomas,

Some Naturalists (only a minority) are moral antirealists. Let's take a look at some of J. L. Mackie's arguments for moral antirealism.[16] First, consider the widespread disagreements about morality, not only between cultures but among those within the same culture or society. If there were objective truths about morality, says Mackie, people would tend to agree over time, as scientists tend to agree over time as they confront empirical facts. Since widespread moral disagreement persists, there must be no objective moral truth.

Second, Mackie emphasized the *strangeness* of moral properties. They are strange in several ways.

1. It seems that we cannot observe wrongness or "oughtness." For example, you can observe people lie, but you cannot (literally)

observe that they *ought* not to lie or that lying is *wrong*. So do we have some sort of extrasensory perception that puts us in touch with moral properties? Moral truths, if they existed, would call for a strange way of knowing.

2. Mackie asserted the following conditional: "If you really believe you ought to do X (e.g., give to charity), then you are automatically and necessarily motivated—at least to some extent—to do X." But as Hume claimed, it seems we need both beliefs *and* desires to be motivated. For example, suppose I believe that the bus is the fastest way to get downtown. Well, that belief won't motivate me to take the bus unless I want (desire) to go downtown. And yet Mackie's conditional statement makes no mention of wants or desires. So, says Mackie, if we accept that moral judgments are sometimes true, we also have to accept that moral properties have a strange, seemingly "magical" power to motivate us, apart from any desires. But surely there can be no properties with such a strange power.

3. Consider the statement "Causing intense pain just for fun is wrong." If this statement is true, then there is a necessary link between the natural property, *causing intense pain just for fun*, and the moral property, *being wrong*. But there seems to be no way to explain that linkage—it's quite mysterious, says Mackie. So if moral judgments are objectively true, then moral properties are strange because they have a totally inexplicable linkage with natural properties. Mackie found the existence of such properties literally incredible.

—Zach

Dear Zach,

I don't buy Mackie's first argument. People have always disagreed about philosophical matters in general, and those disagreements show no sign of going away. So should we say that there is no objective truth about the existence of God, about determinism, about free will, or about whether people have souls? *If* "God exists" is true, then surely it is true whether or not we believe it. (Though I doubt that God exists, I've never supposed for one moment that God's existence might somehow depend on human beliefs! If God does exist, God in no sense owes his existence to human beings; the dependency relations would be quite the other way round.) Thus, long-standing or even ineradicable disagreement on a given topic is not a good reason to conclude that there are no objective truths on that topic.[17]

—Thomas

Dear Thomas,

I think you're right about Mackie's first argument. What do you think of his arguments concerning the strangeness of moral properties? Here are some points to consider.

1. Indeed, moral properties don't seem to be observable, but that can be said about other sorts of properties too. Can one see logical (or metaphysical) necessity? Can one observe that an object is identical with itself? I don't think so, yet we seem to be acquainted with these properties and to know that they are present in the world.

In this connection, it is well to keep in mind that moral evaluations are not the only kinds of evaluations. For example, suppose I say, "If you know that all collies are dogs and all dogs are animals, then you *ought* to believe that all collies are animals." Here "ought" indicates an epistemological requirement, roughly, to believe what follows logically from things one already knows. But we are surely able to know that "oughts" of this sort are present in the world, even if we cannot literally observe (see, touch, etc.) them, so why suppose there is any special problem about moral "oughts"? I don't see a good answer to that question.[18]

2. Regarding Mackie's point about motivation, I agree with him to this extent. If I ought to do X (e.g., give to charity), then I have a reason to do X. And if I'm aware that I ought to do X, then (assuming I am functioning normally) I will be motivated (at least a little) to do X. But I don't see why I must have a desire to do X in order to be motivated to do it. I can be motivated (to some extent) to do X simply by *being aware of a reason* to do X. Or so it seems to me.

3. Like Mackie, I see no way to explain the (apparently) necessary link between (a) causing pain just for fun and (b) doing wrong. But, in my opinion, we are often in a position to see that a truth is necessary even though we cannot explain why it is, for example, "Whatever has color has size," "Red is a color," and "No persons are numbers." At perhaps an even more basic level, can we explain why "Contradictions are never true" is necessary? I think we just see that this is so. (Any attempt to explain it via logic will *presuppose* that contradictions are never true.) So examples of necessary truths about morality, such as "Causing intense pain just for fun is wrong," seem no stranger than nonmoral examples of necessary truths.

—Zach

Dear Zach,

Mackie raises intriguing questions about the nature of moral properties. But it's going to take a really strong argument to get me to deny that there are any moral facts. I don't think Mackie's arguments are all that impressive.

—Thomas

Dear Thomas,

And we haven't yet looked at the downside of moral antirealism. Mackie himself was an *Error Theorist*; that is, he believed that all moral judgments are false. Like other forms of moral antirealism, this one has implausible implications, e.g., that each of following statements is false: "Booth murdered (unjustifiably killed) Lincoln," "Genocide is wrong," "Justice is good," and "Torturing people for no reason is wrong." It's hard to accept the claim that all moral judgments are false.

Most moral antirealists claim that moral judgments are neither true nor false; moral judgments merely express feelings, make recommendations, or the like. This version of moral antirealism has difficulty explaining moral error, for it denies that anyone (ever) has false moral beliefs. Hitler believed that he and his fellow Nazis ought to commit genocide. If Hitler's belief was neither true nor false, how can we say that he was mistaken? If we say that Hitler's view conflicts with a more general norm, such as, "Murder is wrong," what is the status of this more general norm? It too is neither true nor false, so why should we regard it as a standard whereby moral error can be discerned? Once we deny moral truth, it seems we are led to deny the presence of moral error.

Furthermore, if moral judgments are neither true nor false, how shall we understand arguments about moral issues? Many arguments about moral issues appear to be logically valid; i.e., the conclusion follows logically from the premises. For example, consider the following argument:

1. All acts of murder are wrong.
2. Oswald performed an act of murder.
3. So Oswald performed an act that was wrong.

A valid argument is one that preserves truth; that is, if you start with true premises, you'll wind up with a true conclusion, if you argue validly. The point is this: The fact that we regard some moral reasoning as valid indicates that we regard moral judgments as *propositions*, i.e., as either true or false. But most moral antirealists claim that moral judgments are neither true nor false.

Many moral antirealists have held that moral judgments merely express feelings or emotions. Saying "Murder is wrong" is like saying "Murder—boo!" A friend of mine who teaches ethics received a paper defending this thesis from a student. My friend immediately placed an F on the paper and returned it. The student contacted her to protest the grade. The conversation went something like this:

> *Student:* Why did you give me an F? I worked hard on that paper. Was it unclear? Did I leave something out? Was there an error in the logic?
>
> *Prof:* You write well. You have a clear thesis. The paper is nicely organized. The grammar is fine. I didn't spot any fallacies.
>
> *Student:* Well, then, the grade is unfair.
>
> *Prof:* "Unfair." Hmmm. "Unfair" is a moral word, isn't it? But as you point out in your paper, there is no moral truth. People just feel differently about certain things. Well, you and I just *feel* differently about this paper.

The point, of course, was not to stick the student with a bad grade, but to initiate a serious discussion about the foundations of morality. Verbalizing moral antirealism is one thing, accepting its implications is another thing altogether.

—Zach

Dear Zach,

Here's what I think: If Naturalists adopt moral antirealism, the Naturalistic hypothesis becomes very implausible. I find the thesis that there is no objective moral truth extremely hard to swallow. But, of course, Naturalists don't have to be moral antirealists. Won't Naturalists tend to view morality from an anthropological perspective? Each culture or society has a moral code; so can't societal codes *be* the moral standard, from a Naturalistic perspective?

—Thomas

Dear Thomas,

Some Naturalists take that approach. It can be formulated as a version of Ethical Naturalism. (Recall that Ethical Naturalism is the view that moral properties are identical with natural properties.) I'll refer to this view as Normative Relativism, since it posits a moral standard that is relative to societal norms.

**Normative Relativism (NR):** The property of *moral rightness* consists in being approved of by the society in which the act is performed; and the property of *moral wrongness* consists in being disapproved of by the society in which the act is performed.

(Let's stipulate that a society approves of an act if the vast majority of its members approve of that act; and a society disapproves of an act if the vast majority of its members disapprove of that act.) Given this view of rightness and wrongness, a social scientist could determine what is right and wrong by taking appropriately designed opinion polls.

Many people nowadays find NR attractive because it avoids ethnocentrism. It says (in effect) that people should be judged by the standards of their own society, not by standards external to it.

—Zach

Dear Zach,

Regarding certain issues, there may be no consensus within a society. What does Normative Relativism tell us about right and wrong in such cases? For example, do Americans, taken as a group, approve of the death penalty, abortion, affirmative action, and same-sex marriages? Currently, there seems to be no social consensus in regard to these matters.

—Thomas

Dear Thomas,

You've pointed to one problem for Normative Relativism. Given NR, if there is currently no consensus in America regarding the death penalty, abortion, affirmative action, and same-sex marriages, then these acts or practices are *neither right nor wrong* in America at this time. But, of course, when people debate the death penalty, abortion, etc., they normally assume that these acts (or practices) are either right or wrong. Here are some further challenges NR faces.

*Apparently malign rules.* Societal codes often include apparently malign rules or values. For example, some societies approve of cannibalism, wife-beating, and "honor" killings. And historically, many forms of child abuse have been approved of by various societies. According to NR, these acts (or practices) are right when performed in societies that approve of them. That's pretty hard to believe.

*Moral epistemology.* Given NR, the best way to determine what's right or wrong is to take a scientific opinion poll, for such a poll is surely the best way to discover what a society approves of (or disapproves of). Now, consider the implications of this and think historically. Imagine an abolitionist giving a speech against slavery.

The abolitionist summarizes all the arguments against slavery, building an apparently strong case. But someone in the back of the room raises his hand and says, "Well, what's right is just a matter of what society approves. And we all know our society approves of slavery—all the polls indicate this. Therefore, however well intentioned you may be, you are clearly in moral error." The point is that NR implies an implausible view of how to discover moral truth.

*The arbitrariness problem.* Given NR, the approval of one's society determines what's right. But why is *society* the relevant group? Why not one's family, religious group, or some subculture (e.g., the "drug subculture")? On what grounds is *one* of these groups properly chosen as morally authoritative? If there are no grounds, moral relativism seems ultimately arbitrary. We might as well flip a coin to select the group that we will regard as authoritative. But it's hard to believe that something as important as morality is arbitrary in this way.

*Aggression between societies.* Suppose society A approves of shooting a nuclear missile at society B so that nearly everyone in society B will die and society A can annex the territory of society B. Not surprisingly, the members of society B disapprove of the act. What does NR say about shooting a nuclear missile in such a case? Is shooting the missile morally permissible because the members of society A approve of it? If so, NR has very implausible implications. Should we say instead that, since the act has effects in society B, it happens in both society A and society B? But if the act does (somehow) occur in both societies, then does NR tell us that the act is right, that it is wrong, or that it is both? There seems to be no clear answer, but that in itself is a problem, because the act is plainly wrong.

*No standard of moral progress.* NR leaves us without a standard by which to judge that a moral code has gotten better (or worse). Suppose a society approves of slavery at some point in its history. Then there is an antislavery movement, and slavery is abolished. Everyone now disapproves of slavery. Has the society made an improvement in its moral code? From the standpoint of NR, there is no standard above society's approval by which that approval can itself be judged. We can say the moral code has changed over time, but there are no grounds for saying that the code has gotten better. Of course, intuitively, the code *has* improved—that's the problem.

—Zach

Dear Zach,

That's quite a list of objections! I do see that NR is problematic. Perhaps a better approach, from a Naturalistic perspective, would be to view morality from an evolutionary standpoint. Clearly, in order to flourish, humans must live in groups. And in order to live together, humans need a code of behavior that promotes survival and reproduction. Good or right behavior will be behavior that conforms to such a code; bad or wrong behavior will be behavior that violates such a code.

—Thomas

Dear Thomas,

I take it you're suggesting a form of Ethical Naturalism that identifies moral goodness (or rightness) with *conformity to a code that promotes survival and reproduction*. We might call this *evolutionary ethics*. How plausible is this view? Here are some things to consider.

First, Stephen Gould claims that large mammals probably wouldn't have evolved if the dinosaurs hadn't died off. If Gould is right, is the extinction of the dinosaurs good *as a means* to the production of more complex life forms? Could the extinction of humans in principle be good as a means to the production of some unknown life form? In short, even if human survival is a good, is it the sort of good that might be outweighed by other goods and sacrificed for them?

Second, societal codes often favor the rich and powerful, and so the codes often fail to promote every individual's survival (and ability to reproduce). Will evolutionary ethics promote inequality, e.g., by favoring the survival (and reproduction) of the "fittest"?

Third, is mere survival really a good? Mere survival might involve a miserable, just-getting-by sort of existence. But if we go beyond mere survival and talk about the quality of life, won't we find ourselves claiming that many things are good: health, companionship, pleasure, creative activities, and so on? How are these goods related? Are they all to be given equal weight? Should they be combined in certain ways? These are old ethical questions; do facts about biology give the answers?

In short, the proposed evolutionary ethics raises many questions.[19]

—Zach

Dear Zach,

Well, is there a better way for the Naturalist to proceed?

—Thomas

Dear Thomas,

Perhaps. Notice how our discussion of Naturalism and morality has proceeded so far. We have repeatedly appealed to our *considered views* about morality: "Causing intense pain just for fun is wrong," "Genocide is wrong," "Slavery is wrong," and so on. If we are going to think seriously about ethics, we seem to have little choice but to take our considered views about right and wrong, good and evil, as control beliefs. Control beliefs guide our theorizing. If a theory conflicts with our control beliefs, it is to some extent problematic. I'm not suggesting that control beliefs are infallible, but they are very important and should not be abandoned unless we have good reasons (arguments) for giving them up.

Perhaps this is a good place to recall the Starting Principle, which we considered in our discussion of religious experience: "It is rational to accept what seems to be so unless special reasons apply." I believe this principle applies to our thinking about morality. We don't start from a position of radical skepticism. We give the benefit of the doubt to what seems clearly true about right and wrong, good and evil. Of course, what seems to be true can rightly be doubted if "special reasons apply." If our moral beliefs have implausible implications, we may have to give them up.

Now, among our considered moral judgments are judgments about which character traits are virtues. Virtues are morally good character traits, traits we need in order to live well as human beings. Few will deny, for example, that the following character traits are virtues: Being just (or fair), being courageous, being wise, being honest, being self-controlled, and being loving. We regard people who have all of these character traits as morally exemplary. I'm suggesting, then, that Naturalists might adopt as their starting point in ethics such judgments as "Justice is a virtue," "Love is a virtue," "Wisdom is a virtue," and "Honesty is a virtue."

If we are not convinced by the arguments of the moral antirealists, statements such as "Justice is good" and "Justice is a virtue" are plausibly taken as *truths*. And Naturalists can employ such truths as a moral standard, without taking a stand on the metaphysical dispute between Ethical Naturalists and Ethical Non-Naturalists.

—Zach


Dear Zach,

Are you suggesting that "Justice is a virtue," "Love is good," etc., are self-evident moral truths?

—Thomas

Dear Thomas,

I doubt that statements such as "Justice is a virtue" and "Love is good" are self-evident. If a statement is self-evident, then one can see that it is true simply by grasping the concepts involved. The problem is that concepts such as justice and love seem to be rather complex. (Consider that the terms *justice* and *love* are not easy to define or analyze.) And I doubt that we have a sufficiently firm grasp of the concepts to support a claim to self-evidence.

But again, if the arguments for moral antirealism are not strong, then "Justice is a virtue," "Love is a virtue," "Wisdom is a virtue," and "Honesty is a virtue" are plausibly regarded as *truths.* Can we use these statements to develop a general view of what is right and wrong? Some moral theorists have suggested that virtuous persons provide us with a model of reliable moral judgment. We can look to virtuous persons to see what sorts of things to consider in making moral decisions, to see how much weight to give principles when they conflict with other principles, and also to see what should not be taken into account at all.[20] From this perspective, if we can identify the main moral virtues, we have some basis for discerning what is right and wrong in a very wide range of cases.

If we look to virtuous persons for moral guidance, I think we will find that they tend to agree on many points, e.g., that killing persons is generally wrong, stealing is generally wrong, cheating is generally wrong, and lying is generally wrong. There will be unusual situations calling for special exceptions, but I suggest that the resulting moral judgments would support a rather traditional-sounding morality. If that's correct, then an ethical system that starts with claims about the virtues is apt to result in a conception of moral evil that is similar to the conception found among Theists.

—Zach


Dear Zach,

Well, then, why not add another thesis to MUH Naturalism. We can call it the *Moral Standard thesis*: "The following character traits are moral virtues: justice, love, wisdom, honesty, and courage." With the addition of this thesis, MUH Naturalism contains a plausible standard of good and evil.

—Thomas


Dear Thomas,

We can add the Moral Standard thesis to the naturalistic hypothesis. But of course, this will lower the prior probability of Naturalism, at least somewhat. After all, the Moral Standard thesis is a substantive philosophical thesis, denied by moral antirealists. Theism pays a price for postulating a moral standard at the outset (with its relatively complex claim that God is morally perfect); Naturalism must surely pay *some* price (in terms of prior probability) if it adopts the Moral Standard thesis.

The question now becomes "Does Naturalism *with* the Moral Standard thesis explain evil better than Theism does?" I see no good reason to answer yes. Our discussion has revealed many problems in the naturalistic explanation of evil.

1. I have argued that the discussion of fine-tuning ends unfavorably for the Naturalist. If my arguments are on the right track, Naturalism does a poor job of leading us to expect the presence of a universe that contains the chemicals necessary for life. But if Naturalism falters on this point, it falters in explaining all evil. There is no evil in the world unless there are living things who can suffer. In contrast, Theism renders our life-supporting universe unsurprising.

2. Even if Naturalism explains fine-tuning, the naturalistic explanations of the origin of life and of complex life are in varying degrees speculative. Again, the upshot is that Naturalism, unlike Theism, does a poor job of leading us to expect the presence of conscious beings in the world.

3. Regarding free will, the best Naturalists can do is affirm that free agents exist, as a brute fact. Naturalists often take more problematic positions, denying the presence of free agents altogether or affirming the compatibilist view of free will. By contrast, Theism leads us to expect free will, in the incompatibilist sense.

4. MUH Naturalism has a lower prior probability than Theism. And MUH Naturalism *with the Moral Standard thesis added* has a somewhat lower prior probability than MUH Naturalism.

Given these problems, I have a hard time understanding why so many people seem to think that Naturalism has no difficulty explaining the presence of suffering and evil in the world. In fact, the Naturalistic explanation of suffering and evil falters at several key points. And some people might suggest that, although Theism struggles to explain the full range of evils, on the whole it explains suffering and evil better than Naturalism does. For these folks, the "problem of evil" has become (paradoxically!) an "argument from evil" for Theism.

I wouldn't go that far myself. The whole issue is too messy, in my view, to support such a judgment. Instead, as I see it, both Theism and Naturalism struggle in their attempts to explain suffering and evil. I don't see a clear winner. But Naturalism's explanation of evil is at least as open to question as the best Theistic explanations. If that's right, the upshot is quite significant: *The problem of evil gives us no reason to accept Naturalism over Theism.*

—Zach

Dear Zach,

It's true that Naturalism must abandon its original simplicity in order to explain evil. It may have to affirm the presence of the fine-tuned universe, of conscious life, and of free agents as brute facts. But once those claims are added, no amount or type of evil is surprising given Naturalism. By contrast, you've admitted that some types of suffering are surprising, on the assumption that Theism is true.

—Thomas

Dear Thomas,

If Naturalists add all those claims to their hypothesis, they will lower its prior probability still further. (Instead of explaining these phenomena, they would simply be making the phenomena part of their hypothesis.) The cost of adding these claims is hard to calculate—which only reinforces the point I've been making. The quality of an explanation depends on its prior probability as well as on its explanatory power. As Naturalism takes on a series of additional claims, its prior probability must drop, but *I don't see how to specify how far it will drop.* This is *one* reason I think we cannot determine whether Naturalism or Theism provides the better explanation of evil.

Furthermore, if Naturalists are free to assume that fine-tuning, conscious beings, and free agents came into existence *without divine design or guidance*, Theists are free to make some assumptions too. For example:

**Super Theism:** (1) There is exactly one entity that is (2) perfectly morally good and (3) almighty and that (4) exists of necessity. (5) *The almighty and perfectly good being has a morally sufficient reason for allowing (or causing) all the evil that exists.*

Armed with clause 5, no actual instance of evil is surprising, from the standpoint of Theism. Of course, clause 5 is controversial, speculative, and questionable. But the same can be said about the assumptions you've suggested we add to the Naturalistic hypothesis. So, once again, I see no reason to suppose that the Naturalistic explanation of evil is better than the Theistic explanation.

To sum up, Theism and Naturalism both struggle to explain moral and natural evils. Neither emerges as a clear victor in the dispute. What's odd is that people so commonly assume that the problem of evil is a special problem just for Theism. On the contrary, evil is as much a problem for Naturalism as it is for Theism, or so it seems to me.

Where does this leave us? The presence of evil in the world supports neither Naturalism nor Theism. But, as we have already seen, the design argument and the argument from free will provide significant positive support for Theism over Naturalism. Therefore, taking into account all the things we've discussed so far, the evidence favors Theism.

—Zach

# CHAPTER 9

# A Moral Argument

Dear Zach,

Yesterday I got into an argument with some people at work. One of them, a very religious person, was advancing a line of reasoning that went something like this—I'm paraphrasing, of course:

1. There are objective truths about morality, i.e., truths about right and wrong, good and evil, that hold whether humans believe them or not.
2. The best explanation of premise 1 is that God commands human beings to do certain things (e.g., love one another) and forbids humans to do others (e.g., steal, bear false witness, commit adultery).
3. So God exists.

Now, I accept premise 1. As far as I'm concerned, certain things are just wrong, period, whether humans believe it or not—examples: genocide, rape, child abuse, torturing people for sadistic pleasure.

But what is the best explanation of the presence of moral truth? Is it indeed that God commands us to do certain things and forbids us to do others?

—Thomas

Dear Thomas,

Let's get clearer about what a divine command theory of morality is. Is it this?

**Divine Command Theory (DCT):** Whatever is right or good (e.g., acts, character traits, persons) is right or good *simply because* an almighty being approves of it. Whatever is wrong or evil is wrong or evil *simply because* an almighty being disapproves of it.

Two main philosophical arguments might be given in support of the DCT.

*Argument A*

1. Laws require lawmakers.
2. So if there are moral laws, then there are moral lawmakers
3. These lawmakers are either (a) humans as we actually are, (b) some idealized version of us, or (c) God.[1]
4. (a) and (b) are not plausible.
5. So God is the moral lawmaker.

The defense of premise 4 would require a discussion of the constructivist views of ethics, which claim that moral rules are made or constructed by human minds (actual or idealized). Normative Relativism, which we discussed recently, is one form of constructivism. But it would sidetrack us to explore all of these ethical theories, e.g., subjectivism, contractarianism, and ideal-observer theories.[2]

*Argument B*

1. God is almighty.
2. So God has control over what is good and evil, right and wrong.
3. So the DCT is true.

Clearly this argument presupposes that God exists, so it cannot be used to support an argument for God's existence.

—Zach

Dear Zach,

I can see that a religious believer would find argument B plausible. In fact, I'm not sure why any Theist would object to argument B.

—Thomas

Dear Thomas,

Argument B fails if there are necessary moral truths, and I think some moral truths are necessary. Let me explain. If we set aside moral antirealism and assume that there are moral truths, then it is plausible to suppose that some of them are necessary truths. This claim can be defended in at least two ways.

First, we can offer examples of moral statements which, if true, are plausibly necessary, e.g., "It is wrong to torture people for fun" and "Unjustified killing is wrong." It's hard to see how these statements could be false *under any possible circumstances*; hence, it is plausible to suppose that they are necessary truths.

Second, as Swinburne notes:

> Once one has specified fully what it is that makes the action wrong, then it will be (given that it is a truth) an *analytic* [necessary] truth that an action of that kind is wrong. For if it were not it would be coherent to suppose that another action could be just like the first one in all other qualitative respects and the second be right and the first wrong—yet this is not a coherent supposition.[3]

To paraphrase: Pick an action that you regard to be wrong, *clearly* wrong. For me, torturing people just for fun would be a good example. Then make a list of all the natural features of the action that make it wrong. (Leave aside supernatural features, such as divine approval.) For instance, torturing people just for fun involves causing intense pain in humans, *solely* for the enjoyment of the one who inflicts the pain. If your list of natural, wrong-making features is really complete, can you conceive of another action with the very same features that is not wrong? No, says Swinburne.

Now, we saw long ago that a maximally powerful being cannot bring about logical or metaphysical impossibilities. Such a being cannot create circular squares or colorless red rubies or actions that are simultaneously free and coerced. It follows that a maximally powerful being does not have control over necessary truths, for in order to make a necessary truth false, one would have to bring about a logical or metaphysical impossibility. Therefore, if there are necessary moral truths, argument B fails. The inference from "God is almighty" to "God has control over what is good and evil, right and wrong" is invalid. God does not control necessary truths; they cannot be false under any circumstances whatsoever. (In fact, if God could make them false, then they wouldn't be necessary truths after all.)

—Zach


Dear Zach,

I see. And if there are necessary moral truths, argument A fails also, because its first premise is false: "Laws require lawmakers." There surely don't need to be "lawmakers" in order for there to be necessary truths about mathematics, such as, $9 < 10$, $2 + 2 = 4$, or the square of the hypotenuse of a right triangle is equal to the sum of the squares of the two sides. Similarly, if there are necessary moral truths, then there can be "moral laws" without there being moral lawmakers.

—Thomas

Dear Thomas,

Yes, I agree. There seem to be some necessary moral truths, and this throws a wrench into both of the arguments for the DCT.

We should also consider the negative implications of the DCT. First, DCT is a theological version of "Might makes right": Whatever the *almighty* being approves of is right, simply because he approves of it. But "Might makes right" is a principle that nearly all serious ethicists reject. Tyrants are not good people just because they have the power to impose their will on others. To put it bluntly, the fact that someone can "beat you up" doesn't make him a moral authority.

Second, DCT faces a dilemma: Does the almighty being approve of things for a reason or not? If not, then morality is ultimately *completely* arbitrary, given DCT. Had God approved of murder, torture, theft, or hating thy neighbor, these things would have been good or right. But this implication is implausible—even outrageous. Torturing people for fun could not be right, period. Or so it seems to me.[4] On the other hand, suppose the almighty being approves of things for a *reason* (and disapproves of things for a reason). Then surely acts are not right (or wrong) *simply* because the almighty being approves (or disapproves)—the *reason* is at least a contributing factor to the rightness (or wrongness). Either way, DCT seems false.

Third, what does God's goodness consist in, given the DCT? Answer: divine self-approval. That is, the DCT implies that God is good simply because God approves of himself. Now, this is implausible. Tyrants often seem to approve of themselves, and that certainly does not make them morally good. There is no logical connection between self-approval and being morally good.

Fourth, DCTists apparently think the following conditional is a *necessary* truth (cannot be false under any possible circumstance): "If an almighty being approves of an act, then it is right." But it seems obvious to many people that the stated conditional is not a necessary truth, because there is no necessary linkage between *being powerful* and *being right* ("Might does not make right"). Thus, the fundamental principle of the DCT is quite dubious.

—Zach

Dear Zach,

May I suggest a modified version of the Divine Command Theory?

**Modified Divine Command Theory (MDCT)**: To be morally required is to be commanded by a *perfectly good* and almighty being. (In other words, an act's being morally required *consists in* its being commanded by a perfectly good and almighty being.) To be morally wrong is to be contrary to the commands of a *perfectly good* and almighty being.

This is not a theological version of "might makes right." Rather, MDCT stresses that the commands of a *good* God underlie morality.

—Thomas

Dear Thomas,

The MDCT is certainly an improvement over the DCT. But I do have questions about the MDCT. First, I assume that God issues commands freely, not of necessity. (If God does issue commands of necessity, then, it seems to me, the deepest ground of morality is plainly necessity, not divine command.) But if God commands freely and not of necessity, then for any morally required act you can name, God might not have commanded it. And for any wrong act you can name, God might not have forbidden it. Take as an example *torturing people just for fun*: God might not have forbidden this type of action. And if God had not forbidden it, it would not have been wrong, according to the MDCT. But "Torturing people just for fun is wrong" strikes me as a necessary moral truth (i.e., one that cannot be false under any possible circumstances).[5] To suggest that *torturing people just for fun* would not have been wrong if God had not forbidden it is implausible. Let me put the point this way: If there were no God, it still seems to me that *torturing people just for fun* would be wrong—very wrong. The same goes for many other acts, such as killing people for a trivial reason, breaking one's promises for no reason, and punishing the innocent.

Second, note that MDCT, as stated, does not offer an account of God's goodness. In fact, it explains obligations or moral requirements, not other moral properties such as goodness or virtue. But then we must ask, does God control whether propositions such as the following are true: "Love is good," "Love is a virtue," "Justice is good," "Injustice is bad," "Wisdom is good," and so on? If we answer yes, then presumably God can make these propositions false, and an arbitrariness problem emerges, similar to the one that DCT faces. If we answer no, then these propositions must be necessary truths. But if "Love is good" is a necessary truth, is it true independent of God's existence and nature? If so, then MDCT presupposes that the ultimate moral truths are independent of God. I presume that the defenders of MDCT wish to avoid this result. But a necessary thing (e.g., a being or proposition) cannot depend on something that isn't necessary, such as a free choice. (If I can, by a free choice, make a proposition true, e.g., "I am now raising my right arm," that proposition obviously is not a *necessary* truth.) One necessary thing can only depend on another necessary thing. Of course, many Theists hold that God exists of necessity and/or has certain attributes of necessity (e.g., omnipotence and moral goodness). But can these necessities that belong to God's own existence or nature depend on God? It is not easy to see how. Thus, it seems that MDCT's view of divine goodness depends on a resolution of the difficult and controversial issue of God's relation to necessity. And that's a liability.[6]

Third, MDCT may face another dilemma similar to one DCT faces. Does God command acts for a reason? If the answer is no, then, once again, rightness and wrongness seem to be ultimately arbitrary. And this is troubling. For example, if the divine commands regarding sexual ethics might very well have been much less restrictive than Christians traditionally take them to be, then (from that perspective) God has placed unnecessary burdens on human beings, burdens that are hard to bear and that have produced a tremendous amount of frustration. On the other hand, if God does command acts for reasons, then the *reasons* surely contribute to the rightness or wrongness of the action. And perhaps it is the reasons, rather than the divine command, that make the act right or wrong. At least, if the reasons are strong, they will plausibly support a claim to rightness (or wrongness, as the case may be). On the other hand, if the reasons are weak, the problem of arbitrariness may reappear—the reasons don't really ground the command.[7]

To sum up, MDCT has some implausible implications and leaves me with many questions.

—Zach

Dear Zach,

If I understand you correctly, you are saying that there is no need to postulate God in order to explain the presence of moral truth. It surprises me that you would take such a position. Don't Theists generally regard God as (in some sense) the ground of moral truth?

—Thomas

Dear Thomas,

Theists do commonly regard God as the ground of moral truth. Of course, that's often because Theists assume some version of the Divine Command Theory. Some theologians have suggested that moral truth might somehow be grounded in God's nature without being grounded in God's will. This claim seems a bit obscure to me. But I do see a way in which God's commands could ground *some* moral truths.

Consider an analogy. Under normal circumstances, we owe a debt of gratitude to our parents, who brought us into the world, raised us, and helped us in ways too numerous to mention. If our parents place a demand on us, it can become a duty, because we owe them this great debt of gratitude. For example, I recall that your mother recently asked you to help her move some heavy furniture in her home, furniture she could not lift by herself. You were *glad* to oblige, I'm sure. But if you reflect on the matter, I'd guess that you did feel *obligated*. And, unless you'd had some very good excuse, you'd have felt guilty if you had denied her request—you'd have felt that you'd failed in your obligations. Indeed, your feelings signaled a moral truth, according to many ethicists. Now, if the demands of our earthly parents can create obligations, the demands of God surely can too. We owe our very existence to God and all the good things we've experienced come ultimately from God. So if God exists, we owe God a very great debt of gratitude.[8]

But notice that I have not said that God creates morality or obligation in any radical sense. Your mother's demand created an obligation because there is a deep moral truth to the effect that *we owe a debt of gratitude to those who've helped us in important ways*. God's demands would also have purchase because of some truth along these lines, I take it. For example, if God commands a group of people to worship on the sabbath, they would be obligated to do so. But God would not *and could not* create an obligation to torture people just for fun, to "hate thy neighbor," to kill innocent children, and so on.

—Zach

Dear Zach,

I'm puzzled. If you do not regard Theism as the best explanation of objective moral truth, what will you propose as evidence for God's goodness?

—Thomas

Dear Thomas,

Theists have offered several kinds of evidence for the goodness of God, including the so-called "ontological" argument, various moral arguments, and religious experience. Of course, we have already examined religious experience.

I would add that the design argument and the argument from free will also provide evidence of God's goodness. Notice that it is essential to those arguments (in the versions we've discussed) that Theism postulates a *good* God. If God is good, God is generous and has reason to share good things with intelligent, sentient creatures; hence, God has reason to bring such creatures into existence. If God is good, God is loving, and has reason to create beings who can return that love *freely*. Furthermore, we have seen that postulating an evil God is self-defeating; such a postulate would cast doubt on the reliability of all our cognitive faculties. Thus, the design argument and the argument from free will do not provide evidence merely for a powerful Intelligence; they provide evidence for a God who is good.

I'm not saying that the design argument and the argument from free will show that God is *perfectly* good, of course. But, as we have seen, the hypothesis that God is imperfectly good is a rather tricky one. Roughly speaking, the more morally imperfect we suppose God to be, the more we have reason to doubt the reliability of our cognitive faculties. (In general, the more morally imperfect we suppose God to be, the less we can expect God to look out for our interests, including our interests as truth seekers.) So the design argument and the argument from free will work only for Theistic hypotheses that credit God with considerable goodness.

—Zach

Dear Zach,

I'd like to know more about the ontological argument. I've heard some summaries of it. I thought they sounded intriguing.

—Thomas

Dear Thomas,

The ontological argument comes in many versions. The best versions, in my judgment, involve *modal* logic (the logic of possibility and necessity).[9] Unfortunately, this means the logic is a bit tricky.

Recall that a necessary truth is one that cannot be false under any possible circumstances, such as "2 + 2 = 4," "All cats are cats," and "Circular squares do not exist." A contingent truth is one that could be false under different circumstances, such as "I exist," "My house is white," and "There is a book on my desk."

According to proponents of the ontological argument, if God exists at all, then "God exists" is a necessary truth. God wouldn't be

God if "God exists" were merely a contingent truth, for this would imply that God might not have existed at all and that God *could* cease to exist. So if it's possible that God exists, it's possible that "God exists" is a necessary truth. Does that make sense so far? Now comes the crucial step, and I need to do a little explaining.

Take any math statement, such as $233 - 44 + 59 = 248$. Such a statement is either necessarily true or necessarily false: If true, it cannot be false under any possible circumstances; and if false, it cannot be true under any possible circumstances. The same can be said even in the case of mathematical propositions whose truth value is unknown, such as Goldbach's Conjecture (every even number greater than 2 is equal to the sum of two prime numbers): Such propositions are either necessary truths or necessary falsehoods. More generally, if a given proposition is true *only if* it is a necessary truth, then the proposition is either a necessary truth or a necessary falsehood. Furthermore, if a proposition is either necessarily true or necessarily false, then if it is possibly true, it is necessarily true, for if it is possibly true, it is not necessarily false. And this is the essential logic of the modal ontological argument:

1. If God exists, then "God exists" is a necessary truth.

2. So "God exists" is either necessarily true or necessarily false.

3. "God exists" is possibly true, hence not necessarily false.

4. So "God exists" is necessarily true.

The argument seems to be valid; i.e., the conclusion follows logically from the premises.

—Zach

Dear Zach,

Hold on a minute! Suppose we applied that logic to some unknown math statement, such as Goldbach's Conjecture. Suppose I were to argue as follows:

1. If Goldbach's Conjecture is true, it is necessarily true.

2. So Goldbach's Conjecture is either necessarily true or necessarily false.

3. Goldbach's Conjecture is possibly true, hence not necessarily false.

4. So Goldbach's Conjecture is necessarily true.

According to what you're saying, this argument is valid. Maybe so. But now I begin to see that premise 3 is loaded with meaning. It doesn't just say that, *for all we know*, Goldbach's Conjecture is true. It says that Goldbach's Conjecture is not necessarily false. But of course, no one knows that. For all we know, someday some mathematician may show that Goldbach's Conjecture leads to a contradiction.

This suggests a similar problem for the ontological argument. How is premise 3 of the ontological argument known? As the case of Goldbach's Conjecture indicates, even when relatively simple math concepts are at issue, we cannot always know what's possible. How much more cautious we must be when major metaphysical concepts are in play!

—Thomas

Dear Thomas,

I think you make a good point. The third premise, "'God exists' is possibly true," is plausible if it means "For all we know, God exists." But epistemic possibility is not relevant here. We need to know that "God exists" is logically or metaphysically possible. And how can we know that?[10]

In the case of Goldbach's Conjecture, we can know that it is possibly true only by proving that it is true, for there may be some mathematical impossibility buried deeply within it, something very difficult to ferret out. Only a proof of the conjecture can assure us that no such impossibility lurks within it.

And in this context, the claim that "God exists" involves some special complications (beyond those involved in Theism, as I've defined it). To advance the argument, *God* is usually defined as "the most perfect being possible." What is the most perfect being possible like? Omnipotent, omniscient, and perfectly morally good, for starters, but we must add more, to make the argument work. Specifically, *the most perfect being possible must have these attributes (omnipotence, omniscience, and perfect moral goodness) in every possible situation in which it exists*, for a being that could in principle lose these attributes would not be perfect—so the argument goes. Moreover, if the being *can* lack these attributes, then perhaps it lacks them in the actual world. So premise 3 of the ontological argument is very complicated in the end. Made fully explicit it would look something like this:

> (3+) It is logically (metaphysically) possible that there is a *unique* being who is omnipotent, omniscient, and perfectly morally good and who cannot lack these attributes under any possible circumstances.

(3+) is far from obvious. Does an omnipotent being have the ability to give up some of its power or knowledge, *if it so chooses*? No, according to (3+), but one might doubt that. Indeed, even some Christian theologians have suggested that one of the divine persons gave up some knowledge in order to become human (without giving up his divinity).[11]

Also, would an entity be genuinely good (in a moral sense) if it isn't even logically possible for the entity to do evil? Recall that in our discussion of the problem of evil, I suggested that we humans would have an inferior, puppetlike goodness if we did not have a real choice between good and evil. But (3+) denies God any choice between good and evil.

Well, I don't pretend that these brief remarks refute the ontological argument. But I do think they point out some of the obstacles it faces. Since I see these obstacles as pretty daunting, I don't want to push the ontological argument.[12] Instead, I'd like to offer a moral argument.

—Zach


Dear Zach,

If you've got a moral argument to offer, I'm all ears.

—Thomas


Dear Thomas,

OK, here goes. I will refer to my "moral" phenomenon as *the moral order*. It may be summed up as follows:

**The Moral Order**: (a) The strongest reasons always favor doing what is morally required, and (b) the correct moral code is traditional in content.

When I speak of a traditional moral code, I mean one that says killing, stealing, lying, adultery, and so on are wrong, except perhaps in certain special cases, e.g., killing in self-defense.

In our discussion of the Imperfect-Deity hypothesis, I mentioned that most moral theorists hold or presuppose that the strongest or overriding reasons always favor doing one's moral duty. I know of no way to prove that this principle is true, but I think most people believe it or at least find it plausible once they've considered it.

Suppose someone's behavior seems odd to you, apparently irrational. For example, at a great banquet a guest next to the host snatches the host's fork from his hand. A hush falls over the crowd of people. The host is visibly angry. But later it is revealed that the host is highly allergic to the food he was about to eat, the guest next to him knew this (though the host didn't), and so the guest snatched the fork from the host's hand just as he was about to take a bite. The guest was doing his moral duty—his act was fully justified and there was nothing irrational about it.

We tend to reject certain moral theories precisely because they seem to present *as duties* actions that are not backed by the strongest reasons. For example, suppose someone were to advance this moral theory: *One is always morally required to do what is best for others.*[13] ("Love thy neighbor *instead of* thyself.") On this theory, one's own interests are irrelevant to morality—one must do what is best for others regardless of the cost to oneself. Now suppose Smith, a young person in good health, can help Jones, a very old person, live for two more weeks—the catch is that Smith has to donate her perfectly healthy heart. Is Smith morally required to give up her heart so Jones can live two additional weeks? Everyone would answer no, I assume. Well, why not accept this moral theory? One good reason seems to be this: It fails to give self-interest (or self-love) its due and thus yields a situation in which *alleged* moral requirements ("Donate your heart") are overridden by self-interest.

—Zach

Dear Zach,

I find the thesis you call "the moral order" plausible, but I fail to see any theological implications. What prevents someone from simply defining "morally required acts" as "acts backed by the strongest reasons"? Then the first part of the phenomenon ("The strongest reasons always favor doing what is morally required") would be true by definition, hence necessarily true. And we don't need a hypothesis to explain necessary truths—they simply can't be false, end of story.

—Thomas

Dear Thomas,

Well, you won't find your proposed definition in any dictionary. Moreover, "All morally required acts are acts backed by the strongest reasons" does not seem to be a necessary truth. At least, it seems to me that we can easily imagine circumstances in which it is not true, *given that the moral code has traditional content.*

Just to establish the principle, consider an admittedly far-fetched case. Suppose there is an all-powerful but malevolent Deity who delights in making highly morally virtuous people eternally miserable after death.[14] Moreover, the Deity rewards morally wicked and morally "average" persons with eternal happiness. In such a situation, it seems clear that moral reasons would not always be the strongest reasons.

(To avoid eternal misery, one needs to fail in one's duty and/or commit immoral acts, at least occasionally.) So, at some point, when prudential considerations are sufficiently momentous, they can outweigh moral considerations. That much seems clear to me.

—Zach

Dear Zach,

I got your recent letter and I agree with your main point, but I still don't see any interesting theological implications.

—Thomas

Dear Thomas,

Before we consider theological explanations of the moral order, let's consider some explanations that Naturalists can endorse. Why is it that the strongest reasons always favor doing one's moral duty (where *moral* is understood in a traditional way)? Here's one answer:

*Hypothesis 1.* Being moral always promotes one's self-interest.

Hypothesis 1 is questionable. Consider the following case.

*The Case of Ms. Poore.* Ms. Poore has lived many years in grinding poverty. She is not starving but has only the bare necessities. She has tried very hard to get ahead by hard work, but nothing has come of her efforts. An opportunity to steal a large sum of money arises. If Ms. Poore steals the money and invests it wisely, she can obtain many desirable things her poverty has denied her: cure for a painful (but, let's assume, nonfatal) medical condition, a well-balanced diet, decent housing, adequate heat in the winter, health insurance, new career opportunities through education, etc. Moreover, if she steals the money, her chances of being caught are very low and she knows this. She is also aware that the person who owns the money is very wealthy and will not be greatly harmed by the theft. Let us add that Ms. Poore rationally believes that if she fails to steal the money, she will likely live in poverty for the remainder of her life. In short, Ms. Poore faces the choice of stealing the money or living in grinding poverty the rest of her life.[15]

In this case, Ms. Poore has a moral duty *not* to steal the money, and yet stealing it seems to be in her self-interest. Indeed, in order to be moral, she has to make a great personal sacrifice (i.e., live in poverty) even though the sacrifice prevents relatively minor harms. So, this case at least *appears* to be a counterexample to hypothesis 1.

—Zach

Dear Zach,

How about the idea that we should be moral not for some reward but simply because it's right?

—Thomas

Dear Thomas,

I think your point is this: We cannot get people to do their moral duty by appealing to their self-interest, for if they do the right thing for self-interested reasons, they are not really acting morally. One must do the right thing *because it's right*, not for a self-interested reward.

The point you're making seems correct, but it does not explain the Moral Order. No doubt we should do the right thing because it's right and not for a self-interested reward. But what if, in a given case, we have stronger reasons to do the wrong thing? Then doing the right thing is irrational—in the sense that it involves acting on inferior or weaker reasons.

Go back to the Ms. Poore case. Does it really look like the strongest reasons favor doing her moral duty (not stealing)? Assuming, as Naturalists do, that there is no God and no life after death, I think the Ms. Poore case looks like a counterexample to the principle that the strongest reasons always favor doing one's duty. *When considerations of prudence and morality conflict, if the prudential considerations are momentous while the results of behaving immorally are relatively minor, then morality does not override prudence.* In the light of the Ms. Poore case, that principle strikes me as very plausible.

—Zach

Dear Zach,

I'm not sure I agree with your analysis of the Ms. Poore case. Consider this hypothesis:

*Hypothesis 2.* Doing one's duty is the only way one can have peace of mind.

It might seem that Ms. Poore can gain by stealing, but she'll be plagued by guilt if she steals the money. So, in the long run, doing her duty will pay in terms of peace of mind.

—Thomas

Dear Thomas,

Hypothesis 2 is roughly Plato's answer.[16] His answer probably works for some morally upright people. Because such people have a well-formed conscience, they feel very guilty whenever they violate their conscience, "beating themselves up" for even relatively minor moral infractions.

But to test hypothesis 2, we have to consider two other kinds of cases. First, we have to consider people who are not very conscientious, happy-go-lucky folks who do not approach life primarily from a moral perspective. It is not clear that these folks can have peace of mind only by doing their duty at all times. For them, peace of mind can apparently be achieved by relegating conscience to a minor role. Ms. Poore might be one of these folks.

Second, we have to consider the fact that even morally upright people give in to temptation occasionally. Doesn't everyone act selfishly at times? And most of us probably fail at times to stand up for what's right—especially when doing so would be unpopular or dangerous. Now, do these failures necessarily destroy a person's peace of mind? Maybe in the short run, but assuming the moral violations are not egregious, people forgive themselves and "get over it." (Ms. Poore might very well fall into this category.) And depending on the price they would have paid for doing their duty—which can be quite high in some cases, they might even admit that they would probably do the same thing again in similar circumstances. In short, there are worse things than a temporary loss of peace of mind.

For these reasons, hypothesis 2 seems unsatisfactory to me.

—Zach

Dear Zach,

I've been sharing our recent letters with some colleagues at work. One of them just shook his head and said, "Doesn't this guy know that virtue is its own reward?" What do you say about that?

—Thomas

Dear Thomas,

Some moral theorists, such as Aristotle and Aquinas, emphasize character traits—virtues and vices. A character trait is a disposition or tendency to act in a certain way. The virtues include such traits as being wise, just, moderate, and courageous. The vices include being foolish, unjust, immoderate, and cowardly. This approach to ethics suggests the following explanation of the Moral Order:

> *Hypothesis 3.* Virtue is its own reward, that is, having a good moral character (i.e., having the virtues) is necessarily a greater benefit to you than any benefit you might obtain at the expense of your good moral character.

In my view, moral virtue is indeed a benefit to those who possess it. But the claim that *perfect* virtue is *necessarily* a great enough benefit to its possessor to compensate fully for any loss it might entail is implausible. Consider the following thought experiment.

> *The Case of Mr. Gladwin and Ms. Goodwin*. Mr. Gladwin is a morally lukewarm person who happens to be regarded as a paragon of virtue. He is admired by most people, prosperous, loved by his family and friends, and enjoys his life very much. Ms. Goodwin on the other hand is genuinely virtuous—honest, just, and pure in heart. Unfortunately, because of some clever enemies, Ms. Goodwin is widely regarded as wicked. She is in prison for life, on false charges. Her family and friends, convinced that she is guilty, have turned against her. She subsists on a bread-and-water diet.[17]

Now, which of these two people is better off? Which is more fulfilled? To all appearances, it is Gladwin, not Goodwin. And note that even if virtue is of value for its own sake, it isn't the *only* thing of value. In particular, freedom is valuable too. Suppose the warden agrees to release Ms. Goodwin if (but only if) she commits one morally wrong act. (Perhaps her accounting skills enable her to steal a large sum of money for the warden.) Now, it certainly appears that it is in Ms. Goodwin's long-term best interest to act immorally in this sort of case. The choice is roughly between lifelong misery and an action that is immoral but produces relatively minor harms. So it does not seem *necessarily* true that the rewards of *perfect* virtue compensate for the rewards of wrongdoing; nor does it seem *necessarily* true that being *perfectly* virtuous is in the agent's long-term best interest. And thus, "Virtue is its own reward" does not explain how it is that the strongest reasons always favor doing your moral duty.

—Zach

Dear Zach,

Maybe we should just give up on the idea that the strongest reasons always support doing your duty.

—Thomas

Dear Thomas,

To a morally serious person, I think the suggestion that the strongest reasons do not always favor being moral is bound to be profoundly disturbing. If we sometimes have to act on the weaker reason in order to be moral, then (in one clear sense) to be moral is sometimes to be *irrational*. A morally serious person will not find that picture of morality easy to accept. Furthermore, as we've already noted, there seems to be a deep intuition to the effect that morally required actions are *somehow* always supported by overriding reasons. A theory that can "save" (i.e., account for) this intuition ought to be regarded as having significant merit.

So far our discussion has left aside any thought of life after death. But from various religious and philosophical perspectives, life after death plays a key role in explaining why the strongest reasons always favor being moral. We can give a generic version of the answer as follows:

*Hypothesis 4.* Being moral always pays in the long run, where "the long run" includes life after death.

Traditional Theists generally accept hypothesis 4. A perfectly good God clearly would not set up a moral order that ultimately penalizes moral virtue. And an all-powerful Deity is able to raise people from the dead, thus providing a life after death. So even if being virtuous does not always pay in this earthly life, if God exists, God can ensure that no one is ever penalized for being virtuous in the long run, where "the long run" includes life after death. Moreover, from the Theistic perspective, to act immorally is to sin; to sin is to alienate oneself from God; and it is never in one's long-term best interests to alienate oneself from God. In short, if a perfectly morally good and all-powerful God exists, it is never in anyone's long-term best interests to be immoral.[18]

The doctrines of reincarnation and karma also amount to an endorsement of hypothesis 4. If reincarnation occurs, then after one dies, one's soul enters another body, and so one lives another life—a life after death, not in heaven, but on Earth. According to the doctrine of karma, one's degree of moral virtue determines one's circumstances in the next life: *The more virtuous one is, the better one's circumstances in the next life.* Being moral always pays in the long run, from this perspective, and being immoral never pays in the long run.

Notice that hypothesis 4 is similar to hypothesis 1: "Being moral always promotes one's self-interest." Both tell us that *being moral pays*, although hypothesis 1 does not explicitly allow for the possibility of a life after death. Also notice that the Ms. Poore and Ms. Goodwin cases do not give us a reason to reject hypothesis 4. These sorts of cases show only that immoral actions sometimes pay in the relatively "short run," prior to death.

—Zach

Dear Zach,

Instead of accepting hypothesis 4, we could just revise our moral code, couldn't we? We could make it the case that the strongest reasons always favor morality by revising the moral code so that it is less demanding—so that it never requires that we do anything that does not promote our self-interest *in this life* (prior to death).

—Thomas

Dear Thomas,

Well, yes, we could revise the moral code. But here are some things to keep in mind. First, this approach wouldn't explain our phenomenon, the Moral Order. Rather, it would be a denial of our phenomenon, for it denies that the correct moral code is traditional in content.

Second, the idea of revising morality is apt to be disturbing to the morally serious person, for it is apt to allow significant departures from traditional morality. For example, it would tell us that it is morally permissible for Ms. Poore to steal the money. More generally, when prudential considerations are momentous and acting immorally (in a traditional sense) has relatively minor results, the code will be revised, I take it.

Third, moral thinking has its own internal standards of justification and critique. And I very much doubt that virtuous persons—persons who are wise, just, loving, and so on—are going to concur with your proposed revision of morality. The moral thinking of virtuous persons generally agrees with what I've called traditional morality. So, assuming that the moral thinking of virtuous people is generally reliable, your proposed revision of morality doesn't provide a satisfying solution to the problem.

—Zach

Dear Zach,

Well, even if we leave the phenomenon unchallenged in this case, I don't see how it gets us to God. As you yourself pointed out, we might just as well opt for reincarnation.

—Thomas

Dear Thomas,

OK, let's think about reincarnation a bit. We *could* combine Theism and reincarnation. Many Hindus do combine the two. But it's also true that many Hindus (and Buddhists) teach reincarnation but deny Theism—or at least they don't affirm Theism. And, for present purposes, it will be helpful to consider reincarnation (plus karma) as an *alternative* to Theism.

Given that reincarnation and karma hold *in the absence of any Deity*, the universe is governed not only by physical laws (such as the law of gravity) but by *impersonal* moral laws. These moral laws must be very complicated, for they have to regulate the connection between each soul's moral record in one life and that soul's total circumstances in its next life, including which body it has and the degree of happiness (and/or misery) it experiences. Accordingly, these laws must somehow take into account every act, every intention, and every choice of every moral agent and ensure that the agent receives nothing less than his or her just deserts in the next life. Now, not only is the degree of complexity and coordination involved here extraordinarily high, but the complexity *serves a moral end*, namely, justice. Such complexity can hardly be accepted as a brute fact. A highly complex order *serving a moral end* is a phenomenon that calls for explanation in terms of an intelligent cause. And if the order is on a scale far surpassing what can reasonably be attributed to human intelligence, an appeal to divine intelligence seems entirely justified. Thus, the Moral Order postulated by non-Theistic reincarnation paradoxically provides evidence for Theism.[19]

I might add that, in order to explain the Moral Order, we don't need to postulate reincarnation, karma, *and* Theism. Theism alone will be sufficient. So, on grounds of simplicity, it seems to me that Theism provides the best explanation of the Moral Order.

—Zach

Dear Zach,

But does God have to be perfectly good to guarantee the Moral Order? Won't some version of the Imperfect-Deity hypothesis work just as well?

—Thomas

Dear Thomas,

I think not. We need a guarantee that perfect virtue will always be backed by the strongest reasons. No morally imperfect Deity could be counted on to make that guarantee. For by definition such a Deity is itself less than perfect, morally speaking. Such a Deity is apt to let us down on occasion, apt to let the virtuous be penalized in some cases, and apt to let vice pay off in some cases. (I mean even in the long run).

—Zach

Dear Zach,

Fair enough. I also had this thought: How likely is it that an imperfect Deity would secure a life after death for its creatures? The more imperfect the Deity is, the less concerned it would be with righting wrongs, ameliorating tragedies, and securing the ultimate fulfillment of each person. An imperfect Deity might not care enough to secure a life after death or might secure it only for some, play favorites, and so on.

—Thomas

Dear Thomas,

That seems right to me. All in all, the situation seems to be this. *The Moral Order* is a plausible thesis. But Naturalistic attempts to account for it are unsatisfactory. Theism, on the other hand, readily accounts for it. Thus, the Moral Order supports Theism over Naturalism. More formally:

**Premise 1**. Theism has a far higher prior probability than Naturalism does. (I assume the relevant version of Naturalism is at least as complex as MUH Naturalism *supplemented with the Moral Standard thesis*. Premise 1 is established not only by comparing the relative complexity of the two hypotheses, but by taking into account Theism's success in explaining the presence of (a) our life-supporting universe and (b) free will. In other words, fine-tuning and free will now count as part of the background evidence.)

**Premise 2**. Theism does a better job of leading us to expect the Moral Order than Naturalism does.

**Conclusion**: Theism explains the Moral Order better than Naturalism does; hence, the Moral Order provides evidence in favor of Theism over Naturalism.

This moral argument is the last of my arguments for the existence of God. So let me briefly sum up my cumulative case for Theism: A consideration of religious experience and the Cosmological Argument leave Theism and Naturalism on a par. But the design argument and the argument from free will provide significant support for Theism over Naturalism. The phenomenon of evil, commonly thought to provide evidence for Naturalism over Theism, supports neither of these hypotheses over the other. The Moral Order provides further evidence for Theism over Naturalism. Therefore, in the end, it seems to me that the preponderance of evidence favors Theism over Naturalism.

I don't wish to suggest that the evidence *overwhelmingly* favors Theism. I don't pretend to have offered "knockdown" arguments. Such arguments are rare or nonexistent in philosophy. But I do think the evidence favors Theism, all things considered.

Your friend,<br>Zach

Dear Zach,

You've given me a lot to think about! As you know, I'm not a person that changes his mind very easily or often, so, frankly, I'm still in a state of doubt. I can't affirm that the preponderance of evidence favors Theism over Naturalism.

But I will admit this much: You've convinced me that Theism has a lot more going for it than I supposed. In fact, I hope to look back over our correspondence from time to time. And when I do, I'll send you any further reflections or questions that come to mind.

I hope this note finds you in good health and good spirits.

All my best,
Thomas

# Notes

## Introduction

1. This point about a double standard with regard to religious beliefs is made with great force in Peter van Inwagen, "It Is Wrong, Everywhere, Always, and for Anyone, to Believe Anything upon Insufficient Evidence," in Jeff Jordan and Daniel Howard-Snyder, eds., *Faith, Freedom, and Rationality* (Lanham, MD: Rowman and Littlefield, 1996), 137–53.

2. I am not here claiming that a person's religious beliefs *must* be based on arguments in order to be rational or warranted. One issue in this connection is the extent to which religious experience (as opposed to arguments) can warrant religious belief (or make it rational). Another issue is the extent to which religious beliefs may be accepted on authority. The general relationship between "faith" and "reason" is not the subject of this book. But even if arguments are not needed to make religious belief rational (or warranted), I suggest that persons of sufficient intelligence have a moral responsibility to examine such arguments (unless weightier responsibilities make this impossible). It seems to me that with respect to our ultimate commitments, we have a moral duty to seek the truth, and examining the main arguments concerning the existence of God is surely one aspect of such seeking. For a discussion of differing views of the relation between "faith" and "reason," see Richard Swinburne, *Faith and Reason* (Oxford: Clarendon Press, 1981), and Alvin Plantinga, *Warranted Christian Belief* (New York: Oxford University Press, 2000).

3. Two hypotheses might be equal in prior probability and also equal in explanatory power. Does it follow that the two explanations are

equally good? For present purposes I shall assume so, but some would argue that there can be reasons, in addition to prior probability and explanatory power, for preferring one hypothesis to another. These alleged additional reasons do not, in my view, make a difference in regard to the arguments considered in this book, and so I shall ignore such reasons. (An example of such an additional reason is *fruitfulness*, which a hypothesis has if it leads us to new discoveries.) For a brief discussion of what makes a scientific hypothesis good, see Del Ratzsch, *Science and Its Limits* (Downers Grove, IL: InterVarsity Press, 2000), 38–72.

4. To test his hypothesis that mosquitoes spread yellow fever, Reed proceeded by placing volunteers in a mosquito-proof room divided into two spaces by a mosquito net. Reed then released some mosquitoes *known to have bitten persons with yellow fever* into one of the spaces. The mosquitoes bit the volunteer in that space and he developed yellow fever shortly thereafter, but the volunteers in the other space did not develop yellow fever. See Irving M. Copi and Carl Cohen, *Introduction to Logic*, 10th edition (Upper Saddle River, NJ: Prentice Hall, 1998), 509.

5. I am following Richard Swinburne in emphasizing a distinction between scientific and personal explanations. See Richard Swinburne, *The Existence of God* (Oxford: Clarendon Press, 1979), 25–46. Swinburne uses the term *inanimate* rather than the term *scientific*.

# 1. Theism and Naturalism

1. The material in these "lecture notes" appears in the Introduction. Zach and Thomas frequently allude to this material in what follows.

2. For discussions of divine power, see Richard Swinburne, *The Coherence of Theism* (Oxford: Clarendon Press, 1977), 149–61, and Peter Geach, "Omnipotence," *Philosophy*, v. 48 (Jan. 1973), 7–20. The latter is anthologized in William L. Rowe and William J. Wainwright, eds., *Philosophy of Religion: Selected Readings*, 2nd edition (New York: Harcourt, Brace, Jovanovich, 1989), 63–76.

3. For a justly famous discussion of omniscience and freedom, see Nelson Pike, "Divine Omniscience and Voluntary Action," *The Philosophical Review*, v. 74, n. 1 (January 1965). We shall take up this issue in Chapter 6.

4. Some have argued that miracles are impossible, on the following grounds: (1) Laws of nature are true universal generalizations, i.e., of the form "All A are B." (Example: "All people dead for a week stay dead." (2) A miracle is an exception to a law of nature. (3) A universal generalization is not true if there are exceptions to it, i.e., if "at least

one A is not a B." So miracles are impossible. I think this argument fails, at least in part because a law of nature is a generalization about what happens when *merely natural* causes are at work. If a supernatural cause brings about an event, it is thus not an exception to a law of *nature*.

5. It is common enough to meet people who suggest that contradictions may sometimes be true. In my experience, few who make this suggestion realize the enormity of it from a logical and philosophical point of view. Some points to bear in mind: First, in any sort of practical thinking, we always reject contradictions as false. (Just think of jurors evaluating conflicting testimony from eyewitnesses in a court of law.) Second, if we allow that contradictions are sometimes true, on what basis do we say they are usually (or even sometimes) false? How do we tell a true contradiction from a false one? If you are tempted to say, "Just look at the evidence," consider the next point. Third, any examination of evidence presupposes that contradictions are false. Evidence *for* statement A (e.g., "Al stole the TV") is automatically and rightly taken as evidence *against* not-A ("Al did not steal the TV"). Thus, there is no point in basing one's views on evidence unless one presupposes that contradictions are false. Fourth, if you hold that *contradictions are sometimes true*, do you infer that *contradictions are never true* is false? Presumably the answer is yes. But doesn't that inference depend on the assumption that both statements cannot be true because they're contradictory? If so, you've no right to the inference because your premise denies the basis for it. Finally, within classical logic, any contradiction can easily be shown to imply *every* proposition—see C. Stephen Layman, *The Power of Logic*, 3rd ed. (New York: McGraw-Hill, 2005), 289–90, 348.

6. Thomas Nagel, *Mortal Questions* (London: Cambridge University Press, 1979), 183.

7. This characterization of the physical is inspired by a discussion of physical causation in William Hasker, *The Emergent Self* (Ithaca, NY: Cornell University Press, 1999), 62–63.

8. Larry Witham, *Where Darwin Meets the Bible: Creationists and Evolutionists in America* (New York: Oxford University Press, 2002), 272.

9. This is a slightly modified version of a principle formulated by Daniel Howard-Snyder, "God, Evil, and Suffering," in Michael J. Murray, ed., *Reason for the Hope Within* (Grand Rapids, MI: Eermans, 1999), 84.

10. My list of the facets of simplicity is substantially borrowed from Richard Swinburne, *Simplicity As Evidence of Truth* (Milwaukee: Marquette University Press, 1997), 23–27. But I have altered this material for my own purposes, especially as regards the fourth facet of simplicity, and I have also omitted *as irrelevant for present purposes* some of Swinburne's facets of simplicity, e.g., facets concerning the *mathematics* used in certain scientific hypotheses.

11. *Merriam–Webster's Collegiate Dictionary*, 10th ed. (Springfield, MA: 1999), 939.

12. Using "Prob" as shorthand for "the probability of," we can state this principle succinctly as follows: Prob(A & B) = Prob(A) × Prob(B if A). For a short introduction to probability, see Layman, "Probability," *op. cit.*, Chapter 11, 489–516.

13. We can explain this in terms of the general conjunction rule: Let A stand for our hypothesis and B stand for the statement we wish to add to it. If B follows *necessarily* from A, then the probability that (B is true if A is true) = 1. In that case, the probability of "A and B" = the probability of A *times* 1 = the probability of A.

14. Again, we can explain this in terms of the general conjunction rule: Let A stand for our hypothesis and let B stand for the statement we wish to add to it. If the probability of B = 1 and B's probability is unaffected by A, then the probability of (B is true if A is true) = 1. In this sort of case, once again, the probability of "A and B" = the probability of A *times* 1 = the probability of A.

15. My wording of the principle of credulity owes a debt to Richard Swinburne, *The Existence of God*, rev. ed. (Oxford: Clarendon Press, 1991), 254. Here's another example of a principle that appears unprovable but is an important principle of thought: "The future will resemble the past (in such a way as to support inductive inferences)." There seems to be no way to prove this principle, but we presuppose it in making ordinary inductive inferences such as: "All lemons tasted in the past have been sour; hence the next lemon to be tasted will be sour."

16. For a discussion of the difficulties in proving the reliability of sense experience, see William Alston, *Perceiving God* (Ithaca, NY: Cornell University Press, 1991), Chapter 3 ("The Reliability of Sense Perception: A Case Study").

17. This example is inspired by one offered in Swinburne, *Simplicity, op. cit.*, 45.

18. For an excellent recent example of Perfect Being Theology, see Thomas V. Morris, *Our Idea of God: An Introduction to Philosophical Theology* (Downers Grove, IL: InterVarsity Press, 1991). I am not suggesting that Morris claims that Perfect Being theology yields a simpler version of Theism. But this claim has been made in conversations with other philosophers and I think it's worth exploring.

19. Morris, *op. cit.*, 35.

20. See Michael C. Rea, *World Without Design: The Ontological Consequences of Naturalism* (Oxford: Clarendon Press, 2002), 15. For example, Rea claims that Naturalists typically regard their view as one that developments in science could never refute, but, on the other hand, Naturalists "are united at least in part by methodological dispositions that preclude

allegiance to views that cannot be called into question by further developments in science" (51).

21. Alvin Plantinga, *Warrant and Proper Function* (New York: Oxford University Press, 1993), 216–37. Also see Alvin Plantinga, "Naturalism Defeated" (unpublished, 1994), available online at: http://www.homestead.com/philofreligion/files/alspaper.htm. For critical discussion of Plantinga's argument, see James Beilby, ed., *Naturalism Defeated? Essays on Plantinga's Evolutionary Argument Against Naturalism* (Ithaca, NY: Cornell University Press, 2002). Also see Branden Fitelson and Elliott Sober, "Plantinga's Probability Arguments against Evolutionary Naturalism," in Robert T. Pennock, ed., *Intelligent Design Creationism and Its Critics* (Cambridge, MA: MIT Press, 2001), 411–27.

22. Letter to William Graham, Down, July 3, 1881, in *The Life and Letters of Charles Darwin, Including an Autobiographical Chapter*, ed. Francis Darwin (London: John Murray, Albermarle Street, 1887), 1:315–16, as quoted in Plantinga, *Warrant and Proper Function*, 219.

23. Plantinga, *Warrant and Proper Function*, 225.

## 2. Religious Experience and Interpretation

1. William James, *The Varieties of Religious Experience* (New York.: New American Library, 1958), 68.

2. *Ibid.*, 63.

3. *Ibid.*, 302. James ascribes this quotation to a Mr. Trine, *In Tune with the Infinite*, 137.

4. Timothy Beardsworth, *A Sense of Presence* (Oxford: Religious Experience Research Unit, 1977), 121.

5. *Ibid.*, 121.

6. *Ibid.*, 121–22.

7. *Ibid.*, 121.

8. *Ibid.*, 122.

9. Evelyn Underhill, *Mysticism: The Nature and Development of Spiritual Consciousness* (Oxford: Oneworld Publications, 1999 [first published, 1910]), 242.

10. *Ibid.*, 242–43.

11. Simone Weil, *Waiting for God* (New York: Harper, 1951), 24.

12. *Ibid.*, 69.

13. Brother Lawrence, *The Practice of the Presence of God* (Springdale, PA: Whitaker House, 1982), 17.

14. My suggested Principle of Credulity is inspired by Richard Swinburne, *The Existence of God*, rev. ed. (Oxford: Clarendon Press, 1991), 254.

15. For detailed discussion of the circularity of attempts to prove the relia-
    bility of sense experience, see William Alston, *Perceiving God* (Ithaca,
    NY: Cornell University Press, 1991), 102–45.

16. The importance of avoiding an arbitrary, unjustified double standard
    in thinking about sense experience and religious experienced is em-
    phasized by Alston, *op. cit.*, 249–50.

17. Coherentists claim that we do need arguments (inferential support)
    for all our beliefs. But a discussion of coherentism would take us too
    far afield. For a defense of coherentism, see Laurence BonJour, *The
    Structure of Empirical Knowledge* (Cambridge, MA: Harvard University
    Press, 1985). If all our beliefs must be justified by inference from other
    beliefs, then if any belief is justified, we must apparently accept either
    (a) an infinite regress of supporting beliefs or (b) circular reasoning.
    Both (a) and (b) seem problematic. Be that as it may, even coherentists
    will agree that, for practical purposes, we have to start somewhere
    when we argue. So they can view my proposed Starting Principle as
    appropriate for practical purposes.

18. My suggested Principle of Testimony is inspired by Richard Swin-
    burne, *Faith and Reason* (Oxford: Clarendon Press, 1981), 40–41.

19. Throughout the remainder of this chapter, I borrow heavily from Al-
    ston, *op.cit.* However, I have modified this material to suit my own
    purposes, and so I must take responsibility for any errors in the pre-
    sentation.

20. *Ibid.*, 35–43, 186–87.

21. *Ibid.*, 59–60.

22. Isaiah 6:1–5 provides a classic example of a religious experience in-
    volving visual imagery.

23. The key points in this paragraph are due to Alston, *op. cit.*, 44–45.

24. For the main point in this paragraph I'm indebted to Alston, *ibid.*, 96.

# 3. Is Religious Experience Reliable?

1. Here and throughout this chapter I often borrow points from William
   Alston, *Perceiving God* (Ithaca, NY: Cornell University Press, 1991). The
   example of the musically gifted person is borrowed from Alston, 254.

2. *Ibid.*, 203. Alston attributes the criteria to Joseph de Guibert, S.J., *The
   Theology of the Spiritual Life* (New York: Sheed and Ward, 1953).

3. My reasoning concerning an evil God owes a debt to Alvin Plantinga,
   *Warrant and Proper Function* (New York: Oxford University Press, 1993),
   216–37. See also Alvin Plantinga, "Naturalism Defeated" (unpublished,
   1994): http://www.homestead.com/philofreligion/files/alspaper.htm.

4. The example of epiphenomenalism is borrowed from Plantinga, *Warrant and Proper Function*, 223.

5. Thomas' objection here is similar to one offered by W. J. Talbott, "The Illusion of Defeat," in James Beilby, ed., *Naturalism Defeated? Essays on Plantinga's Evolutionary Argument Against Naturalism* (Ithaca, NY: Cornell University Press, 2002), 153–64.

6. The example is borrowed from Alvin Plantinga, "Reply to Beilby's Cohorts," in Beilby, *op. cit.*, 207.

7. Andrew Newberg, Eugene D'Aquili, and Vince Rause, *Why God Won't Go Away: Brain Science and the Biology of Belief* (New York: Ballantine Books, 2001).

8. *Ibid.*, 121–22.

9. William James, *The Varieties of Religious Experience* (New York: New American Library, 1958), 322.

10. *Upanishads*, trans. M. Muller, ii, 17, 334, as quoted in James, *op. cit.*, 321.

11. Sarvepalli Radhakrishnan and Charles A. Moore, *A Source Book in Indian Philosophy* (Princeton, NJ: Princeton University Press, 1957), 508, 545–46, 555–71.

12. *Ibid.*, 550. Ramanuja offers a series of arguments against the idea that no distinctions are real, 543–55.

13. *The Koran*, trans. J. M. Rodwell (London: Everyman, Orion Publishing Group, 1909, 1994), 429.

14. If we believe that quarks exist, we do so, not because anyone has directly observed them, but because the theories involving quarks have tremendous explanatory power.

# 4. A Cosmological Argument

1. This definition is adapted from Laurence BonJour, *In Defense of Pure Reason* (New York: Cambridge University Press, 1998), 32.

2. It is often supposed that quantum mechanics involves the claim that some events occur uncaused, e.g., the decay of a particular atom of radium. But even the smallest physical particles presumably behave as they do because of built-in tendencies. Although these tendencies may not *guarantee* a particular result, it seems to me that they must be counted as controlling (hence causal) factors within the physical realm.

3. This formulation of the link between *necessary being* and *necessary truth* is borrowed from William L. Rowe, "The Nature and Attributes of God," William L. Rowe and William J. Wainwright, eds., *Philosophy of Religion: Selected Reading*, 2nd ed. (New York: Harcourt Brace Jovanovich, 1989), 2.

4. David Hume, *Dialogues Concerning Natural Religion*, ed., Richard H. Popkin (Indianapolis, IN: Hackett, 1980), Part IX, 55.

5. Saul A. Kripke, *Naming and Necessity* (Cambridge, MA: Harvard University Press, 1972), 116–29.

6. Strictly speaking, the necessary truth in question is "If water exists, then water is $H_2O$," since it seems logically possible that there be no water at all. But with this understanding, Kripke's examples show that Hume's view of necessity is highly dubious, at best.

7. Hume, *op. cit.*, 55.

8. Paul Davies, "A Naturalistic Account of the Universe," in Michael Peterson, William Hasker, Bruce Reichenbach, and David Basinger, eds., *Philosophy of Religion*, 2nd ed. (New York: Oxford University Press, 2001), 240.

9. Hume, *op. cit.*, 56.

10. Davies, *op. cit.*, provides some elaboration along this line, e.g., "empty space itself exploded under the repulsive power of the quantum vacuum" (236). In this highly speculative work, Davies seems to regard the fundamental laws of physics as the ultimate reality: "the physical universe blossomed forth spontaneously out of nothing, driven by the laws of physics" (240). This is puzzling because laws of nature are typically regarded as grounded in the tendencies of physical entities (objects, states, fields, energy, quantum vacua, etc.). What would make such laws true in the absence of any physical reality? Moreover, to put it mildly, it is deeply puzzling how the mere presence of abstract truths could account for the existence of physical objects. Finally, if the claim is that the fundamental laws of physics are necessary truths, then the claim is emphatically philosophical and not within the province of science—no observation or experiment could possibly show that the laws of nature are necessary truths. In addition, various current cosmological hypotheses, such as some forms of the many-universe hypothesis, presuppose that the laws of nature may differ from one universe to another (and hence are not necessary).

11. Hume, *op. cit.*, 56.

12. This response is due in its essentials to William L. Rowe, *Philosophy of Religion: An Introduction*, 2nd ed. (Belmont, CA: Wadsworth, 1993), 24.

13. My response here owes a debt to Robert C. Koons, "A New Look at the Cosmological Argument," *American Philosophical Quarterly*, v. 34, n. 2 (April 1997), 197–98.

14. The distinction between contingent facts and contingent beings was suggested to me by the discussion of facts in Koons, op. cit., 194–95. However, I've modified this material for my own purposes and must take responsibility for any errors in the reasoning.

15. The idea that a cosmological argument need not employ the Principle of Sufficient Reason is well worked out in Bernard D. Katz and Elmar

J. Kremer, "The Cosmological Argument Without the Principle of Sufficient Reason," *Faith and Philosophy*, v. 14, n. 1 (January 1997), 62–70. For a critical discussion of the Principle of Sufficient Reason, see William J. Wainwright, *Philosophy of Religion* (Belmont, CA: Wadsworth, 1988), 44–47. Also see Peter van Inwagen, *An Essay on Free Will* (Oxford: Clarendon Press, 1983), 202–03. The gist of van Inwagen's argument is as follows: If the Principle of Sufficient Reason is true, then there is a sufficient reason for every fact. If $x$ is a sufficient reason for $y$, then $x$ necessarily implies $y$. And no contingent fact is a sufficient reason for itself. Now, let $P$ be a giant conjunction of *all* the contingent truths. $P$ is a contingent fact. Is there as sufficient reason for $P$? Such a sufficient reason must be either a necessary truth or a contingent truth. It cannot be a contingent truth, because all the contingent truths have been included in $P$. And the alleged sufficient reason cannot be a necessary truth either: If a necessary truth necessarily implies $P$, then $P$ is a necessary truth. But $P$ is contingent. Hence, there is no sufficient reason for $P$ and the Principle of Sufficient Reason is not true. (*Note:* Some of the inferences here belong to modal logic, the logic of necessity and possibility. For an introduction to modal logic, see my "Modal Logic" at www.mhhe.com/layman2. Click on "Student Resources" and then on "Modal Logic Chapter.")

16. Process theologians hold that God did not create the universe *ex nihilo* (out of nothing). Rather, God forms a preexisting and recalcitrant material into the universe we observe. God's power over this preexisting material is limited, and the limitations of God's power explain the presence of suffering and evil.

# 5. A Design Argument

1. Paul Davies, *The Accidental Universe* (Cambridge: Cambridge University Press, 1982), 89–91. $1/10^{60}$ may also be written $10^{-60}$.

2. Paul Davies, *Superforce: The Search for a Grand Unified Theory of Nature* (New York: Simon & Schuster, 1984), 242.

3. This point and the next are taken from Ernan McMullin, "Fine-Tuning the Universe?," *Science, Technology, and Religious Ideas*, eds., Mark H. Shale and George W. Shields (New York: University Press of America, 1994), 113.

4. Max Tegmark, "Parallel Universes," *Scientific American* (May 2003), 46.

5. McMullin, *op. cit.*, 113.

6. Hugh Ross, *The Creator and the Cosmos*, 3rd expanded ed. (Colorado Springs, CO: NavPress, 1993). For a more rigorous and detailed discussion of fine-tuning, see John Leslie, *Universes* (New York: Routledge, 1989), especially Chapters 2 and 3. Here's a partial list of the

parameters: the mass of the electron, electron-neutrino, up-quark, and down-quark; the mass of the muon, muon-neutrino, charm quark, and strange quark; the mass of the tau particle, tau-neutrino, top-quark, and bottom-quark; the mass of the gluon, photon, and weak gauge bosons; and the relative strengths of the strong, electroweak, and gravitational forces. The precise number of independent parameters listed in the literature varies, depending on the theoretical orientation of the author.

7. Brian Greene, *The Elegant Universe: Superstrings, Hidden Dimensions, and the Quest for the Ultimate Theory* (New York: Norton, 1999), 122.

8. The list that follows is borrowed from Del Ratzsch, *Science and Its Limits*, 2nd ed. (Downers Grove, IL: InterVarsity Press, 2000), 92–99.

9. Some would include the Strong Anthropic Principle (SAP) in this list. According to SAP, *any actual universe must contain observers* (and hence life). The idea is that quantum events (e.g., the motion of a quark) are indeterminate unless observed, and universes involve many quantum events, so universes can be actual only if, at some point in their histories, conscious observers are present. I think SAP is fundamentally misguided, for at least two reasons. (1) The laws of physics do not presuppose *conscious* observers. Unconscious detection devices can play the role of a conscious observer in any of the experiments used to support contemporary physical theory. (2) SAP implies that cosmic events in general depend on observers. After all, the motions of stars and galaxies, and presumably the origin of the universe itself, involve quantum events. But it strains credulity to suppose that cosmic events in general could not occur in the absence of human (or similar) observers. Many cosmic events occur at distances beyond the range of human observation and many of them occurred billions of years before humans evolved. For more about SAP, see John A. Peacock, *Cosmological Physics* (Cambridge: Cambridge University Press, 1999), Section 3.5, available at http://nedwww.ipac.caltech.edu/level5/Peacock/Peacock3_5.html.

10. Recall that clause 4 is needed if Naturalism is to compete with Theism as an explanation of contingent beings. Since "the form our universe takes" includes quantum physics, clauses 2 through 4 of Single-Universe Naturalism ensure the existence of contingent beings. For example, the atoms in radioactive substances are contingent since they decay at a specifiable rate.

11. The objection summarized in this paragraph is developed in detail in Gilbert Fulmer, "A Fatal Flaw in Anthropic Principle Design Arguments," *International Journal for the Philosophy of Religion*, 49 (2001), 101–10. The crux of Fulmer's objection is that the "APDA [Anthropic Principle Design Argument] depends on the claim that we can know it is very improbable that other universes, with different laws or constants, could support life. Therefore, to refute the APDA I need only

show that we cannot know this" (104). While many proponents of design arguments do make the claim Fulmer indicates, my argument does not depend on it.

12. If the number of possible universes is *infinite*, there is an initial technical problem in speaking of a large percentage of the possible universes. Suppose we assign a natural number {1, 2, 3, . . .} to each universe. If the even-numbered universes are life-supporting, we might be tempted to say that half the universes are life-supporting. But that's not right, for a little reflection reveals that the "number" of even integers is the same as the "number" of integers—infinite. (In other words, the set of even integers is not half the size of the set of integers, but the same size.) However, mathematicians have ways of putting a measure on an infinite set, so we need not get bogged down in this technical issue.

13. Tegmark, *op. cit.*, 46.

14. Del Ratzsch, "Saturation, World Ensembles, and Design: Death by a Thousand Multiplications?" *Faith and Philosophy* (forthcoming, 2007), 6. Compare John Polkinghorne, *Science and Theology: An Introduction* (Minneapolis, MN: 1998), "[In] Many-universes quantum theory . . . worlds differ only in the outcomes of quantum processes and not in basic physical laws," 39.

15. Polkinghorne, *op. cit.*, 39.

16. Tegmark, *op. cit.*, 41–42.

17. *Ibid.*, 50.

18. Greene, *op. cit.*, 368.

19. In scientific writing the distinction between *being directly observable* and *being empirically testable* is not always kept clear. Quarks are not directly observable, but the hypothesis that they exist generates predictions involving observable phenomena; in that sense the existence of quarks is open to empirical tests. Similarly, universes distinct from ours are not directly observable, but conceivably the hypothesis of other universes might predict observable phenomena.

20. To the charge of contrivance, a reviewer noted that at least one philosopher, David Lewis, has postulated an infinity of universes in an attempt to explain modal phenomena (necessity and possibility). However, very few philosophers have found Lewis' ontology compelling. Here's one reason why. Presumably, President G. W. Bush *could* have been a marine. To employ the philosophical idiom, there is a possible world (universe) in which Bush is a marine. But Lewis is forced to deny this. According to Lewis, there are other universes containing persons similar to, but not identical with, Bush. With different bodies in distinct locations (universes) as well as various additional differences (e.g., in thoughts or actions), these so-called *counterparts* of Bush could be his "twins," but they could not be numerically the same person. (Indeed, the assumption that Bush's counterparts are identical

with Bush leads to contradictions such as "Bush is a marine while not being a marine.") According to Lewis, to say that *Bush could have been a marine* is to say that he has a counterpart in some actual universe who is a marine. But this is clearly mistaken, like claiming that "You could be a marine" means (or is equivalent to) "You have a twin who is a marine." Thus, Lewis' attempt to explain modal concepts by postulating an infinity of universes does not look promising. See David K. Lewis, "Counterpart Theory and Quantified Modal Logic," *Journal of Philosophy* 65 (1968), 113–26.

21. That Theism can be modified in this way was pointed out to me by Robin Collins in email correspondence.

22. In this paragraph I am borrowing heavily from Ratzsch, *op. cit.*, 4. Ratzsch briefly describes four contemporary hypotheses regarding a universe generator: "The first involves Hugh Everett's many-worlds interpretation of quantum mechanics, according to which each possible alternative at each quantum juncture is actually realized, each 'world' splitting at that point into distinct paths, each path characterized by one of the alternative values of the quantum event in question. The second involves John Wheeler's oscillating-universe model, with a new universe (or family of such) emerging out of each collapse of the preceding cycle. The third involves Edward Tryon's picture of universes being generated as quantum bubbles out of vacuum nonhomogeneities within a larger quantum vacuum domain. The fourth involves inflationary cosmologies, e.g., Andrei Linde's chaotic-inflation model, in which multiple independent, isolated, and variant domains ('universes') coalesce out of different symmetry breakings in the early instants of cosmic inflation" (4).

23. Chapter 3 ("Is Religious Experience Reliable?") explains how hypotheses concerning morally flawed deities can undermine human knowing.

## 6. An Argument from Free Will

1. Marilyn McCord Adams, *Horrendous Evils and the Goodness of God* (Ithaca, NY: Cornell University Press, 1999), 180.

2. My characterization of free will is borrowed in its essentials from Peter van Inwagen, *An Essay on Free Will* (New York: Oxford University Press, 1983), 8.

3. *Ibid.*, 2.

4. Throughout this chapter I use phrases such as "governed by the laws of nature" and "the operation of the laws of nature." This sort of language is admittedly loose. Strictly speaking, laws of nature are propositions, generalizations about the behavior of physical objects. But pre-

sumably these generalizations are true because of inherent tendencies of the fundamental physical entities. So I employ phrases such as "governed by the laws of nature" and "the operation of the laws of nature" as shorthand for the operation of the mechanistic causal powers of the fundamental physical entities (whatever those entities turn out to be). Recall that mechanistic factors are nonpurposive and nonvolitional, such as the force of gravity and the positive charge of a proton.

5. For example, John Martin Fischer, *The Metaphysics of Free Will: An Essay on Control* (Cambridge, MA: Blackwell, 1994), 163.

6. The argument here is borrowed from van Inwagen, *op. cit.*, 56.

7. I wish to thank Noel Hendrickson for advice in characterizing what I call *mechanism*. However, because I have adapted his suggestions, I must take responsibility for any flaws in the presentation.

8. This letter owes a debt to Timothy O'Connor, "The Agent as Cause," in Peter van Inwagen and Dean W. Zimmerman, eds., *Metaphysics: The Big Questions* (Oxford: Blackwell, 1998), 375.

9. I do not claim that all our moral beliefs would be false if we lack moral responsibility. For a careful discussion of which moral beliefs could still be true even if we lack moral responsibility, see Derk Pereboom, *Living Without Free Will* (Cambridge: Cambridge University Press, 2001), 141–57.

10. My response here owes a heavy debt to Pereboom, *op. cit.*, 94–100.

11. Marcia Johnson, "Genetic Technology and Its Impact on Culpability for Criminal Actions," *Cleveland State Law Review* (Cleveland, OH: Cleveland State University, 1998), 11. Available online at: http://www .law.umkc.edu/faculty/projects/ftrials/leoploeb/darrowclosing.html http://64.233.167.104/search?q=cache:TjOygLGVqL0J:www.earlcarl .org/publications/geneticTechnology.pdf+%22determinism+defense %22&hl=en.

12. The computer example is borrowed from Daniel C. Dennett, "Mechanism and Responsibility," in Gary Watson, ed., *Free Will* (New York: Oxford University Press, 1982), 150–73.

13. See van Inwagen, *op.cit.*, 109.

14. The example is a slightly altered version of one described by John Locke, *An Essay Concerning Human Understanding*, ed. Peter H. Nidditch (Oxford: Clarendon Press, 1975), Book II, Chapter XXI, 238.

15. Harry Frankfurt, "Alternate Possibilities and Moral Responsibility," *The Journal of Philosophy*, v. LXVI, n. 23 (Dec. 4, 1969), 829–39. Many different Frankfurt cases appear in the literature, developed by different philosophers. Pereboom's discussion of the Frankfurt cases is especially clear and insightful, as is the treatment found in William Hasker, *The Emergent Self* (Ithaca, NY: Cornell University Press, 1999), 86–94.

16. Pereboom, *op. cit.*, 18.

17. The analysis here is borrowed in its essentials from Robert Kane, *The Significance of Free Will* (New York: Oxford University Press, 1996), 42.

18. Leon Glass and Michael C. Mackey, *From Clocks to Chaos: The Rhythms of Life* (Princeton, NJ: Princeton University Press, 1988). My response here owes a debt to Kane, *op. cit.*, 129.

19. Pereboom, *op. cit.*, 85. Kant's noumenal selves are not in space and not in time. And since there is no causal relation between Kant's noumenal selves and events in the phenomenal realm (the physical world), any coincidence between our mental states (e.g., choices) and events in the physical world seems an amazing piece of luck.

20. *Ibid.*, 86.

21. Timothy O'Connor, *Persons and Causes: The Metaphysics of Free Will* (New York: Oxford University Press, 2000), 114.

22. Necessity Naturalism says: (1) There is a self-organizing physical reality, (2) some part (or aspect) of physical reality exists of necessity, (3) the necessary part (or aspect) of physical reality generates additional parts or aspects of physical reality in a contingent manner (not of necessity), and (4) leaving aside possible special cases (e.g., sets or numbers), all entities are physical entities.

23. If the statement added to a hypothesis has a probability of 1, then it can be added without decreasing the prior probability of the hypothesis. Similarly, if the statement added is logically entailed by other statements in the hypothesis, then it can be added without decreasing the prior probability of the hypothesis. See Chapter 1, notes 13 and 14, for an explanation of these points about probability.

24. I am not here (implicitly) denying the *possibility* that free will evolved. But the question is not whether free will is possible, given Naturalism, but whether Naturalism *leads us to expect* the presence of free will in the world.

25. The argument here is a simplified version of a very influential argument put forward by Nelson Pike, "Divine Omniscience and Voluntary Action," *Philosophical Review,* v. 74 (1965), 27–46.

26. I am here assuming that what a maximally powerful being knows, it knows infallibly. The foreknowledge argument never gets off the ground if God's knowledge is regarded as fallible.

27. Those concerned with traditional Theism might consider this type of scenario in the light of certain Bible passages, such as, Exodus 11:10, where God is said to "harden Pharaoh's heart" (apparently causing Pharaoh to refuse to let the children of Israel leave Egypt).

28. It's worth noting here that divine infallible foreknowledge is not taught in any of the official creeds of the Christian faith. For a thorough defense of Open Theism, see William Hasker, *God, Time and*

*Knowledge* (Ithaca, NY: Cornell University Press, 1989). Also see, Richard Swinburne, *The Coherence of Theism* (Oxford: Clarendon Press, 1977), 162–78.

29. This point is borrowed from Alvin Plantinga, "On Ockham's Way Out," *Faith and Philosophy*, v. 3, n. 3 (July 1986), 239.

30. Scott Davison, "Divine Providence and Human Freedom," in Michael J. Murray, ed., *Reason for the Hope Within* (Grand Rapids, MI: Eerdmans, 1999), 233.

31. Philosophers call such conditionals *counterfactuals of freedom* because (a) the if–clauses are contrary to fact and (b) the then–clauses describe an act that an agent would perform freely.

32. Throughout this paragraph I have borrowed heavily from Davison, *op. cit.*, 232–33.

33. Richard Swinburne, *Providence and the Problem of Evil* (Oxford: Clarendon Press, 1998), 133. Also see Hasker, *op. cit.*, 96–115, for a thorough critique of the middle knowledge solution.

34. Proponents of middle knowledge may claim, however, that certain Biblical passages indicate that God has it, for example, "Woe to you, Bethsaida! for if the mighty works done in you had been done in Tyre and Sidon, they would have repented long ago," Luke 10:13 (RSV). But (1) this passage may be taken as a vivid rhetorical device rather than as a literal assertion of middle knowledge, and (2) it plainly concerns actual historical peoples, with a moral track record, as opposed to as-yet-nonexistent persons or merely possible persons who will never exist.

35. Swinburne, *op. cit.*, 256.

## 7. Theism and Evil

1. A plant can be damaged, of course, but I assume that plants cannot feel pain, since they lack a nervous system.

2. The strategy employed in this chapter and the next may be called the *comparative approach* to the problem of evil, since it essentially involves comparing Theistic and Naturalistic explanations of evil. See C. Stephen Layman, "Moral Evil: The Comparative Response," *International Journal for Philosophy of Religion*, v. 53 (February 2003), 1–23, and "Natural Evil: The Comparative Response," *International Journal for Philosophy of Religion*, v. 54 (August 2003), 1–31.

3. Here I am borrowing from Daniel Howard-Snyder, "God, Evil, and Suffering," in Michael J. Murray, ed., *Reason for the Hope Within* (Grand Rapids, MI: Eerdmans, 1999), 84.

4. In developing my Theistic explanations of evil I borrow heavily from Richard Swinburne, *Providence and the Problem of Evil* (New York: Oxford University Press, 1998), 125–59. However, I am adapting this material for my own purposes, and so I must take responsibility for any errors.

5. According to certain forms of Theism, God *fully* causes everything that happens in the created realm. These forms of Theism deny that creatures have free will, in the incompatibilist sense, and special problems result. For example, if God fully causes everything that happens in the created realm, then God fully causes each instance of moral wrongdoing. But moral wrongdoing is also sin, i.e., offense to God. Now, if I *fully* cause Val to kill Pete, I'm the one to blame, not Val; Val is just a tool in my hands. So a God who causes humans to sin would seem to be morally blameworthy and hence not perfectly good. Furthermore, such a God causes sin while (presumably) condemning it, which seems both hypocritical and irrational. Finally, if such a God holds the creatures accountable for sin, he seems unjust. For an intriguing exploration of theological determinism and the problem of evil, see Derk Pereboom, "Free Will, Evil, and Divine Providence," in Andrew Chignell and Andrew Dole, eds., *God and the Ethics of Belief: New Essays in Philosophy of Religion* (Cambridge: Cambridge University Press, 2005), 77–98.

6. For a discussion of the Augustinian and Irenaean accounts of the fall, see John Hick, *Philosophy of Religion*, 4th ed. (Englewood Cliffs, NJ: Prentice Hall, 1990), 41–48.

7. For the Biblical narrative of the fall, see Genesis 2:15–3:24. Religious attitudes toward evolution may differ, of course. For an interesting exchange, see Alvin Plantinga, "When Faith and Reason Clash: Evolution and the Bible," and Ernan McMullin, "Plantinga's Defense of Special Creation," in *Christian Scholar's Review*, XXI:1 (September 1991), 8–32, 55–79.

8. The idea that the thinking of virtuous persons is a reliable process for arriving at truth about how to act in particular circumstances is borrowed from Russ Shafer-Landau, *Moral Realism: A Defence* (Oxford: Oxford University Press, 2003), 267–302.

9. See Swinburne, *op. cit.*, 139, and Howard-Snyder, *op. cit.*, 88–89.

10. That God is vulnerable through the vulnerability of creatures is suggested in some well-known Biblical texts, e.g., "And the King will answer them, 'Truly, I say to you, as you did it to one of the least of these my brethren, you did it to me'" Matthew 25:40 (RSV). It might be suggested, however, that the doctrine of the incarnation renders God's vulnerability through creatures gratuitous. (According to the Christian doctrine of the incarnation, the second person of the Trinity took on human nature, i.e., a divine person became human. The doctrine of

the Trinity says that there is one God but three divine persons, Father, Son, and Holy Spirit.) Of course, I am presently exploring the resources of Theism, as explicitly formulated, which does not include the doctrines of the Trinity and the incarnation. But I don't think the doctrine of the incarnation renders God's vulnerability through creatures gratuitous, for several reasons: (1) God is more vulnerable if vulnerable both directly and indirectly. (2) It's rather hard to see how one man could be constantly subject to direct harm by all persons over long periods of history. (3) In some views, becoming incarnate involves giving up some knowledge (hence power) temporarily and voluntarily; so if all three divine persons became incarnate at once, God would cease to exist. For a brief philosophical discussion of the doctrines of the incarnation and the Trinity, see Thomas V. Morris, *Our Idea of God: An Introduction to Philosophical Theology* (Downers Grove, IL: InterVarsity Press, 1991), 159–84. For a more detailed treatment of these issues, see Ronald J. Feenstra and Cornelius Plantinga, Jr., *Trinity, Incarnation, and Atonement: Philosophical and Theological Essays* (Notre Dame, IN: University of Notre Dame Press, 1989).

11. I am not here endorsing consequentialism, the view that the *consequences* of an act are what make it right (or wrong). But one doesn't have to be a consequentialist to hold that wrong acts *tend* to be destructive or harmful in some way. For an introduction to the major moral theories, see Fred Feldman, *Introductory Ethics* (Englewood Cliffs, NJ.: Prentice-Hall, 1978).

12. Robert Nozick, *Anarchy, State, and Utopia* (New York: Harper, 1974), 42–45.

13. Here I'm borrowing from Swinburne, *op.cit.*, 242–43.

14. Marilyn McCord Adams, *Horrendous Evils and the Goodness of God* (Ithaca, NY: Cornell University Press, 1999), 55 (see also 20–21).

15. This is so even if humans are identical with their bodies; see Peter van Inwagen, "The Possibility of the Resurrection," *International Journal for the Philosophy of Religion*, v. 9 (1978), 114–21.

16. Judging from the great literature of the world, even humans in the best of this-worldly circumstances have profound but unsatisfied yearnings and deep unfulfilled longings. With this in mind, clause 5 seems to predict an afterlife for all humans, if God exists.

17. See Chapter 1 ("Theism and Naturalism"), especially endnote 14, for an explanation of the point regarding statements with a probability of 1.

18. My reflections on the link between natural evil and the moral life are inspired by Swinburne, *op. cit.*, 166. However, I am adapting this material for my own purposes, and so I must take responsibility for any errors.

19. The value of being of use is particularly emphasized by Swinburne, *op. cit.*, 101–05.

20. In the Bible, the book of Job warns against interpreting suffering and misfortune as divine punishment. See also John 9:1–3.

21. It is one thing to doubt whether certain kinds of animals can feel pain and another thing altogether to justify acts that may, for all we know, cause them pain. While there is much that we do not know about animal pain, morality often tells us to err on the side of caution. So nothing I've said here justifies acts that, for all we know, inflict pain on animals. On the other hand it would clearly be fallacious to argue, "It is wrong to do X to an animal because doing X *might* cause the animal pain. Hence, the animal can feel pain."

22. H. David Baldridge, *Shark Attack* (New York: Berkeley Medallion Books, 1975), 222.

23. *Ibid.*, 204.

24. Hugo and Jane van Lawick-Goodall, *Innocent Killers* (Boston: Houghton Mifflin, 1970), 13. Italics added.

25. This paragraph owes a debt to Swinburne, *op. cit.*, 171–72.

26. John Wesley, "The General Deliverance" (Sermon 60), in Albert C. Outler, ed., *The Works of John Wesley*, v. 2 (Nashville, TN: Abingdon Press, 1985), 436–50. John Wesley was the founder of Methodism.

27. For an approach to the problem of evil that involves postulating a God of limited power, see John B. Cobb, Jr., and David Ray Griffin, *Process Theology: An Introductory Exposition* (Philadelphia: Westminster Press, 1976), esp. 69–75. Though I do not accept process theology *in toto*, I think that process theologians have offered deep insights into the nature of divine goodness.

28. See Chapter 3 ("Is Religious Experience Reliable?") for an explanation of this point.

# 8. Naturalism and Evil

1. This strategy may be called the *comparative approach* to the problem of evil, since it essentially involves comparing Theistic and Naturalistic explanations of evil. C. Stephen Layman, "Moral Evil: The comparative response," *International Journal for Philosophy of Religion*, v. 53 (February 2003), 1–23, and "Natural Evil: The comparative response," *International Journal for Philosophy of Religion*, v. 54 (August 2003), 1–31.

2. See Chapter 5 ("A Design Argument") for a detailed discussion of the various Naturalistic attempts to explain fine-tuning.

3. Paul F. Lurquin, *The Origins of Life and the Universe* (New York: Columbia University Press, 2003), 7–8; Sylvia S. Mader, *Inquiry into Life*, 6th ed. (Dubuque, IA: Wm. C. Brown, 1991), 59–60; Charles B. Thaxton,

Walter L. Bradley, and Roger L. Olsen, *The Mystery of Life's Origin* (NewYork: Philosophical Library, 1984), 2–4; and Michael J. Behe, *Darwin's Black Box* (New York: Free Press, 1996), 257–58. Eukaryotic cells, which compose multicellular organisms, have a much more complex structure than prokaryotic cells (see, e.g., Behe, 258–59).

4. For a recent, sympathetic discussion of the various scientific, origin-of-life hypotheses, see Lurquin, *op. cit.*, 62–173.

5. Stanley L. Miller, "A Production of Amino Acids Under Possible Primitive Earth Conditions," *Science*, v. 117 (1953). I am here relying on summaries by Lurquin, *op. cit.*, 94–99, and Thaxton, *op. cit.*, 22–24.

6. For a more detailed discussion of animal pain, see Chapter 7 ("Theism and Evil").

7. This statement concerns what Naturalists will grant with regard to life as we know it on Earth. I am not suggesting that Naturalists are committed to any particular view on the subject of artificial intelligence or life in other galaxies. Our question here is how well Naturalism explains the presence of conscious life on Earth.

8. For an argument to the effect that the evolution of humans (or some similarly complex animals) was inevitable, see Simon Conway Morris, "The Paradoxes of Evolution: Inevitable Humans in a Lonely Universe?" in Neil A. Manson, ed., *God and Design: The Teleological Argument and Modern Science* (New York: Routledge, 2003), 329–47. For the view that human (or similar) intelligence is utterly unpredictable on evolutionary theory, see Stephen Jay Gould, *Wonderful Life: The Burgess Shale and the Nature of History* (New York: Norton, 1989), 45–52. Michael Denton argues in effect that if evolution is not guided by an intelligence, then it involves a series of extremely improbable transitions; see Michael J. Denton, *Nature's Destiny: How the Laws of Biology Reveal Purpose in the Universe* (New York: Free Press, 1998), 265–389.

9. Gould, *op. cit.*, 14. Gould speaks of "the 'pageant' of evolution as a staggeringly improbable series of events," 14.

10. *Ibid.*, 313.

11. *Ibid.*, 311–18.

12. For example, Paul Churchland, "Eliminative Materialism and the Propositional Attitudes," *Journal of Philosophy*, v. 78, n. 2 (1981); reprinted in Paul Churchland, *A Neurocomputational Perspective: The Nature of Mind and the Structure of Science* (Cambridge, MA: MIT Press, 1989), 1–22.

13. See Chapter 6 ("An Argument from Free Will") for a discussion of the relationship between free will and moral responsibility.

14. The issues briefly summarized in this paragraph are discussed in detail in Chapter 6.

15. For an excellent discussion of a wide range of views within the metaphysics of morals, see Russ Shafer-Landau, *Moral Realism: A Defence* (Oxford: Clarendon Press, 2003). Works defending moral antirealism include: Alfred Jules Ayer, *Language, Truth and Logic* (New York: Dover, 1946), Chapter VI; J. L. Mackie, *Ethics: Inventing Right and Wrong* (New York: Penguin Books, 1977), and Bernard Williams, *Ethics and the Limits of Philosophy* (Cambridge, MA: Harvard University Press, 1985). Some utilitarians are Ethical Naturalists, holding (very roughly) that moral rightness is identical with the property of promoting the general welfare. John Stuart Mill, *Utilitarianism* (1861), ed. George Sher (Indianapolis, IN: Hackett, 1979), held a more sophisticated utilitarian version of Ethical Naturalism. For a discussion of Mill's view, see Stephen Darwall, *Philosophical Ethics* (Boulder, CO: Westview Press, 1998), 110–22. Shafer-Landau provides a sustained and rigorous argument for Ethical Non-Naturalism.

16. Mackie, *op. cit.*, 36–41.

17. In this letter and the next I am borrowing from Shafer-Landau, *op. cit.*, 260–65, 80–98. I am, however, adapting this material for my own purposes and so am responsible for any errors.

18. This point about epistemic properties is borrowed from Terence Cuneo, *The Normative Web: A Defense of Moral Realism* (forthcoming, Oxford University Press, 2007). Note that, "You ought to believe A" here seems at least partially analyzable along these lines: "You *have a reason* to believe A, namely, in order to get truth." So understood, "ought" statements may seem less strange and mysterious. Is "You ought morally to do $X$" at least partially analyzable as "You have a reason to do $X$, namely, in order to ___"? Different moral theorists might fill in the blank differently, e.g., "promote the general welfare," "do God's will," "satisfy the categorical imperative."

19. For an insightful discussion of the relation between evolution and ethics, see James Rachels, *Created from Animals: The Moral Implications of Darwinism* (New York: Oxford University Press, 1990), 62–98.

20. This idea is developed in considerable detail in Shafer-Landau, *op. cit.*, 265–302.

# 9. A Moral Argument

1. The wording of the argument to this point is borrowed from Russ Shafer-Landau, *Moral Realism: A Defence* (Oxford: Clarendon Press, 2003), 45. Shafer-Landau is not arguing for the DCT, but using the argument to structure a discussion of constructivist views of ethics.

2. For a discussion of constructivist views, see Shafer-Landau, *op. cit.*, 39–52. See also Fred Feldman, *Introductory Ethics* (Englewood Cliffs, NJ: Prentice-Hall, 1978).

3. Richard Swinburne, *The Existence of God*, rev. ed. (Oxford: Clarendon Press, 1991), 177. In the context of Swinburne's writing, *analytic* should here be understood as "necessary." In Capter 4 ("A Cosmological Argument"), I offered a more standard characterization of these concepts.

4. The arbitrariness of the DCT has troubled many Theists. C. S. Lewis remarks, "There were in the eighteenth century terrible theologians who held that 'God did not command certain things because they are right, but certain things are right because God commanded them.' To make the position perfectly clear, one of them even said that though God has, as it happens, commanded us to love Him and one another, He might equally well have commanded us to hate Him and one another, and hatred would then have been right. It was apparently a mere toss-up which He decided on. Such a view of course makes God a mere arbitrary tyrant. It would be better and less irreligious to believe in no God . . . than to have such an ethics and such a theology as this." C. S. Lewis, *Reflections on the Psalms* (New York: Harcourt, Brace, and World, 1958), 61.

5. It might be suggested that "Torturing people just for fun is wrong" is not necessarily true, because it's not necessary that people exist. We can easily accommodate this concern by slightly altering the example: "If there are any people, then it is wrong to torture them just for fun."

6. For a defense of the claim that necessity is grounded in God, see Thomas V. Morris and Christopher Menzel, "Absolute Creation," *American Philosophical Quarterly*, v. 23 (1986), 353–62; reprinted in Thomas V. Morris, *Anselmian Explorations: Essays in Philosophical Theology* (Notre Dame, IN: University of Notre Dame Press, 1987), 161–78.

7. I certainly do not pretend that my brief discussion of the MDCT is definitive. For a sophisticated defense of a MDCT, see Robert Merrihew Adams, *Finite and Infinite Goods: A Framework for Ethics* (Oxford: Oxford University Press, 1999), esp. Chapters 1 and 10–12.

8. My argument in this paragraph is borrowed in its essentials from Richard Swinburne, *The Coherence of Theism* (Oxford: Clarendon Press, 1977), 203–09.

9. For a short introduction to modal logic, see www.mhhe.com/layman2; click on "Student Resources" and then on "Modal Logic Chapter." The validity of the ontological argument is treated in Section 12.5.

10. For a discussion of epistemic and metaphysical (or logical) possibility, see Chapter 4 ("A Cosmological Argument").

11. Some Christians hold that the second person of the Trinity, the divine Son, temporarily and voluntarily gave up some knowledge (without

giving up his divinity) when he became incarnate. See Ronald J. Feenstra, "Reconsidering Kenotic Christology," in Ronald J. Feenstra and Cornelius Plantinga, Jr., eds., *Trinity, Incarnation, and Atonement: Philosophical and Theological Essays* (Notre Dame, IN: University of Notre Dame Press, 1989), 128–52.

12. For a defense of the ontological argument, see Alvin Plantinga, *God, Freedom, and Evil* (New York: Harper & Row, 1974), 85–112.

13. The example is borrowed from Sarah Stroud, "Moral Overridingness and Moral Theory," *Pacific Philosophical Quarterly*, v. 79 (1998), 170–89.

14. As we have seen, the hypothesis of a malevolent Deity in fact creates serious epistemological difficulties, but this does not destroy the point of the example.

15. The case is borrowed from C. Stephen Layman, "God and the Moral Order," *Faith and Philosophy*, v. 19, n. 3 (July 2002), 307.

16. I'm speaking loosely here. According to Plato, a person's soul consists of reason, the appetites, and the spirited element. Reason includes the conscience, the faculty through which we know what's right and wrong. The appetites are bodily desires, e.g., for food, drink, and sex. Through the spirited element we are competitive or willing to strive and struggle. For Plato, reason (hence, conscience) must govern the soul, otherwise the soul will be disordered and lacking in harmony. So harmony of soul (or peace of mind) is possible only if one is moral.

17. This thought experiment is borrowed in its essentials from Richard Taylor, "Value and the Origin of Right and Wrong," in Louis Pojman, ed., *Ethical Theory: Classical and Contemporary Readings* (Belmont, CA: Wadsworth, 1989), 115–21.

18. It is not here being asserted that traditional Theists hold that people can *earn* heaven—i.e., the eternal enjoyment of right relations with God and other creatures. The point is simply that moral wrongdoing will never promote a person's self-interest *in the long run* if God exists. Traditional Theists offer various theories about how people can enter heaven—that's another topic.

19. The main point of this paragraph is borrowed from Robin Collins, "Eastern Religions," in Michael J. Murray, ed., *Reason for the Hope Within* (Grand Rapids, MI: Eerdmans, 1999), 206.

# Index

273